At Play with Krishna

At Play with Krishna

At Play with Krishna

Pilgrimage Dramas from Brindavan

John Stratton Hawley

IN ASSOCIATION WITH

Shrivatsa Goswami

MOTILAL BANARSIDASS PUBLISHERS
PRIVATE LIMITED • DELHI

First Indian Edition: Delhi, 1992

ISBN: 81-208-0945-9

Published by arrangement with Princeton University Press

Also available at:

MOTILAL BANARSIDASS

41 U.A. Bungalow Road, Jawahar Nagar, Delhi 110 007

120 Royapettah High Road, Mylapore, Madras 600 004

16 St. Mark's Road, Bangalore 560 001

Ashok Rajpath, Patna 800 004

Chowk, Varanasi 221 001

PRINTED IN INDIA

BY JAINENDRA PRAKASH JAIN AT SHRI JAINENDRA PRESS, A-45 NARAINA INDUSTRIAL AREA, PHASE I, NEW DELHI 110 028 AND PUBLISHED BY NARENDRA PRAKASH JAIN FOR MOTILAL BANARSIDASS PUBLISHERS PVT. LTD., BUNGALOW ROAD, JAWAHAR NAGAR, DELHI 110 007

to Śrī Rādhā Ramaṇ Jī
and
for Laura and Sandhya

Contents

List of Illustrations

All photos are the author's except those credited to others.

Preface

More than one book has been written to tell the story of Krishna, but in this one he will speak for himself, as he does year in and year out to audiences all over India. Only a small proportion of India's vast population has ever been literate and even those who could read have never been satisfied that a tradition can be learned from the page of a book. Commentaries must enrich a text; and more than that, one needs a living relationship with a teacher to bring the tradition to life in oneself. Westerners, by and large, are more comfortable with the notion that religious truth comes from books, but in India religion is not an extraction from the past. The gods surround you. Through their images — now cinematic as well as static — they are visible; and through various media they speak.

In the case of Krishna this is especially so. The life he adopted was neither the stuff of distant legends nor a tale of inaccessible Himalayan heights. He pitched his tent with common cowherd folk. On the whole, Krishna's world is perfectly familiar to most Indians today. Exact replicas of the bullock cart he kicked over as a tiny child creak down every country road in India. His speech, too, is that of the common people. They call it Braj Bhāṣā, the dialect of the Hindi family that is spoken in the Braj region just to the south of Delhi on the river Jumna. This is where Krishna chose to live, and he lives there still today. He infuses himself as a living presence into a dramatic tradition called the *rās līlā*, in which native Brahmin boys take on the roles of Krishna and his lovers and friends. Led by singer-directors who as boys played the principal roles themselves, these *rās līlā* troupes are at home in Braj during the rainy season. Pilgrims from all over India come to see them, especially in Brindavan, which is today the spiritual center of Braj and the most important place of pilgrimage for Krishna in all of India. In other seasons the directors take their art to the people, traveling with their troupes to every corner of the subcontinent.

I have translated four of these *rās līlā*s here. These four are selected from the mammoth repertoire not only because they are among the most commonly performed but because they present the full span of Krishna's sojourn in Braj, from his arrival to his departure. They ignore the mature Krishna who teaches the *Bhagavad Gītā* and heroically conducts affairs of state in his role as king of the western city of Dvaraka. For all the renown the *Gītā* has attained in the last century both in India and in the West, it is Krishna in Braj that people know and love best, Krishna in his youth; these plays present four important moments in that story. One of them, "The Birth of Krishna," has an additional significance because of its intimate relation to a principal festival in the annual calendar; another, "The Great Circle Dance," incorporates a version of the dance sequence that daily introduces these plays, and without which they would not have the ritual force they do. By exploring such matters in the introductions to each of the plays I hope to give the reader a sense not only of the narrative line but also of the ambiance that makes it possible for those who see these plays to enter into the story themselves. The first chapter, on Brindavan, has that as its entire aim.

One question that outsiders immediately ask—who wrote these plays?—does not occur to anyone in Braj. These are not individual compositions, but a collective forum in which Krishna makes himself available to those who love him. In most cases it would be extremely difficult to ascertain the author. This is a dramatic tradition at least five centuries old, and although in every generation new plays are added at the initiative of inspired persons, including the *rāsdhārī*s themselves, the singer-directors who literally "bear" or "hold together" the *rās līlā*s, in most instances the author, if there ever was one, has long been forgotten. Furthermore, the plays are constantly being recomposed as *rāsdhārī*s introduce new songs into the music that undergirds and embellishes the *līlā*s, and omit old ones. Each *rāsdhārī* possesses his own written list of songs, but the dialogue is entirely an oral tradition, and although the *rāsdhārī*s remember the lines from past performances and teach them to their companies, there is also a measure of independence: performers often invent new lines on the spot. Similarly, most plays retain a very traditional plot structure, but others, like "The Great Circle Dance" included here, are more modern attempts to bring tradition to life. All this being the case, it has been essential to translate these dramas from actual performance rather than from any written text. I have occasionally summarized a scene or two in the interest of brevity, but the dialogue that appears, save for the omission of a few interjections and rhetorical repetitions, is an unabridged rendering of what I actually heard.

One important element, however, is missing—the music—and its absence sometimes has the effect of leaving exposed what is not very good verse, lines intended more to structure the drama than to be savored for a poetic timbre and density of their own. On occasion, in fact, the removal of the melody almost totally robs the poetry of its aesthetic effect, and when that happens it has seemed wise to supplement the literal sense slightly so as to compensate for the loss. Otherwise it would scarcely be possible to convey the charm that the alternation of song and speech continually lends to these dramas. There are other times—when the compositions of the medieval poets Sūr Dās or Raskhān are quoted, for example—when one can expect much more, but on the whole one should remember that this is largely a folk idiom, in which songs are intended to be understood by many at a single hearing rather than pondered by a few connoisseurs.

These four plays were performed in the summer months of 1976 by a single company on a single stage. The troupe is unusual in that two *rāsdhārīs*, or *svāmīs* as they are popularly called, have joined forces to create it. Their cooperation aptly symbolizes the fact that, while ancient, this tradition is constantly changing. In every generation it is infused with new blood as handsome and clever boys are recruited from outside the old *rāsdhārīs*' immediate families to play Krishna or his beloved Radha when there are no suitable candidates in the family itself. Svāmī Natthī Lāl, who plays the drums, comes from an old line of *rāsdhārīs* and hails from Kamain, one of the villages in which the *rās līlā* tradition is the oldest, whereas Svāmī Śrī Rām, who leads the musicians in singing the narration, was the first in his immediate family to enter the *rās līlā* tradition. The troupe of Śrī Rām and Natthī Lāl is neither the most famous in Braj nor the least, though recently it has gained in reputation as it has come under the patronage of one of the great religious leaders of Brindavan, Puruṣottam Gosvāmī.

I am grateful to all three of these men for permitting and encouraging me to tape these plays, and to Murārī Lāl Varmā for transcribing them. Premānand, the best known and most prolific composer of *rās līlā*s in Brindavan today, was kind enough to correct the texts in a number of instances. Michelle Nguyen, Linda Konishi, Barbara Schuster, Georgia Lo Cornett, and Libby Sandusky have provided meticulous typing assistance, and my wife Laura Shapiro has improved the manuscript with a myriad of editorial suggestions. Norvin Hein and Rādhā Dāsī have also offered helpful corrections and comments, and to Mark Juergensmeyer I owe, after many hours of patient labor, most of what is poetic in the verse. The traditional stencil drawings come from the hands of Nārāyaṇ Dās and Cain Sukh Dās of Mathura. The Foreign Area Program of the Social Science Research Council and the American Council of Learned Societies, Harvard University, and the National Endowment for the Humanities have all provided generous grants for research.

Projects in pursuit of intercultural understanding often presuppose a great deal of personal interdependence, and this book is a case in point. It could scarcely have been undertaken without the help of Shrivatsa Goswami, son of Puruṣottam, who first welcomed me to Brindavan and introduced me to the *rās līlā*s, and who has aided me in various stages of my study ever since. I have tried to acknowledge my debt to him by including his name on the title page. By answering my questions as I translated, and by reviewing the final product, he has saved me from innumerable errors, and his understanding of the theological perspectives that undergird these dramas has greatly amplified and often corrected my own. I remain responsible for the text, however, and it will be evident to the reader that the commentary, aimed at outsiders, is also the work of an outsider. I can only hope that I have heard enough of the music of Krishna's flute to prevent me from grossly distorting a tradition that is precious beyond telling to those who preserve it.

TRANSLITERATION

SINCE THIS WORK reproduces oral speech more than written, and deals with vernacular literature more than classical, I have often departed from conventions designed primarily to facilitate the transliteration of Sanskrit texts. Sanskrit words are transliterated in the standard fashion if they occur in Sanskrit quotations or figure in a context that mainly concerns Sanskrit rather than the vernacular. Otherwise I have attempted to convey Hindi, or Braj Bhāṣā, as it sounds. The transliteration of the neutral vowel (ə) is therefore omitted when it is not heard (Kāmdev). Normally this happens at the ends of words, but if a preceding glide or consonant cluster renders it audible I note it in transliteration (Bhāratīya, Nanda). The nasalization of vowels is indicated by ṃ before sibilants and h (*saṃsār, siṃh*) and by the tilde at the ends of words (*bhaktõ*). Often, however, vernacular speech neutralizes what would in Sanskrit usage be a nasalized vowel (Kans).

This emphasis on oral speech will sometimes make names that are familiar to Sanskritists look odd (Rūp Gosvāmī), and I regret the necessary adjustment. I also apologize for words whose form changes somewhat according to context. Sometimes, for instance, it seems more natural to repeat a more familiar Sanskrit form (Duryodhana) when a word is spoken only rarely (Duryodhan) than to enforce the rule of speech with utter consistency. And there are words that have become so well known in their Sanskrit form (Śiva) that I have not attempted to alter them.

The word Brindavan presents a special problem: the town's name is spelled in half a dozen different ways. The Sanskrit option, Vṛndāvana, is at obvious variance with common speech, but even the simplified spelling that is currently official, Vrindaban, fails, in my opinion, to record the way the name is actually pronounced. To my ear it seems that the labial consonants are usually reversed, hence I have settled for the spelling Brindāvan, or, more simply, Brindavan.

Brindavan is one of several very common names that are

treated as if they had come into standard English usage and are given without diacritical marks (Krishna, Radha, Brindavan) unless they occur in compounds (Rādhā Ramaṇ, *kṛṣṇajanmāṣṭamī*, Brindāvanbihārī). The same rule applies to place names and other proper nouns that have a conventional English form. Dāūjī is the exception, and is given in its marked form because the name of the town is equivalent to that of Krishna's brother. In general I have retained the diacritical markings in order to guide pronunciation.

The long vowels *ā*, *ī*, *ū*, *e*, and *o* are pronounced approximately like the corresponding vowels in the English words f*a*ther, mar*i*ne, r*u*le, pr*ey*, and m*o*w. The diphthongs *ai* and *au*, though sometimes given the length of the vowels in English str*i*de and tr*ou*t, are more usually shortened, yielding the vowel sounds contained in m*a*d and cr*aw*l. The vowels *a*, *i*, and *u* are short and are pronounced like the vowels in the words b*u*t, f*i*ll, and b*u*ll. Vocalic *ṛ* is also short; in modern speech it is rendered as if it were *ri*, as in *ri*b.

The consonant *c* sounds like *ch* in the English word *ch*arm, except that it has less aspiration; the consonant transliterated as *ch* has correspondingly greater aspiration. The aspirated consonants *th* and *ph* should be pronounced like the clusters in goa*th*erd and she*ph*erd rather than their counterparts in *th*ing and mor*ph*ium. The distinction between the sibilants ś and ṣ is not usually made in modern Hindi usage; both sound like *sh* in English *sh*ort. For the retroflex consonants, produced by curling the tip of the tongue toward the roof of the mouth (*ṭ*, *ṭh*, *ḍ*, *ḍh*, *ṇ*), there are no genuine English equivalents. To some, they sound as if the corresponding English consonants had been preceded by an American *r* (ha*r*d, hea*rt*), though the placement is slightly farther back in the mouth.

At Play with Krishna

CHAPTER I

Pilgrimage to Brindavan

Temple and Drama: Two Ritual Foci

AMONG THE THOUSANDS of lanes and alleys of Brindavan one is my favorite. It ties together two sites of the ritual action that makes Brindavan what it is: at one end is a temple and at the other end a place where the *rās līlā* is performed. Symbolically, it forms an axis upon which the life of the town turns.

This alley has no name. It uncoils from the small square before the temple gate and angles its way down toward the milky, muddy Jumna like a lazy snake in the afternoon sun. At the last moment it turns abruptly aside, curling past salmon and yellow facades before it leads at last through many other turns to the steps that bank the holy river. The shallow gutters that escort it along on both sides follow a more direct course, becoming a sewer at the bend and emptying into the river not far away. Sometimes there is a back-up of refuse at the bend, just outside the door to the *rās līlā* compound, and contented families of prickly-haired, long-nosed pigs often glut the little thoroughfare at that point, sifting through the stream and filtering it before it joins the Jumna.

The alley has other residents, too. Just next to a rough, mud-floored room where a little family often sits there is an even tinier room where their calf is tethered. Across the way an old widow from Nepal cooks her midday meal over a fire of sticks and dungcakes, sheltered from the weather by the hollow that is left from a brick dwelling that once stood there. The rest crumbled in monsoon rains long ago. Farther up the gentle incline, you can step up over the gutter onto a platform scarcely four feet wide and then look behind you: you find yourself at the door of a doctor of indigenous medicine. His head is bald and round, and as he sits cross-legged, his body spills to the ground with the generosity of a waterfall. They call him Fat Potato, and his eyes crescent with smiles when he hears the name.

It is a quiet alley, barely wide enough at the middle for a well-fed cow to pass, but more open at the ends, and the ends account for the traffic it bears. At the upper end people come and go from the temple of Rādhā Ramaṇ. This is a temple to Krishna, and the name indicates that he is understood from a certain perspective, as the lover (*ramaṇ*) of his playmate and soulmate, the beautiful Radha. No one in Brindavan is so coarse as to label a temple simply Krishna's: he has a hundred names, and each bears some affectionate twist. Rādhā Ramaṇ's temple is not the busiest, but it is notable for housing the image that has remained in Brindavan for the longest continuous period of time. Because the idol is only a foot tall, it could be hidden from the iconoclastic Muslim ruler Aurangzeb,who ravaged much of Brindavan in the seventeenth century, when other images had to be spirited away to safer places. Rādhā Ramaṇ has resided on this spot for almost five hundred years now, ever since the town was first established.

A magnet for pilgrims, Brindavan was established by pilgrims, and the temple of Rādhā Ramaṇ forms an integral part of that history. The man to whom Rādhā Ramaṇ manifested himself in image form had been born in the south of India, where his father was chief priest in the enormous and prestigious temple of Viṣṇu/Krishna at Srirangam. His own life fell under the spell of one of the most remarkable men of his day, the entrancing and entranced Caitanya, who experienced a radical

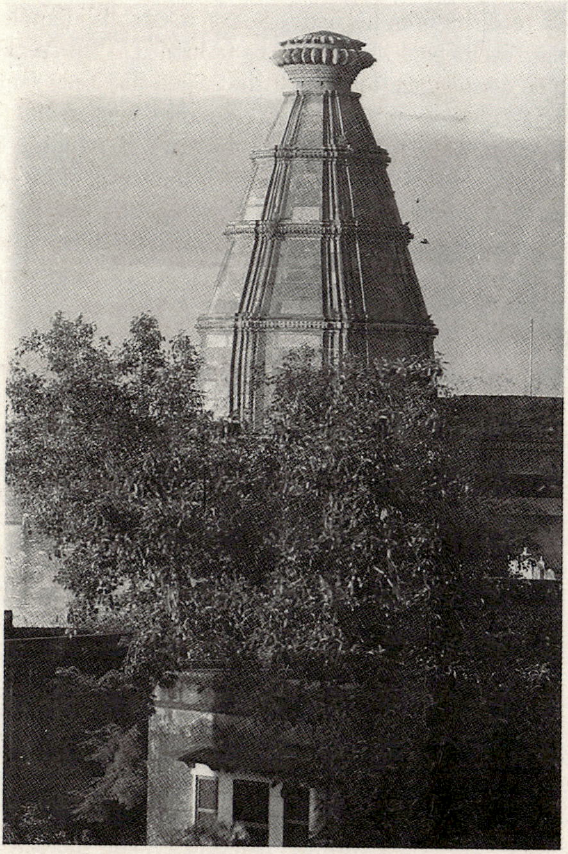

1. Spire of the temple of Yugal Kiśor

conversion to Krishna and dedicated his life to singing and dancing the simple glories of his name. Caitanya had already visited Brindavan—it was only a forest then—and had established through divine clairvoyance that this was indeed the place where Krishna had become incarnate and lived a life of uninterrupted love.[1] Caitanya's followers came to hold that it was because he himself was a further incarnation of Krishna, in conjunction with Radha, that he knew so perfectly just exactly how and where it all had happened. Already he had instructed two scholarly brothers from his native Bengal to establish temples in Brindavan; theirs were the first to be fashioned of the speckled, coral-colored sandstone for which the region had been famous for millennia. He renamed these two disciples Sanātan and Rūp, and they came to bear the family title *gosvāmī*, which is normally interpreted as meaning one who is in control of his sense faculties. The sound of the word, however, and one possible interpretation, associate it naturally with Krishna, who is Govind or Gopāl, protector and herder of the cows among which he lived.

Gopāl Bhaṭṭ, our south Indian Brahmin, was the next *gosvāmī* that Caitanya recruited, and his particular charge was to care for the ritual life of the fledgling community of worshipers of Krishna in Brindavan. It was to him that Rādhā Ramaṇ revealed himself by emerging as a perfectly shaped idol from the mysterious fossilized *śālagrām* stone.[2] Gopāl Bhaṭṭ's descendents have served the deity ever since. Devotees consider that the image lives, but it—or rather he—grants to this chosen family the privilege of assisting him in the daily schedule he maintains.

It is a cowherd's life he leads, eternally. Tradition says there was a time some five thousand years ago, at the beginning of what Hindus calculate to be the present world age, when Krishna made this life manifest on earth for all to see. Now, however, he has returned to his subtle and heavenly cowherd realm, Golok, and the naked eye can no longer perceive his movements.[3] Yet they continue, perennially, and the object of life is to become aware of them. Here in pastoral Brindavan, where Krishna chose to dwell, it is easier than in other places. If one could but see, one would realize that he plays here still, and he has made himself available in the form of an image to aid that vision.

The *gosvāmīs* in the temple of Rādhā Ramaṇ and the other

great temples of the city facilitate this learning to see. At Krishna's bidding they assist him, in his image, in his daily round. He awakes much before sunrise, or rather, he invites his *gosvāmī* servants to awaken him, which they do with the sweet-

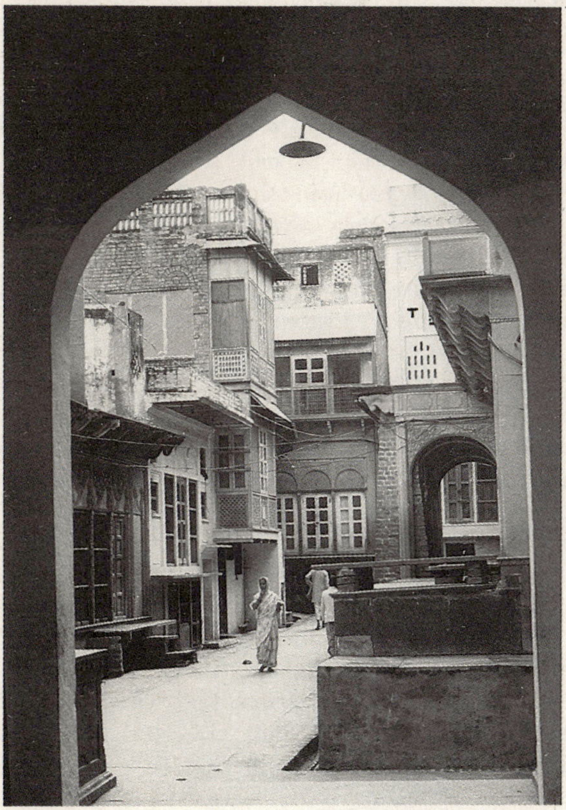

2. Looking into the temple compound of Rādhā Ramaṇ

est songs and the tinkling of bells. He performs his toilet functions, brushes his teeth, has a rubdown, bathes and dresses. Then he is ready for the morning meal of butter, fruit, sweets, and milk that his foster mother Yaśodā delights to serve him, and soon he joins his cowherd friends and takes the cattle out to graze. His image remains in the temple, but the worshipers understand that in reality Krishna is spending the day in the groves of Brindavan — the name literally means the forest *(van)* where the holy basil *(brindā)* grows. By noon it is time for him to sit for the big meal of the day; Yaśodā sends it out to him in the fields. All this is manifest in the temple. Although he (in image form) eats in private, as is the Indian custom, he receives his worshiping guests directly afterward, so that they can receive the leftovers from his table at this as at all meals. But then, as his friends rest in the shade, he is sure to slip off into one of the thickets to join some of his favorite girlfriends, perhaps Radha herself, for a midday tryst and a little nap. At that point it would be unseemly for anyone to watch, and the priests of the temple retire the image to a private chamber behind the dais where it has just been visible.

It is not long before Krishna wakes and reappears among his cowherd friends, his absence unnoticed. Since cowherding is not such a demanding occupation, he joins them in whatever games come to mind; and he is forever playing his rustic flute. All this is left to the worshipers' imagination so as to heighten their sense of welcoming him when he comes back from the forest. For soon it is time to herd the animals home to be milked. As his father watches anxiously from the pen and his mother stands ready at the door with a snack, so the *gosvāmī* priests offer him fruit and sweets and open the door of his chamber to receive him back into the company of whatever worshipers have gathered. They excuse him once again from his public audience and help him wash off the dust of the day, change into comfortable clothes, and relax for his evening meal. Before he goes to bed they bring him his evening repast and his warm milk, as his mother faithfully does. And then sweet sleep. He retires once for his mother's satisfaction, nursed by affectionate lullabies the faithful raise in her name, and as the believers almost see his eyelids droop, the *gosvāmī*s usher him back into his private room. Then, when no one is looking — not even his *gosvāmī* servants, for they by now have closed the door to his inner chamber to allow him complete privacy — he sneaks out again to join the girls for a still sweeter slumber. Yaśodā suspects nothing, and the worshipers can only imagine the subtleties of this love play; but that they do.

As the day proceeds, then, Krishna's primordial time in Brindavan is replicated in the temples he has filled with his presence; his companionship with the herder boys and girls of eternal Brindavan is reflected in the interaction between his image and the people who come to attend it, many of them cowherds still. Most stream into the temple in the dark and silent hour before dawn, before the day becomes tarnished with the tasks of the world. They crowd its inner courtyard with singing, and when the curtain is drawn back and they can see Rādhā Ramaṇ they break into shouts of welcome. Often there is high-pitched ululation from the women and sometimes a little dancing: Krishna makes people happy.

Then the majority must go their way. The priests look after the needs of Rādhā Ramaṇ and the people of Brindavan, having set their lives in his context, look after their own cares. But they are fortified, not only by the sight of him, which Hindus call *darśan*, but also by sharing in the food he eats. Little bits of his leftovers are passed out to them as his grace, *prasād*. These are sweets for the most part, but in the temple of Rādhā Ramaṇ, *tulsī*, a relative of basil and Krishna's favorite plant, is also offered. Those who can, find their way back into the temple from time to time during the day, when there is a chance to see him appear on the dais at one of the eight "watches" *(yām)* of the day, but everyone returns at evening. Krishna is back home by then and everyone else's work is done, too; it is time to revisit the spiritual source of the day. Since there is not one but a number of old temples in Brindavan where Krishna has especially manifested himself, many people make a little tour just after sunset. The priests in each temple will have attended meticulously to his dress and jewelry, and the *darśan* will be different in every one, varying from day to day and season to season.[4]

The opening and closing of the day, then, are special times. All over India these threshold times are honored with particular care, but in Brindavan they are woven into a fabric of story in a way one scarcely finds outside a Vaiṣṇavite context. It is at

3. Rādhā Ramaṇ, dressed for an early morning *darśan* in the hot season (credit: Pravin Photo House, Brindavan)

these times particularly that worshipers are present to see the priests make him the ancient offering of light. They hallow these twilight hours by waving trays of little lamps before the images in graceful circular motions, roughly tracing the devanagari notation for the syllable OM, and drawing attention to the head, waist, and especially the feet of the deity: he emerges from darkness into a mysterious glow. They follow this *ārati*, as it is called, by offering water with the same sinuous motion: they wave a rare right-handed conch before the image and then scatter the water it holds over the heads of the crowd. As the worshipers had received the light that mediated the divine presence by waving their hands before their eyes in humble welcome, symbolically prostrating their heads at the feet of the deity, where the light had tarried longest, so now they continue their bow until a few drops of water sprinkle their heads and shoulders. And then, having received grace *(prasād)* in these ways as well as in Krishna's food, they depart, clogging the little lane. In the hot season the relative cool of these dark hours is a blessing, and the flow of strollers is relaxed. In winter, people shuffle by with hurried steps, hunched under a single gauzy blanket and trembling with the cold. Whatever the season, they daily link their stories with Krishna's, seeking to understand how their lives follow from his grace, and trying to forget everything that seems inconsistent with his realm. By giving such careful attention to his daily needs, whether at the temple or in their own little altars, they sanctify their own routines, transforming repetition into ritual.

There is one season in particular when pilgrims from all over India swell their ranks, weaving hundreds of thousands of other stories into Krishna's tale. In the monsoon, in July and August, the Jumna swells abruptly from a steaming, desolate trickle to a bursting flood. The alley is awash in mud and whatever else the rains manage to uproot, and all the smells of earth and humanity clog the air. At one end of the alley great crowds surge into the temple to catch sight of Rādhā Ramaṇ; but now the traffic moves both ways as the other end of the alley emerges from dormancy.

Down by the pigs' haven there is a little door through a long brick wall; stepping across the sloshing gutter, many feet follow each other into a large compound on the other side. There in recent years a huge building has been constructed by the man who is currently the leader of Gopāl Bhaṭṭ's lineage, Puruṣottam

4. Krishna

Gosvāmī. It is called the Śrī Caitanya Prem Sansthān, an Institute of Love dedicated to the memory of Caitanya, and the auditorium on its ground floor is filled with pilgrims from far and wide jammed together with people native to Braj.[5] They sit cross-legged on the floor, the women on one side and the men on the other. As many as two thousand people may be gathered, and all eyes are on the stage, which pulses with music and dance and vivid, shining costumes.

5. Radha

This is the *rās līlā.*[6] Krishna and his friends and Radha and hers shout out their deliberate lines in high childish voices from the stage, just as they have done for centuries in more traditional settings, simple circles cleared away in forest and town. The roles of Radha, Krishna, and the cowherd girls *(gopīs)* are sanctified and dignified with the title of *svarūp*, which means that the Brahmin boys who adopt them are thought to take on the very form of the personnages they portray once their costumes are complete. The term applies quintessentially to Radha and Krishna, and once the boys who play these two don the crowns appropriate to their roles, they are venerated as the divine couple itself. Radha's crown is a triangular jeweled tiara. Krishna's, too, is laden with gems to whatever extent the troupe can afford, but it bears more obvious references to Krishna's pastoral environment, for it trails a long snake-like tail down the back and culminates in a spray of peacock feathers.

Peacocks, for all their varicolored brilliance, are predominantly a deep blue, and by tradition Krishna, too, is dark in hue. His skin is the deep, velvety blue of peacock and lotus; in the oldest texts he is even described as black, the literal meaning of the term Krishna. But more than color ties Krishna to the peacock; there is also the mating dance. This is the rainy season, and all over Braj one hears the peacock's piercing, hollow call. The male is a proud bird, and on rooftops and hillocks everywhere he struts his colors, fanning out his tail and rotating himself this way and that to attract the females, who come around pecking at the ground in their more modest way. Krishna's moves are similar. With his haunting flute he summons the women of Braj away from their mundane occupations to come out to the forest and dance with him the mating dance, the dance of love, the *rās*; and as the peacock rotates so that his plumage will be visible to every eye, so Krishna multiplies himself to be available with an equal intimacy to every girl he summons.

The *rās līlā* imitates this eternal dance every day in the monsoon season. Its first half, the *rās* proper, reenacts the sequence that begins with the invitation to the dance, presented nowadays not as Krishna's initiative but that of his most intimate partner Radha, so intimate as to be considered a very part of him. As the couple steps down from the throne on which they sit, the little *gopīs* join them and they move through a repertoire of song and dance that does not vary greatly from one performance to the next. There are balances, swings, and circles in the fashion of country dancing, and a number of steps are drawn from the brisk *kathak* tradition of North Indian dance. But the climax draws one directly back to the analogy with the peacock, for in it Krishna drops to his knees and speeds around in a great circle, pivoting from knee to knee as the *gopīs* emit the high-pitched howl of the peahens. Here Krishna, the master peacock, traces the circle in which the *gopīs* will join him, and once they enter the swirl this first section of the *rās līlā* comes to an end.[7]

At this point Krishna and Radha return to their throne, posing for the adulation of the crowd, which is often allowed to come forward at this point to perform many of the same gestures of adoration, purification, and submission that are customary in temples. The people will bring monetary offerings, circling them before the faces of Radha and Krishna in a gesture *(nyauchāvar)* that is somewhat reminiscent of the *āratī*, and placing them at the deities' feet, as one might make an offering in a temple. Then they touch their heads to the *svarūps*' feet in a gesture that recalls the bows and prostrations they offer in temples, and signifies recognition of the superior status of the deities and their own need of divine help. Often they stop just to gaze at the charming couple before others in the crowd push them aside to have access themselves, for this is a living vision that even the finest, most sensitively decorated images in the temples cannot quite convey. These are the gods themselves.

The second part of the *rās līlā* is, as the term implies, the *līlā*. The word means "play" in all senses, and each day the play describes a particular event in Krishna's childhood in Braj, some *geste*, some little moment, episode, or plot. These vary from day to day, and if the company performs the full cycle — which customarily extends from the new moon of the month of *śrāvaṇ* (July-August) to the eighth day of the waning half of the succeeding month of *bhādrapad*, which is the festival of Krishna's birthday — there will be time for twenty-three *līlās*, twenty-three separate episodes in the pastoral story. A few more may be added afterward if there is sufficient audience, and there is one place in Brindavan dedicated to the performance of the *rās līlā* on every day of the year; no pilgrim should come without being able to see the *rās līlā*. Normally, however, one sees it in the rainy season or at Holī, the great spring festival of love and societal inversion. At other times the better-known *rās līlā* companies, called *rās maṇḍalīs*, tour the rest of Braj and India, while simpler troupes disband until the festival season commences again. At monsoon time some fifty or more *rās maṇḍalīs* are active in Braj, most of them in Brindavan itself.[8]

The *rās līlā* is not just drama, it is liturgy; its two parts, *rās* and *līlā*, bear analogy to the fixed and varying parts of Christian liturgical life. The *rās* is repeated with the same regularity as the eucharist, and it has the same sacramental force: to see the *rās* is to participate in the great act of sharing that lies at the heart of tradition. Sharing, indeed, is the root meaning of the word Hindus most often use to describe the relation of loving devotion they feel for God: *bhakti*. The *līlā* expands upon the meaning of this central symbol in much the same way as sermons and lections amplify the connotations of the eucharist: it provides the narrative context that enriches it and makes it intelligible. The *rās* and the eucharist tell their great stories in a nutshell, emphasizing their communal and sacramental aspect; *līlās* and lections make them accessible to various fields of memory and activity.

As we have already hinted, the analogy between the *rās līlā* and temple worship is even stronger. Daily temple worship recapitulates Krishna's diurnal schedule, just as the *rās* presents its narrative focus: an open secret, his trysts with the girls of Braj. The yearly temple calendar amplifies this by allowing participation in particular incidents in Krishna's life history, and the span of *līlās* does the same. The *āratī* ceremony opens and closes every day in Krishna's temple life, and every *rās līlā* begins and ends with the *āratī*. Furthermore, there are historical analogies, for the *rās līlā* owes its present form to the same period that produced the great temples and *gosvāmī* lineages of Brindavan and Braj, though traditions vary (as they do in regard to the establishment of temples) as to which community provided the most crucial inspiration.[9]

All this is more than analogy, in fact. Rightly understood, temple worship and the *rās līlā* are but two arenas of a single dramatic activity, for in the Vaiṣṇavite understanding God himself is an actor. In descending to earth from time to time he plays various roles: these are his avatars. It is true that there is something altogether special about his role as Krishna; that is conceived as his natural form, an intimacy he undertook precisely to escape the hierarchial distance that had separated him eternally from the human beings whose love he shared, and to provide himself a context for experiencing at the same time the complementarity of his own nature, as masculine and feminine, Krishna and Radha.

This role involves, precisely, gaming and play: Krishna and Radha must act out their duality in order to experience their union. Radha does so by expressing herself in the multiple forms of the *gopīs*. And both she and Krishna experience this loving complementarity as well by playing one another, by taking one another's roles. In temples this duality in oneness is expressed in the fact that in every sanctuary where Krishna's image stands alone Radha is understood to dwell within him: her throne, which one sees alongside his, and which is served with the same elaborate attention that is lavished on him, appears empty to the naked eye, for he and she are not so separate as to occupy two distinct places. In the *līlās* this intimate interconnection is acted out in the form of their explicitly adopting one another's positions, dress, and manners. And just as Krishna reveals himself in the temple image, offering himself for the dramatic reenactment of his daily round, he does the same in investing himself in the *svarūps* who perform the *rās*. In the *rās*, however, this tradition of role play is even more firmly rooted, for the residents of Braj (Brajbāsīs) hold that the *rās* began when Krishna disappeared from the *gopīs*' presence, leaving them crazed and bereft. The only solace they could find was to imitate his presence, to play Krishna in his various childhood sports, and to anticipate his circle dance in imagination. Thus the *gopīs* themselves were the first to perform the *rās līlā* or, more accurately, to imitate it. The Braj tradition simply carries on what they began. For this reason, the *rās līlā* is properly called *rās līlānukaraṇ*, the imitation of the *rās*.

The Vaiṣṇavite tradition, then, is totally unembarrassed about the role imagination plays in the religious life. If the worship of images sounds like playing with dolls, let it: it is the spirit, the affection, the *bhāv*, as they say, that counts; and it is the dramatic situation that makes this flow of emotion possible. If the actors in the *rās līlās* seem in reality to be only children, let them: Krishna incarnated himself as a child in order to make this childish identification with himself possible. Vaiṣṇavs see that the world is intrinsically dramatic: without the symbolic shape we give it, it simply does not exist for us. God, Krishna, is merely the master and focus of symbol and drama. The ancient Sanskrit tradition holds that drama is the completest form of art, incorporating all the rest, and Vaiṣṇav religion makes the statement that drama is all of life.[10]

The worship of (or should we say "through"?) images and the adoration of the *svarūps* is hardly credulity. Everyone knows that the images do not actually eat the food that is offered in temples. As I was recently reminded in a Brindavan tea stall, if God ate food such as we eat, there would scarcely be any way to satisfy him! Rather, he allows us the game of feeding him for our benefit: it is symbolic action and would have no value but for the belief, the mood with which it is infused. God dines on our love, not our food. And so it is with the plays. People do not believe in the *svarūps* in the way that children believe in Santa Claus; they know perfectly well that these are normal children. In fact they must be local children, born in Braj, to qualify for their roles—hence, entirely unmystified, completely normal. The mystery is quite the other way around. These are plays in which children enact the naturalness of childhood in order to stir the imagination of adults: tne best Krishna is the one who acts most like himself, a child unbridled.

It is true, nonetheless, that the boys in whom the roles of Krishna and to an extent Radha are invested at any given time are apt to be the recipients of special deference and affection even when they are not on stage. This is particularly true for the more well-known companies. People will bow to such boys in the street, and the *rāsdhārīs* may keep them a little aloof from the normal crowd. If one enters their houses they are invariably introduced with a particular pride; they are plied with the finest food available, offered every attention, even massaged all night as they sleep. Because of people's desire to worship, to serve, and to imagine, the distinction between child and divinity is not observed with the rigidity that the presence or absence of the

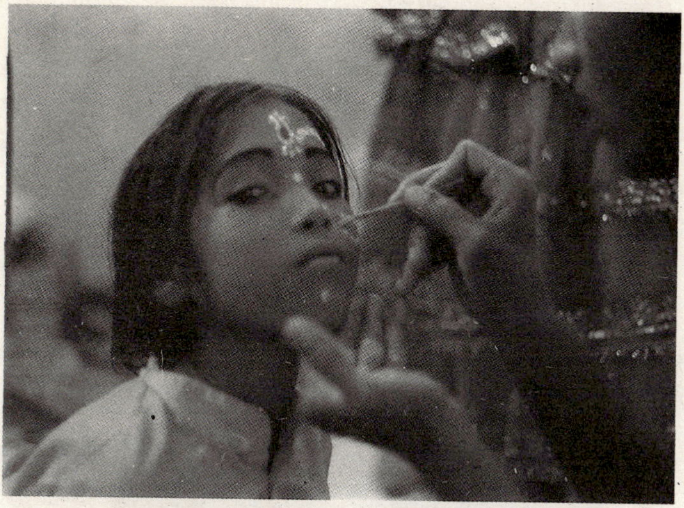

6. Applying facial decorations to a boy who will play a *gopī*

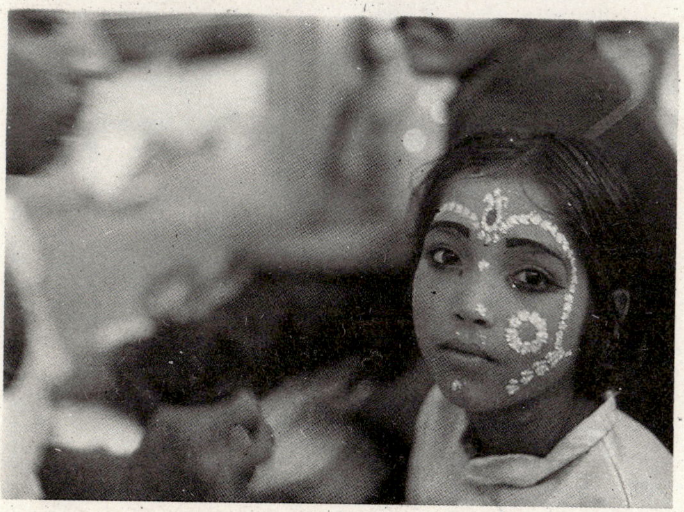

crown by rights signifies. Indeed, the "worship" of children precisely because of their innocence—a normalcy of disposition as yet undistorted by formal rules of conduct—is a general feature of Indian life. Wherever it is economically possible in India, the

7. *Svarūps* of Radha and Krishna

playful among us, the children, are encouraged to play; adults play through them. How much more then do they live through the *svarūps* of Radha and Krishna, whose whole vocation is to play the role of the God who plays.

The Pilgrim's Experience

Brindavan is a national pilgrimage center, and travelers come from all corners of India—great numbers from Bengal, some from beyond the border in Nepal, a trickle from the south, and now, especially with the establishment of a temple and school by the International Society for Krishna Consciousness, from the Western world as well. But insofar as one can say without exact figures, it seems the main catchment area includes all of Braj, and extends eastward a hundred miles or so into Uttar Pradesh, dips far to the south in Madhya Pradesh, and comprehends most of Rajasthan and a great deal of the Punjab.[11]

A typical group of pilgrims in the rainy season may come from a village somewhere beyond Jaipur in Rajasthan, fifty or sixty men and women of various ages who have chartered a rickety bus at an expense of some three thousand rupees for a week (about four hundred dollars). For some this is the first trip to Braj; others return as often as once a year. Brindavan will be their base as they tour Braj, and along with three or four thousand other pilgrims they will stay in the huge, ornately facaded guest house constructed by a wealthy merchant from Mirzapur as an act of piety at the beginning of the century. They will spend three days or so in Brindavan itself, and use the rest of the week to see the other principal sights of Braj—Krishna's birthplace in Mathura and the great Vaiṣṇav temple there; Gokul across the river, where he is supposed to have spent his early infancy; the nearby shrine to his brother Balarām (Dāū Jī, as he is called in Braj); and the other village reputed to have been his early home, Nandagaon, the village of his adoptive father Nanda.[12] They will not miss a trip to Radha's town, Barsana, and most certainly they will make a trip to the sacred mountain near the western perimeter of Braj, Govardhan. Perhaps they will even have time to circumambulate it, as pilgrims have done from time immemorial, and would always have done in the days when most came by foot. This year even the Taj Mahal in nearby Agra is on the schedule.

As they make their way up the road from Mathura to Brindavan, their bus removes them somewhat from the sounds and sights that surrounded pilgrims of earlier generations from their village. The bus is big enough to be intimidating: it clears the road itself, so they will no longer have the task and pleasure of threading their way through the huge herds of cows that clog the road, especially at milking time. There are several large homes for retired cows (*gośālās*) along the way. The most impressive goes by a name that gives a foretaste of what the pilgrims will experience in Brindavan: Hāsānand, named after one of its founders; it means literally "the fun of laughing." The bus may stop at a temple recently built by one of the wealthiest

8. Rajasthani pilgrim and his charge at the Mirzapur guest house

families of India in honor of Krishna as he is known in the *Bhagavad Gītā*—the heroic Krishna who is otherwise altogether absent from Braj. Other buildings to catch the pilgrims' eye will include a number of educational institutions. Again the names are significant—Prem Mahāvidyālay Polytechnic, for instance: Love Polytechnical Institute. Farther up the road comes a mammoth temple just being completed, with a marble facade designed to rival the Taj Mahal. It is dedicated to a certain Pāgal Bābā, or Crazy Saint, who lived in Brindavan until his death and earned his name from his proclivity for riding through the streets tossing money to the crowds. His temple is a sign that Brindavan is still growing, as, indeed, pilgrimage all over the non-Western world seems to be growing, taking advantage of

9. Pilgrims arriving in Brindavan

modern transportation.[13] The little temple to the welcoming elephant god Ganesh has also grown recently: a rude shrine has been expanded to a tidy brick monument. All this is evident from the bus windows, but the turbaned and veiled Rajasthanis inside will scarcely be able to hear the voice of the man who for years has sat in a hut alongside the road at the very outskirts of town announcing Brindavan's sacred perimeter to the visitor with the same gravel-voiced greeting: *Bansīvāle kī jay*, "Hail the One who plays the flute."

Once the bus finds the Mirzapur guest house, however, our pilgrims mix with others who have come in more traditional conveyances—rickshaws, horse carts, and camel-drawn vans; many, of course, have come by foot. Indeed, from here on everyone goes by foot, touching the holy dust of Braj the way one ought. It takes a little while to settle in, and the travelers may want to buy some cowdung cakes from the woman who vends them on the street and light up one of the mudcaked brick stoves to cook a simple meal before they venture out into the town. They are careful about their possessions: already they have heard that someone's briefcase was stolen the night before and a cabinet was found unlocked in the morning.

As evening approaches, they may well head for the most famous temple in town, that of Bānke Bihārī, Krishna the lithe playboy. It is in the center of town, and if they have arrived on *tīj*, the third day of the month of *śrāvaṇ* and traditionally the day on which swings are suspended from trees all over north India for the beloved swinging season that lasts a fortnight, they are in for an experience they will not forget. For Krishna and Radha swing, too; and at Bānke Bihārī's temple the swing stretches all the way from one side of the inner courtyard to the other and is made entirely of purest silver and gold. As they get close, their movements are no longer their own. Slowly, sweating, bubbling with excitement, the crowd sweeps them up the lane toward the temple. Its towers loom ahead. The police keep total confusion at bay by directing traffic one way into the temple, one way out, but there are knots of people from the "out" line struggling against the current to retrieve shoes they left outside the temple on their way in. As the crowd crosses the threshold its mood is increasingly jubilant, and as people pour into the sanctum itself and six massive peppermint-twisted pillars of gold and silver suddenly flash out from behind the dark and musty walls of the vestibule they raise a great shout. It rings in waves through the swirling throng and each word bears an accent: *Bānke Bihārī Lāl kī jay*, "Hail our dear lithe playboy!"

It is the green season, when the rains have brought the earth to life, and the golden *gopīs* who flank the central image of Krishna on its monumental swing are all decked in green, as is

10. Swinging in *śrāvaṇ*

he. The priests, dressed in flashy velvet costumes of all colors or stripped down to sweaty undershirts, flash curtains back and forth in front of the central image in a huge free-form peek-a-boo show, and every time the image reappears there are great cheers from the worshipers. Coins rain in the direction of the swing, but Bānke Bihārī is shielded by a little net, and the priests reciprocate these gifts with *prasād* in the form of perfumed water, which they spray over the unruly mass with great silver syringes. The scene has all the decorum of a homecoming rally for a victorious football team, and the pilgrims know immediately that they are in the right place. Here in Braj no one stands on formality: this is the town where Krishna sports and enjoys himself.

This is only one of Brindavan's moods, and if the pilgrim has the time and energy to visit a few other temples he or she will sample others. The pilgrim with some experience might expect, for instance, that things will be more serene in the great temple of Rādhā Vallabh, where the graceful and charming Radha is understood to be supreme over Krishna, but there is as much confusion there as at Bānke Bihārī's temple because there are no police directing traffic. People enter and leave by the same doors, and there is a constant tug of war around them. Someone is pushed out of the line of vision after having waited a long time for the curtain to be drawn and the image of Krishna revealed, and it is too much for him. He begins swinging his fists, right there in the temple of the community that is explicitly dedicated to celebrating the sweet and constant love represented in the figure of Radha.[14] It is clear that most of the people here tonight are not from Braj, because one hears the cry go up, *Rādhā Vallabh Bhagavān kī jay*: "Hail God, Radha's Joy." Brindavan sentiment would never allow this; Krishna came here precisely in order to get away from people calling him God. He would rather people call him "dear" or "sweetheart."

If the pilgrim walks on to the temple of Rādhā Ramaṇ, which is a little distance away, he or she will experience a much quieter celebration of *śrāvaṇ*. Here the presiding *gosvāmī* gently rocks the great swing of antique, filagreed silver back and forth, as pilgrims come and go lighting little lamps and bowing their heads at the altar. In the back of the temple, opposite the image, hands fly on the drums and an old Bengali man sings songs for the swinging season; some devotees quietly circumambulate the *tulsī* trees in the corners of the courtyard, others prostrate themselves fully on the floor and wait long to rise. The swinging season suggests wild freedom and delight, a swing ride in the sky while luscious clouds gather to relieve the draught and heat of May and June, but it also suggests rhythm and balance as the swing passes back and forth over the ground. This is the season of homecoming, the one time in the year when a woman can leave the duties and oppressions of the family into which she

11. The silver swing of Rādhā Ramaṇ, set in motion by one of the Caitanyite *gosvāmīs*

has been married and return to the sympathies of brothers and sisters and parents. It is also a lover's homecoming: the traveler must return for the rains, since it is no longer easy to move about. Old loves, family loves, will be relived on the swing, whether raucously as in Bānke Bihārī's temple or meditatively as in Rādhā Ramaṇ's.

It is an exhausting first night for our pilgrims, but an exciting one, and they have had a chance to catch a glimpse of the *rās līlā*, too. Some of our company stopped at a street corner to watch a simple troupe portray Krishna as a thief of butter. Others found their way into the crowd at the Śrī Caitanya Prem Sansthān in time to see the *līlā* that specifically depicts the joy everyone feels when Radha returns to her family for *śrāvaṇ*.[15] She rocks back and forth with her brother Śrīdāmā on a swing whose ropes are decorated from top to bottom with the greenery of the season. Krishna, represented as if he were her newlywed husband and jealous at her departure, disguises himself as a girl so that he can join her unnoticed in her native Barsana: he swings with her, too. In the end, then, the *līlā* presents both *śrāvaṇ* reunions, the reuniting of both families and lovers. Tired but satisfied, our pilgrims return to the guest house to join the others who are packed in that night, perhaps as many as five thousand. The vast courtyard is clogged with sleeping bodies, and many sleep sitting up.

When morning comes and the group gathers again, a young father tells with some pride that despite yesterday's crowds and confusion his little son has already been pestering him to know what *darśans* they will see today. The time has come to negotiate a more systematic exposure to Brindavan, and local Brahmin guides called *paṇḍās* or simply Brajbāsīs, "Braj people," are on hand to make it possible. They are a crusty lot, very insistent about what the pilgrims should and shouldn't do in the course of their stay, but pilgrims expect this peremptory attitude: *paṇḍās* everywhere are the same. Like the renowned *paṇḍās* of Benares, many of these Brindavan *paṇḍās* have ledgers in which they and their ancestors have recorded the visits of generations of pilgrims, and by virtue of which each *paṇḍā* claims responsibility for the families of a certain area and caste. They know pilgrims' genealogies with an accuracy that makes the newcomers feel at least known in a strange place, if not positively preempted. But in Brindavan there is a tendency for *paṇḍās* to be freer and more relaxed than their counterparts elsewhere, even in other Braj sites such as Gokul and Dāūjī across the river; and traditional divisions are less rigidly observed. So one finds *paṇḍās* of all sorts, from toothless veterans to slick young men,

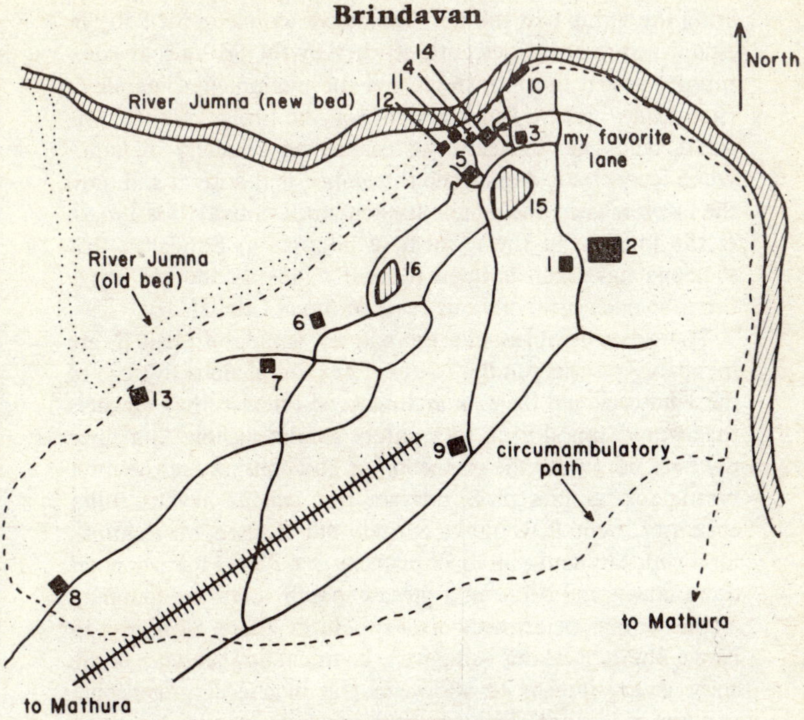

Temples

1. Govindadev
2. Rañg Jī
3. Rādhā Ramaṇ
4. Brindāvanbihārī
5. Shāh Jī
6. Rādhā Vallabh
7. Bānke Bihārī
8. International Society for Krishna Consciousness

Other Sites

9. Mirzapur Guest House
10. Keśī Ghāṭ
11. Cīr Ghāṭ
12. Kāliya Ghāṭ (new site)
13. Kāliya Ghāṭ (old site)
14. Śrī Caitanya Prem Sansthān
15. Nidhi Ban (Hari Dās's grove)
16. Sevā Kuñj (grove of the *rās*)

negotiating with groups of all sizes, arranging everything from a personal tour for an urban, middle class family of three or four, to a traditional round for a group of fifty peasants like ours.[16]

Routes vary with individual *paṇḍās*, but the general direction is set by the fact that every pilgrim wants to go to the Jumna in the morning to bathe. From the Mirzapur guest house this will bring the group past the tall, impressive temple of Śrī Rañg Jī, established in the nineteenth century by the Śrī Vaiṣṇav community rooted in south India, and the monumental temple of Govindadev, where Rūp Gosvāmī was the first priest. The presiding deity, Govindadev, was carried off to safety in Jaipur when iconoclastic Auraugzeb threatened to destroy it and until the last few years the temple has remained unused. It is a mark of the increase in the number of pilgrims to Brindavan that someone has taken it upon himself to install another image there, so once again one can have *darśan* at Govindadev.

These two temples, like the courtly temple of Shāh Jī, are inevitably on the *paṇḍās*' routes. They are obvious features of the landscape and have an architectural interest; they are sites that would appeal even to a purely secular visitor. And since they are not under the protection of *gosvāmīs*, as are the most prestigious temples of Brindavan, the *paṇḍās* have a fuller authority there. It would be entirely out of place, for example, for a *paṇḍā* to herd a group of pilgrims into Rādhā Ramaṇ, quiet them down, and bark out a precast speech about the founding of the temple. Sentiments are too delicate there. Similarly, in Bānke Bihārī or Rādhā Vallabh the commanding presence of the deity is too intense to allow for the practiced, professional remarks of a *paṇḍā*. Though much of what a *paṇḍā* says has to do with Brindavan's specific environment as Krishna's playground, there is nothing about the *paṇḍā*'s craft that is peculiar to Brindavan. Every pilgrimage place in India has its *paṇḍās*. And that debases them in the eyes of the old *gosvāmī* families, whose service is to Krishna and Radha in the special and self-revealed forms they have taken here. *Gosvāmīs* look upon themselves as hereditary servants; by virtue of the prestige of the images they attend, they have little need to bargain for their livelihood. The *paṇḍā*'s lot is different. He is a broker, and though his family may have lived in Braj long before some of the *gosvāmīs* arrived five hundred years ago, his position is distinctly lower.[17] No one comes to him to be initiated into the following of a particular community; no theological tradition finds its center with him, as it does in the various *gosvāmī* lineages. He is a merchant of the sacred, a guide, and he demands his price.

All this comes clear when the *paṇḍās* guide their groups into the temple popularly called that of Nanda Bābā, Krishna's father. It is so named because the *paṇḍās* who run it claim that on this site Nanda established his house in Brindavan, but there is no ancient tradition to support this claim, and the only people who visit the site are those that the *paṇḍās* bring. The more official name of the place and that of its central image, Brindāvanbihārī, suggests something else. The title "Bihārī," of course, recalls that of the greatest temple in the city: the intent seems to be to borrow some of its glory. And the qualifier "Brindāvan" is meant to imply that the temple is the only one in the city under the direct sponsorship of the municipal government. Actually it is not: it was built in the early eighteenth century by King Jai Singh of Jaipur to house his private divinity, Nṛtya Gopāl, and is now owned by the government of Rajasthan. But the pilgrims will never know. Here the *paṇḍās* array themselves under an imagined umbrella of state and plead their common cause, attempting to distinguish themselves not negatively but positively from the *gosvāmīs*.

The first thing pilgrims are told when they enter—after their *paṇḍās* crowd them together on the floor to make sure they get the full effect of the *darśan* when it becomes visible—is that in this temple there will be no throwing of coins at the images. In an effort to buttress their status, the *paṇḍās* make it clear that they look down on such enthusiastic indiscretions, even if the *gosvāmīs* allow them. The weary young *paṇḍā* priest who is resident in charge of the temple goes on to say that here pilgrims can be sure their offerings will count for something—not, by implication, get lost in the *gosvāmīs*' pockets. And the young man who flanks the shrine, sitting just opposite, will make it all possible. He holds a huge account book.

First, however, the man in charge pulls back the frayed curtain and reveals the images. At the center is an image patterned after Bānke Bihārī, and in honor of the place this is supposed to commemorate, we see at his side images of his adoptive father and mother, Nanda and Yaśodā. On the other side a dark Krishna, a child this time, peers over a unique plaster representation of the potful of butter he was always finding his way into; and on the back wall of the shrine, equally unprecedented among temple images, are mammoth representations of Nanda and Yaśodā again, great parental figures surveying the whole affair.

This is no accidentally contrived tableau. As the presiding *paṇḍā* begins his unvarying speech, one senses what force he hopes their unblinking glance will convey. He explains in a casual, matter-of-fact way that whatever gifts one presents at this temple will insure that the donors' desires will be fulfilled, whatever they be: for money, for entertainment, for the grant-

12. Sanctum in the temple of Brindāvanbihārī attended by priest and accountant

ing of a son. He goes on to say that they will be systematically distributed and systematically looked after. An amount of thirteen and a half rupees, an apparently arbitrary number, but one he stresses repeatedly as if it were the one fixed and honest price in an unruly bazaar, will provide for four kinds of pious work in Brindavan over the course of the year — the feeding of cows, the provision of food for ascetics and widows who live here, the support of Brindavan's Brahmins, and the feeding of images on great festival days like Krishna's birthday and the day he first led out the cows, days on which these pilgrims are not likely to be present themselves. It is a system of offering that resembles a trust fund, and the listeners are assured that it will be properly administered, like a bank account. They are meant to feel that unlike the usual temple gift, it goes beyond piety to philanthropy. Hence to provide a little fodder for a home for cows is dignified by the title *godān*, the gift of a cow, as if one were providing that gift to an officiating Brahmin after one of the great sacrifices described in India's oldest scriptures. The *paṇḍā* also places heavy emphasis on filial piety. Not only will the name and provenance of the donor be recorded in the great book when he makes his gift; the *paṇḍā* will insist upon knowing the names of his parents, in whose name and memory he will be making his contribution. Nanda and Yaśodā may well look on with satisfaction at this act of devotion not only to their son but to parenthood in general.

The pilgrims are not apt to respond with the spontaneous fervor that filled Bānke Bihārī's court the night before, and further urgings are sometimes required. The officiant assures his silent listeners it would be a great sin to spend so much money on one's own trip to Brindavan without leaving something behind for the welfare of the place; if they have faith they will surely give. And, indeed, someone soon pledges his thirteen and a half rupees. The *paṇḍā* in charge of this particular donor echoes the pledge with all the ceremony of an auctioneer, and litanizes his name and his village's and his parents' (whether living or dead) before God and the company. It is hoped that other bids will be stimulated, for it is no mystery to anyone that the Brahmins who will be fed with twenty-five percent of the proceeds are the *paṇḍā*s themselves; and according to some accounts the actual figure is much greater, as high as eighty percent. When the formal response has died down and people rise to go, some woman is sure to come over to the men's side and whisper a word to her husband, hiding her face modestly in the corner of her sari. He smiles and relents and gives his permission for her to add a rupee or two to the kitty. It may not be the official amount, but it will be accepted and duly recorded. She will get her receipt and both she and her husband will acquire the merit that belongs to those who revere their elders and keep holy places holy.

If the group has not already done so, it moves on to the banks of the Jumna at this point. Three or four spots along the river are hallowed by incidents in Krishna's life story. From earliest childhood aunts and grandmothers have told these Rajasthanis how as a little boy Krishna was playing ball with his friends by the banks of the Jumna when their ball bounced into the water at the swirling hole where the dread black snake Kāliya lived. Or perhaps they know the version that says the evil king of Mathura specifically required Krishna to retrieve a thousand lotuses from the fearful place. Whatever the story, the outcome was the same. With complete unconcern Krishna climbed into the branches of the *kadamb* tree that overhangs the pool and jumped in to do battle with the great coiled monster, until he emerged victorious on the surface of the turbulent water. As a sign both of his conquest and of the serpent's relief that the miraculous boy would not destroy him altogether—only banish him to make the waters safe—he danced with abandon on the snake's several plumed heads. "And this is where it happened," the *paṇḍā* concludes, gesturing toward a fragrant green tree on the bank and to the backwater nearby, where a number of people are bathing. "Here is the *kadamb* and there is the hole."[18]

A few steps down the bank there is more to see—another *kadamb* tree, in fact. This one is the setting of a different tale. Here, the *paṇḍā* reports in a few simple sentences, is the place where in the month of *kārttik* (actually the *Bhāgavata Purāṇa* specifies the month of *mārgaśīrṣ* instead) the *gopīs* undertook their vow to the goddess Kātyāyanī. He refreshes the travelers' memories by recalling how every morning for a month they went to the river in the chill before dawn to bathe and ask the goddess to grant them Krishna as their husband. One day they were discovered in the course of their austerities by the figure who had inspired it all, and once he was on the scene piety turned to disaster. He gathered the garments they had left on the shore and climbed the *kadamb* once again, this time decorating its branches with his varicolored loot. Shivering in the river the girls demanded that he return their saris, but to no avail: as far as he could see these were just the extravagant flowerings of the *kadamb* itself. Finally he struck a bargain. If they would raise their hands above their heads and come out on the bank in full nakedness, he would be glad to throw their saris back down to them, and despite many protests they ultimately had no other course. Theologians like the writer of the *Bhāgavata Purāṇa* have justified our hero's naughtiness by insisting that the girls were immodest to bathe naked.[19] Another suggestion, more substantial, is that this is the test of nakedness that

13. Krishna in the *kadamb* tree at Cīr Ghāṭ, surrounded by pieces of cloth

every soul must endure if it is to come before the intimate presence of God.[20] But one rarely hears *paṇḍās* explore such points. Their simple aim is to connect the place with the story, and to assure their charges that they are retracing Krishna's steps.

At every spot there is something the pilgrims can do to solidify the connection and add their own contribution to the generations of faith that have kept the story alive, and they can do so here as well. This time it is not just a coin or rupee they can offer to an image: they, like Krishna himself, can hang bits of cloth from the branches of the tree. A Brahmin who claims that his family has supervised the spot for five hundred years[21] sits in its shade tending the recently modeled image of Krishna that rests in one of the crotches, and offers varicolored scraps of silk for sale at a rupee or two apiece. The buyers, who are almost always women, perform a memorial, but it is more than a memorial. Their ritual action recapitulates the *gopīs'* vow; they hope for Krishna's presence in their lives. Yet what they do has a much more general significance, as well, for it is an ancient practice all over India and beyond into the Himalayas to bind bits of cloth to trees to signify the hope that a wish be fulfilled. And here, as anywhere, the wish may be whatever is uppermost in the pilgrim's mind. It is entirely possible, in fact, that the pilgrim has undertaken the trip specifically so that this pious journey and the closer contact it brings with a sacred place will make his or her wish heard more clearly in the heavens. Perhaps some family problem needs solving, perhaps debt is unbearable, perhaps no son has been born.

The priest in charge has a way of tying all this back into the narratives of Krishna. He recalls that in another incident when clothes were stolen Krishna played the role not of the thief but of the savior. It is the story of Draupadī, wife of the five protagonists in the great Indian epic *Mahābhārata,* whose modesty they bargained away in a game of dice. As one of their wicked opponents tugged at the bottom of her sari—only fifteen feet of cloth hid her nakedness—she prayed to Krishna to help her in distress, and miraculously an infinite amount of material was added to the other end. As hard and fast as Duḥśāsan might pull, she remained completely clothed.[22] The priests and the *paṇḍās* assure the pilgrims that if they leave a bit of cloth for Krishna at this spot, they will never in their lives lack for garments. It is a simple fact, they say: it has never been falsified. Other wishes carry, by extension, the same hope of fulfillment.

It is noteworthy that two stories of stealing clothes, both of which involve Krishna and both of which bear the same title in Hindi, *cīr haran,* can be woven together in such a way as to provide a narrative bridge between the story that sanctifies the spot and the ritual practice it supports. Otherwise the story of

Draupadī, though everyone knows it, has no connection with the child Krishna of Braj. And indeed, it is only introduced as a convenience. In the realm of the *paṇḍā*, as distinct from that of the *gosvāmī* or *rāsdhārī*, it is entirely legitimate to mix the specific memories of Krishna in Braj with practices that would be at home in any place of pilgrimage in India.

Keśī Ghāṭ provides another example. This is the spot on the bank of the Jumna at which residents of Brindavan and pilgrims alike most often bathe. When the whole town was spread out along the banks of the river, there were many good accesses, called *ghāṭs* or steps; at that time the Jumna, flowing down from the north, turned abruptly east and wound around half the town. Now it has changed its course, however, and Keśī Ghāṭ is the best place to bathe. Here the current flows even in the dry season, for this is now the place where the Jumna first washes against the town as it comes from the north. As always, a story is associated with the place. Here it was that Krishna fought off the advances of the wild and demonic horse Keśī ("the hairy one") by thrusting his elbow in the animal's mouth until one jaw snapped from the other.[23] The Jumna is not even involved, yet the accidents of time have rendered this the principal bathing *ghāṭ* of Brindavan, and the river is worshiped here as nowhere else. Once again, however, the veneration expressed here is not entirely specific. Those who have lived in Brindavan for a long time or who are steeped in the mythology of Braj by some other means will have a sense for the Jumna's special associations with the magic of Krishna, but they along with everyone else worship it also as a river in the generic sense, a river that in principle comprehends all rivers. As the priest who sits at Keśī Ghāṭ leads pilgrims through the mantras they should say as they gather there, he puts into their mouths the names of the seven principal watercourses of India—the Jumna, the Ganges (who is thought of as the Jumna's sister, and with whom it joins downstream at Allahabad), and all the rest. This is reverence not only for a single great river but for water itself, which purifies as it flows and provides symbolic passage from the grinding difficulties of life on this shore to the peace one hopes to find beyond it.

As the pilgrims dip into the rushing, swollen, gray waters of the Jumna, they perform acts that would be appropriate in any river from the Ganges to the thousands of streams that are transformed by mantras into the Ganges for people in whatever corner of India they live.[24] There is the bath itself, a vigorous affair with much rubbing the body, and one, as Krishna reminded the *gopīs*, that should never be undertaken in full nakedness: a change of clothes should wait on the bank, at least enough to wear temporarily until one's others have dried. But it is a ritual occasion, as well. Bathers cup their hands so that if the water runs out one way it is an offering to the sun, if another way an offering to one's forebears, and if still another way an offering to the river itself. There is a great consciousness of misdeeds and the belief that the Jumna, particularly here at sacred Brindavan, can wash away their ill effects. This is accompanied by the familiar Indian sense that it is the ritual action itself, including the proper mantra (which Brahmins available on the spot can be paid to provide), that cleanses the deed; but in Brindavan there is a countervailing emphasis on faith as well, on the disposition of one's sentiments that amplifies these rites with an interior dimension they might not otherwise have.

It is a complex scene. Here some women from Uttar Pradesh—one knows by the way they wear their saris—offer incense to the Jumna, wedging the little burning sticks in the crevices between the stones. Just below, a man fills a bottle with water he will take with him, perhaps for use in worship here in Brindavan, or for a family altar far away. If the latter, the water will be dispensed as sparingly as gold, a drop at a time, when someone is sick or someone in the family dies. Another woman asks a priest for a glass so that she can drink this holy water: she downs two, even three cloudy glassfuls. (There are the usual stories about how, contrary to appearance, the waters of the Jumna are inordinately pure.) Still another woman, this one a widow, splashes Jumna water on the amulet she wears around her neck, adding purity to protection.

The people here are of all descriptions, and the *ghāṭ* is not narrowly sectarian. A shrine to Hanumān, established some two hundred years ago, draws a considerable number of worshipers.

14. Praying to Sūrya Nārāyaṇ, the sun, at Keśī Ghāṭ

Hanumān is associated with Krishna as the monkey servant of his earlier incarnation, Rām. But Śiva is present here, too, and with him a whole other side of Indian religiòn that is often reviled in Brindavan's official theologies; yet no attempt is made to reconcile the worship of his symbol, the *liṅga*, and his vehicle, the bull, with the rest of the scene. It simply fits, and one is almost as apt to hear people mumble "Har Har Mahādev," repeating the titles of Śiva, as to hear some reference to Krishna.

15. Washing the mouth in the Jumna at Keśī Ghāṭ

Rivers in India are not really subject to sectarian reduction, in part at least because they flow, and tie the entire sacred geography of India into a single whole.[25]

Brindavan among the Tīrthas

In following *paṇḍā* and pilgrim to Keśī Ghāṭ, we have come to Brindavan's most cosmopolitan corner, the part that least distin-

16. An offering of water to the *liṅga* of Śiva in his shrine at Keśī Ghāṭ

guishes it from other places of pilgrimage in India. The standard term for such places is *tīrtha*, which derives from the Sanskrit root meaning "to cross," and means a fording place. Broadly speaking, there are two sorts of *tīrtha*s, those established on mountains, where the crossing is from earth to heaven, and those established on rivers, where the two shores provide the basic metaphor and there is a transition of mediums, land to water. Keśī Ghāṭ is of the latter category, of course, but the other natural *tīrtha* in Braj is a mountain, and it is symbolically present here, too. A boulder from Mount Govardhan stands beside the carved marble feet that are said to represent the Jumna just beneath the bell at the central plaza opposite Keśī Ghāṭ; and in the shrine to the Jumna herself, a few steps closer to the river, the two objects of worship are once again a picture of the river personified and a stone brought from Govardhan. These two are

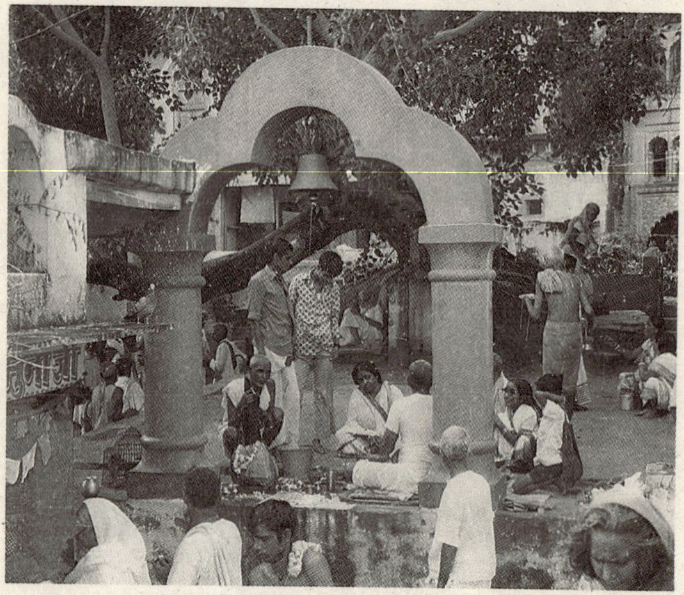

17. *Pīpal* tree, temple to the Jumna, and Brahmin priest officiating for pilgrims at Keśī Ghāṭ

the ancient common denominators of pilgrimage in Braj.[26] Instinctively the one has been brought into the other's presence, and taken together they suggest the entire class of *tīrtha*s throughout the subcontinent, pilgrimage in its totality.

If one wandered into Brindavan without much sense of its specific associations one would soon find one's way here. This happened in the case of two young men I met at Keśī Ghāṭ, who had only that morning arrived in Brindavan. They were from Delhi, and as urbanites were not part of Brindavan's normal flow of pilgrims. Although they lived less than a hundred miles from Brindavan, they knew very little about it—people in Delhi have given me the wildest answers when I ask them if they know where Brindavan is; many have heard of a garden by that name near the city of Mysore some thousand miles away, without realizing that it has a prototype near at hand.

This particular pair of young men had come to Brindavan on vacation from their menial office jobs. They had started out on a trip to Bombay that would ultimately end at the mountain shrine to Vaiṣṇo Devī, a Kashmiri site currently very popular in Delhi. Despite their ultimate destination, however, they felt uneasy about starting their trip in a secular vein, and two-thirds of the way to Bombay they turned back in order to begin their journey at a place of pilgrimage. They chose Brindavan: they knew enough to know that *śrāvaṇ* is the great month to come, but their motive was general indeed. One had had a dream that disturbed him, and which he felt bore in some unknown way on the possibilities for his marrying a young woman he had come to love. He wanted interpretation and advice, and was in search of some wise and holy man who could offer it. The priest beneath the bell at Keśī Ghāṭ bullied him into a conversation, and before long he had referred him and his friend to an ascetic who, he assured him, would satisfy his thirst for a guru. Threading their way through the alleys to an address written on a slip of paper, they found the sage at home: such men are sprinkled here and there throughout the town, as are a much greater number of ascetics, some with specific sectarian ties to Vaiṣṇavism and some without, who cluster in the various ashrams to which Brindavan plays host.

This was a thin, energetic man of sixty. Enthroned cross-legged on a simple bed, and attended by a pensive woman who cooked for him and a couple of well-fed devotees from Jodhpur who had brought tape recorders to preserve his spontaneous discourses, he immediately ascertained why the two young men had come. He pushed aside any hesitation the one with the dream felt in telling all, and proceeded to talk for an hour, placing the young man's particular concern in the context of the general necessity to wean oneself away from the desires that bind. It was the message of yoga, and yogic meditation was specifically recommended, even here in Brindavan, where yogic austerities are held in deep suspicion. By a process of increasingly concentrated and subtle awareness, he explained, one could penetrate through eight layers of reality to a level of perception in which all dualities are revealed as only apparent in nature. In the last analysis, even the great division between male and female, which permeates the world from its subtlest to grossest levels, disappears. But long before this awareness would overtake the perceptions of our young man, his meditations would have freed him from the desires and contradictory emotions generated by the love he thought he felt.[27]

My young friends avowed that they were much satisfied to have been taken so directly in hand; evidently the old man's insistent, doctrinaire manner satisfied their expectations of how authoritative advice is to be proferred. But they continued on to another teacher whose name had been given them, pursuing their personal odyssey, and had heard enough about the particular glories of Brindavan by then to have planned to see a *rās līlā*, as well.

Most who come to Brindavan have a much more specific sense of what awaits them than did these men, but their newfound master directed even them to make use of the atmosphere into which they had unwittingly wandered. They could best begin their yogic ascent, he said, by attending to the great mantra (it is so called: *mahāmantra*) that Caitanya spread abroad:

Hare Krishna Hare Krishna
Krishna Krishna Hare Hare
Hare Rām Hare Rām
Rām Rām Hare Hare.

These words, he insisted, were of value not primarily because they denote three names of Krishna (Krishna, Rām, and Hari) but because each of the syllables has a purificatory value. "Ha," for instance, carries the cleansing force of the wind. If they would return to Keśī Ghāṭ and join the loving company of the pundit who had sent them here, and taste the environment with enough sensitivity to pronounce the great mantra correctly just once, just for a second, their complexions would glow and they would be launched on the road to permanent transformation. Since this man's teaching had to do with interiority and refinement, he had nothing but contempt for the ceaseless repetitions of the great mantra on the part of the Western devotees of Krishna who had recently arrived in Brindavan. Imagine how you would feel, he said, if someone constantly shouted your name at you to get your attention. But to experience it once, fully, interiorly—that was a different matter, and something Brindavan makes possible to an unusual extent by attracting to itself people who are persuaded by the message of love.[28]

The members of the International Society for Krishna Consciousness, however, are not the group most responsible for filling air with the constant ring of the *mahāmantra*. That honor, a dubious one from our yogi's point of view, would have to go to the twelve hundred widows who chant the great mantra eight hours a day at an institution called Bhajan Āśram. Every day they come in from all corners of the town, wherever they have been able to find a tiny room for two rupees a month, to sit in long rows and sing the names of Krishna; every so often a lead singer varies the tune, but the point of the whole exercise is repetition. There are other assemblies in Brindavan where the *mahāmantra* is sung with joy and verve, but not here. An air of boredom and confinement pervades the hall. Eyes look up as strangers come in; there is little sense of community evident. The reason is that the motivation is largely economic. For eight hours of song, each woman is entitled to 250 grams of rice—sometimes there are lentils as well—and forty pice, enough money to buy a simple vegetable or a few chilis. There are officers to make sure that everyone sings the allotted time. Bhajan Āśram is sustained by contributions from the wealthy Marwari community that owns businesses all over India, and they see it not as a prison but as an organ of charity. They, after all, are responsible for the fact that Brindavan is filled with such auspicious sounds, not for the fact that—particularly in Bengal—a woman becomes an outcaste in her own home when her husband dies. Her presence is ominous in the absence of the man whose service provided her a place in society, and in an extremely poor society she is an economic drain as well.

Perhaps a quarter of the population of Brindavan is composed of widows, almost all of them Bengalis or Nepalis, and the great

18. Widows chanting the *mahāmantra* at Bhajan Āśram

majority near destitution. They have come to spend their last days—almost whole lives in the case of some of the younger widows, of whom there are quite a number among the Nepalis—sheltered at the feet of Krishna and Radha. It is not easy to praise their condition—the colorless, borderless white saris and absence of jewelry and shaven heads that spell widowhood—but here at least, far from Bengal, they are relieved of the burden of their own inauspiciousness. They join the ranks

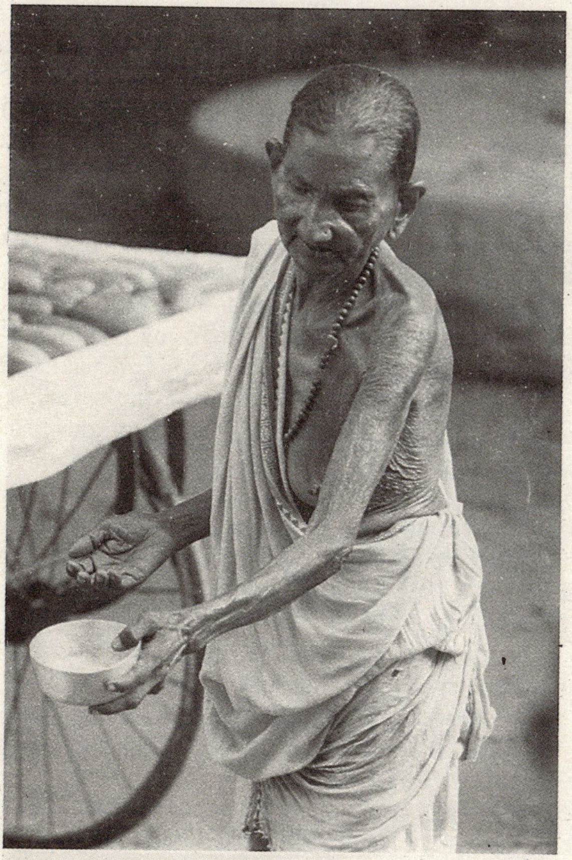

19. Widow begging

of all the *gopīs*. Some, the more wealthy, are provided for by some pension, and come by choice. Others come because here they can beg. Still others are not really widows at all; perhaps they have taken their children and fled a husband who beats his wife. Whatever the reason, they come for refuge, and Brindavan offers it because its holiness absorbs the inauspicious and because its central myth, the *rās*, expresses the vision of an alternative to society rather than a validation of the ways of the world. The *gopīs* who come to Krishna leave house and home, pulled into the forest against their will by the call of his flute. These women, often at least equally unwilling, swell their number—superannuated *gopīs*, many of them, and bent with age. And many do find solace in giving up their lives to Queen Radha's will.

There are a substantial number of other Bengalis who follow Caitanya's exhortation and come to Brindavan, and for them too Brindavan is no ordinary place of pilgrimage. More than any other group, Bengalis are known for the refinement of their religious sentiment (*bhāv*.) For instance, a relatively high proportion of Bengalis, probably more than any group other than Brajbāsīs themselves, undertake the circumambulation of the holy precinct, a walk that takes them through the sandy groves surrounding the town, and provides them with the chance to taste firsthand the sleepy, luxuriant wooded atmosphere that still prevails moments after one has left the pavement and bricks. For Bengali villagers, by far the majority, this rural environment has a natural charm, but residents of crowded, sophisticated Calcutta find it, if anything, more appealing. It was an urban man, after all, a Rajput prince named Nāgarī Dās, who is renowned for having left the world behind to come here and write poetry in which he, like many others, praised each cow and bird, each mole and ant that is privileged to inhabit the trees and thickets of Brindavan, where Krishna and his women dance eternally.[29] Even inside the town itself the unspoiled forest remains part of the sacred landscape—the tree where Krishna especially loved to flute; the grove where he liked to retire with Radha; the shady area where Hari Dās, the saint to whom Bānke Bihārī first revealed himself, sang so many of his songs.

If enjoyment of this rustic atmosphere, particularly as communicated in the plays, by rich merchant families from Calcutta and Bombay smacks of Marie Antoinette in her peasant enclave safe inside the grounds of Versailles, one must remember that the lack of pretension in Brindavan is not so calculated for all. Part of the special attraction of Brindavan for everyone who comes is the air of simplicity that surrounds it, and the rough habits for which Brajbāsīs are legendary help keep it from being overly refined and idealized. Peasants from Rajasthan and Madhya Pradesh may well feel at home in the presence of a god who is tired of the life of the heavenly court. Pilgrims often say that they particularly like the butter-thief *līlā* because it is so natural and so much a part of the particular atmosphere of this place; and when a well-off farmer from near Indore says he comes to Brindavan to forget the rest of the world, he does not mean that he substitutes city sophistication for country ways. Rather, this is a country-city, a place where idealized rural values like simplicity and love are enshrined: that is what makes him forget the rest of the world, and he comes especially to taste it.

In Brindavan, then, there is a special tension between rusticity and refinement. On the one hand the open, artless, even crass behavior of Brajbāsīs provides the standard. Krishna came here because he knew he would not be inundated with etiquette, and Brajbāsīs count themselves lucky that they have been included among the people with whom Krishna came to dwell. They don't have to impress anybody. On the other hand, Krishna was a connoisseur of love, a *rasik*, able to taste its thousand moods, and there is in Brindavan a healthy respect for the fact that it takes some refinement and attention to work one's way back to the simple, unclouded emotions of which the *gopīs* were so naturally capable. One must sit in groups where the songs of Krishna are sung, one must recite the *mahāmantra*, one must imbibe the plays, one must have *darśan* so often and in so many seasons and moods that one knows Krishna and Radha in their every guise, and the sight of them comes as second nature. Then and only then does one stand a chance of seeing them simply present in the groves and rivers of Brindavan, as they eternally are. The *gosvāmīs* of Brindavan, the *rāsdhārīs*, even the jolly and raucous priest at Keśī Ghāṭ see it as their purpose to be of assistance in this refinement. Whether by the arrangement of perfect *darśans*, the presentation of vivid plays and tableaus, or the repetition of mantras, the object is to transport the worshiper behind the encrustation's of this world to a state of loving simplicity.

In that, Brindavan contrasts with the other *tīrtha*s of India. It is a forest in essence, not a city. The perennial urbanity of Benares endears it to Śiva, but Krishna escapes to the forest. Poised timeless on Śiva's trident, Benares is the archetypal *tīrtha*: one goes there to die, to be ferried to a transcendent level, to be released. It is not so in Brindavan. One comes here not to die but to live (even the widows—particularly the widows), to thrive in the perennial presence of Krishna and Radha, and according to the dominant sentiments of Brindavan, that is not a state beyond the world but a secret hidden in its midst. It waits just beneath the shouts of civilization, in the forests of childhood that nourished it.

This is clearly expressed in the mythology of the place. One story tells how the principal *tīrtha*s of India held a conference at the court of the king of all *tīrtha*s, Allahabad or Prayāg, where the Ganges and the Jumna and an invisible spiritual river called the Sarasvatī flow together. Brindavan, however, was not in attendance; perhaps the story is intended to explain the historical fact that although Mathura is included in the ancient documents that list India's principal places of pilgrimage, there is no mention of Brindavan, whose existence as a city goes back only five hundred years.[30] Why was Brindavan absent? It simply didn't belong in their company. Forests have no concourse with cities, and Brindavan, the forest *tīrtha*, does not speak the same language as the others. What would it have had in common with the supercilious boasts of Benares and Mathura and Prayāg? Its claim to fame rests on its humility. It was for that reason that Krishna chose it as his home.[31]

Indeed, the other *tīrtha*s would have found Brindavan an eccentric colleague, for the figure who makes his home in Brindavan is more than a little crazy himself. The *rās līlās* ask us time and again to imagine a potentate who would give up all the comforts and adulations appropriate to his regal station and all the culture of his court to make common cause with a bunch of rowdy herder boys; who would trade in the finest chords the heavenly musicians can produce for the ring of a simple country flute; who would rather endure the insults and curses of irate village women than enjoy the caresses and flatteries of heaven's perfumed goddesses. What kind of a god is it, they ask, who would trade in the glories of lordship in Vaikuṇṭha, the city of heavenly order, for a glass of bitter, watery buttermilk left over after the butter is churned out of curd—and even that administered with laughs and taunts? There can only be one answer: this god is crazy.

But that is the testament of Brindavan. Its mythology, if not always its reality,[32] designates it as a place where every advantage of hierarchy is sacrificed to the joys of intimacy, where insults taste better than the most extravagant praise because they are offered so unselfconsciously. There is, after all, an inner logic in the fact that Krishna was expelled from urban Mathura in the first moments of his life in this world.

For the person who can forget the world's concerns, its questions of status and right and wrong, Brindavan is a haven of blessing. It offers a kind of sanity unrecognizable as such elsewhere in the universe, the unreserved sanity of love. But for those who cannot forget such things, it is an anomaly and a threat. Brindavan would not have been welcome in the assembly of *tīrtha*s even if it had chosen to come. One and all, they facilitate a crossing, an orderly transition across the sea of life's confusion, from this shore to what lies beyond. Brindavan is not like that; it is a *tīrtha* of a different sort. As a song often sung in the *rās līlā* says, its streets swirl with the floods of love: no order there. And once the unwary traveler is caught in the tide, there is no hope of escape. Safe passage is hardly what one expects at Brindavan. One comes not to cross but to drown, to drown in love's uncharted sea, and to find in that drowning a tranquillity unknown on dry land.

CHAPTER II

The Birth of Krishna

Introduction

IT IS THE STORY of a wondrous birth. Prophets had long foretold it, an evil king rallied all his resources to prevent it, and when the child was born all heaven graced the humblest setting earth had to offer. One would suppose that the prophets were Hebrew, but they might well have been Hindu. Nor need the king have been Herod; he could as well have been a despicable tyrant called Kans. And the child might be Jesus, but might also be Krishna.

These are just the broadest contours; a myriad of details are shared as well. In both cases a star portends the birth; in both cases the crucial hour comes in the middle of the night as the evil potentate sleeps; in both cases the realm is bathed in the blood of innocent infants once the king awakes, but in Braj as in Israel the parents of the divine babe have been forewarned and spirit away their tiny charge to a place that lies safely beyond reach of the despot's wrath. Both births take place at a time when it seems the fortunes of earth can sink no lower, and in both cases this extemity is symbolized by the fact that the ruler of God's chosen people is a half-breed imposter.

Herod the Great, who had usurped the throne of Hasmonean Jerusalem, was regarded by the orthodox as only half a Jew because of his Idumean origins. Similarly Kan's claim to the ancient and holy city of Mathura was only half justified by birth; for though his mother was the queen, he was fathered by a demon who deceived her by assuming the appearance of her true husband, and raped her. Like Herod, his acts confirmed his origins. Kans was patently cruel, and he introduced changes in the religious life of the realm that were hateful to the populace, repugnant to their tradition. Although Herod erected a magnificent temple, he also countenanced the introduction of a number of strictly Roman practices in and around his capital. Kans went further, not merely disestablishing but banning the worship of Viṣṇu in favor of Śiva, Viṣṇu's chief male rival to hegemony over the Hindu pantheon, and at least on the surface a far more threatening personality. Worse than that, Kans, like Herod, was a man of great pride—a pride so overweening that he understood his own person and rule to be everything the scriptures had ever foretold. Yet for all his bravado and apparent strength, Kans was as inwardly insecure as the Gospel of Matthew portrays Herod to have been. And his point of vulnerability is a child. When Herod hears that messengers from the East have come to pay tribute to a remarkable baby to be born in his realm, he immediately interprets the event as a threat to his own throne. The annunciation to Kans is at once more interior and more ominous. It comes in the form of a voice from heaven, and it foretells, quite specifically, his own death. And the one to bring about that downfall, of course, is Krishna.

As the time of his birth draws near, he is announced again, as it were, in the form of an older child, much in the same way that John the Baptist heralded Jesus. All the gospels work this theme into their accounting of Jesus' mature career, starting with his baptism, but Luke goes further, telling the story of how

Mary went to John's mother Elizabeth with the news of her pregnancy, and Elizabeth's baby leapt in the womb at the tidings. For centuries afterward the two infants were portrayed in Christian art as if they were brothers, in numerous paintings such as Leonardo's "Virgin of the Rocks" and "Virgin and Child with St. Anne and the Infant St. John." John amplifies the holy family by his presence. Similarly, Krishna's way is prepared by his brother Balarām, and Vaiṣṇav sculpture has offered its version of this amplified holy family, mother and father and two infant boys.[1]

The story is this. Balarām and Krishna are the seventh and eighth sons of Devakī, the sister of Kans. By the time Balarām is to be born, the evil king has already murdered six of Devakī's offspring. He is playing it safe: a voice from heaven has told him that the eighth will be his death. Vasudev, father of the as yet unborn Krishna, senses that things can only go from bad to worse for his family, and takes the precaution of sending another of his wives, Rohiṇī, to Gokul, a cowherding settlement located in the forest and grazing land across the river.[2] There is no question of sending Devakī herself, since she and Vasudev have long ago been clapped in the royal dungeon by Kans. Rohiṇī, however, can go, and once in Gokul she is taken in by Nanda, a dear friend of Vasudev. There she is safe from Kans, whose hegemony extends only along the right bank of the Jumna; and her safety becomes the basis and token of other safeties to come.

As the time for a seventh pregnancy draws near, earth herself cries out to Viṣṇu at the weight of the burden of injustice that the reign of Kans places upon her, and the great God responds with a timely intervention. According to the story as told in the *Viṣṇu* and *Bhāgavata Purānas*, he removes one white hair from the head of the great snake that symbolizes his primordial energy, and one black one from his own. The latter he holds in readiness: it will become Krishna, whose very name means "black." With the former he penetrates the womb of Devakī, heralding a miraculous if not altogether virgin birth: the white Balarām. In a second act of mercy he transfers the fetus out of the womb of Devakī and across the river to that of Rohiṇī. Back in the jail of Mathura, this appears as a simple miscarriage, and no one is the wiser.

All this lays the groundwork for the impending birth of Krishna. The escape route will be the same, but this time the suspense is far greater, for the journey to safety does not begin until the last minute. Krishna is conceived, and Kans keeps anxious watch over the pregnancy. As the time for delivery draws near, the prison guard is doubled and vicious animals from the royal menagerie—lions and dogs—join the palace guard. But at the eleventh hour a divine sleep descends upon the whole compound, creating a magical space within which the birth can safely take place—swaddling clothes of cosmic dimensions. Krishna is born in his majestic four-armed form, and all the gods rain blessings, but the only mortal awake to watch the spectacle, Vasudev, is awestruck and terrified. He begs the Lord to assume a more accustomed appearance. In a flash the blinding light of divinity is blackened: Krishna is a mere infant now, and Vasudev strikes out in the dead of night past the dozing guards to remove his imperiled son from danger. He lifts him high above his head and somehow manages to ford the river, even though it is swollen to overflowing with monsoon rains and made almost black by the eroded soil it carries along. Some accounts say he is able to make the impossible crossing because the touch of the infant's foot calms the water; indeed the river had risen to spate only in its desire to experience that touch. Others hold the spirit of Balarām responsible, for Krishna and his father are protected as they go by a great snake; that same serpentine energy that was the source of Balarām accompanies Krishna. One thinks of the miraculous fording of the Red Sea—a major element of Hebrew lore long before Jesus was carried across—and of Moses, whose own birth, initially imperiled, was made safe by a water crossing.

Vasudev's destination is, once again, Gokul and the household of Nanda. There Nanda's wife, Yaśodā, has just given birth to a girl, and Vasudev exchanges the infants.[3] That done, he can return to his cell in Mathura, secure in the knowledge that Krishna will have a chance to escape the wrath of the king, whatever may happen to the poor girl who is to take his place.

Once he departs, the news goes out that a son has been born, and Yaśodā, who has been enveloped in the same magical blanket of sleep that has descended over Mathura, has no inkling that the son is not her own.

Nor, once the plot resumes, does Nanda. He too forgets the midnight incident and returns to his simple duties as head of the cowherds' encampment, though as the centuries have passed his status has risen. Just as in the course of time *vraja*, the old word for a nomadic settlement, has come to be Braj, a fixed and nonnomadic cowherd realm, so Nanda and Yaśodā have gone from being leaders of a wandering tribe to sedentary, though still rustic, king and queen. Thus Krishna's royal identity will be hidden as he begins life in Braj, much as that of Jesus was disguised by the stables of Bethlehem and the carpenters' stalls of Nazareth. And those who celebrate the birth itself will be simple cowherd folk. They form a wonderstruck audience as all the gods of the Hindu pantheon fly to Gokul on their celestial vehicles and the heavenly musicians rain down songs of praise and torrents of flowers, just as Bethlehem's shepherds were startled by the angels' glorias.

This array of similarities between the nativity stories of Jesus and Krishna intrigued some of the British missionaries in India who discovered them, but it rankled the sensitivities of others. By the end of the nineteenth century, the issue had aroused enough heat to burn its way into the sober pages of the *Journal of the Royal Asiatic Society*, the greatest scholarly forum for Indological studies in its day. The debate was introduced by George Grierson, the most eminent vernacular linguist of the period. Grierson had long objected to what he considered the facile and stupid analogy implied by Britishers when they characterized the triadic formula relating three great gods of the Indian pantheon, Viṣṇu, Brahmā, and Śiva, as "the Indian Trinity."[4] Alas, one still hears this analogy today. As far as Grierson could see, the only thing the two triads had in common was the number three. But he was impressed with the common elements in Vaiṣṇav devotional religion and Christianity as he knew it: an emphasis on the efficacy of faith per se, a reliance on the power of the name of God, and the sharing of a ritual meal. And of course Grierson was struck—though, to be fair, not overawed—by the parallels between the nativities of Jesus and Krishna.[5] His was not yet a generation that could see these as two examples of a much larger class that emerge without any apparent relation in various cultures, for reasons common to all. That would have to wait for the folklorists and psychologists of the following generation, who were much less deeply disturbed by debates like these.[6]

In an argument too involved to repeat in full, Grierson proposed that one story was in fact derived from the other. Not surprisingly, Christ came first, Krishna second. As for the general similarities between the Vaiṣṇavite piety of north India and its Christian cousin, Grierson emphasized the fact that the major Vaiṣṇav communities of north India trace their ancestry (rightly or wrongly, we might add) to the south. And the south, he recalled, had been the home of a Christian community from the early centuries A.D. That was the well, he proposed, from which these Vaiṣṇavs had drunk, knowingly or not, and the hidden stimulus for the waves of devotional piety that had swept into north India. The theology of this early Christian settlement is not known, but Grierson supposed it must have been Nestorian, and that encouraged him to see in Vaiṣṇavism a truer version of the Trinity he had so rightly discounted before. This time, however, it was a Nestorian Trinity—Father, Son, and Virgin Mary—that he saw replicated in three aspects of Vaiṣṇav teaching. These he trinitized as: "Supreme Deity, His incarnation, and His *Śakti*, or energic power."[7] And then, in a vivid stroke of creativity, he suggested that buried in the great *Mahābhārata* was a remembrance of an overland encounter between Indians and Nestorians. For him the journey it described to a White Island, or White Continent as he called it, where the inhabitants were white-skinned and worshiped a single resplendent God, could only have terminated in one of the Nestorian cities of the Near East.[8]

Grierson's contemporary and colleague, James Kennedy, also a contributor to the *Journal*, went a few steps further. He rigidly separated the wily adult Krishna who became king of Dvaraka, far to the west of India, from the charming child who was reared in the environs of Mathura, holding the former to be indigenous to India and the latter imported. He extended Grierson's thesis by proposing that it had been the Gujars that brought the religion of the child Kṛishna to India, herdspeople who had wandered in Central Asia and entered India between the time of Christ and the sixth century A.D. or so; and they, in turn, had borrowed from the Nestorians. Thus India had become heir, "however imperfectly," to "the divinity of childhood . . . an idea which the world owes to Christianity." [9] Kennedy went on to assert that details of the narrative of Krishna's birth were necessitated by the Gujars' desire to accommodate the Gospel stories to their own narratives: Balarām, for instance, had to be Krishna's foster brother—"for the occasion," as Kennedy pointedly notes—because John the Baptist was born to Elizabeth rather than to Mary.[10] He did not consider why this detail added to the cogency of the tale in its own terms.

For all the ingenuity and conviction in such constructions, there were severe problems, and another contributor to the *Journal*, Arthur Berriedale Keith, was quick to point to a number of them.[11] Subsequent research has indicated that the debt of north to south, though real, was not exactly as Grierson pictured it—insofar as we can reconstruct it at all[12]—and that though the Gujar hypothesis is not yet totally discountable, it is a significant fact that the first reports of the story of Krishna as a child come from around the time of Christ, not, as Kennedy had thought, the sixth century A.D.[13] Christian influence would have had to predate the advances of the Nestorians by a good bit to be active in this mythology, and that seems unlikely.

More thought-provoking is the fact that the Christian nativity stories themselves were in all likelihood not part of the original synoptic core, but additions made from common folkloric traditions to suit the needs of theological narrators such as Luke and John. Such currents of story do seem to have flowed through the trade routes connecting the Hellenistic world and the Han dynasty with enough force that in some respects the birth stories of Krishna and Christ may have been genuine but distant cousins. One doubts, however, that specific documentation for such a hypothesis will ever be truly satisfying. In any case, such superficial resemblances as that in some dialects the name "Krishna" is pronounced vaguely like "Christ"—fascinating to the linguist Grierson—are of no weight whatever.[14]

In the years since 1908, we have heard very little about this debate in the West, but it continues to fire the Indian imagination. I have many times been assured by Indians who are aware of the outlines of Christian belief that there must be some truth to the legend that Jesus traveled to the northwest reaches of the subcontinent, to Kashmir, to spend his childhood and early manhood. Why else would one not have stories in the Bible relating the events of those hidden years? And how else to explain the manifest connections between his teachings and those of India? Jesus becomes, then, an avatar not only in the formal sense—a descent of Godhead into human form—but also in the historical sense, related in some tangible way to India and all the sacred geography of the other avatars.[15]

For others, however, the connection need not be terrestrial. The puranas and the *Bhagavad Gītā* speak of the fact that Viṣṇu/Krishna, supreme above all, descends to earth from time to time when the burdens of injustice become intolerable. I have heard this doctrine transposed from its original temporal context into spatial or communal terms: God cares for each of the great traditions of the world by vouchsafing it a revelation understandable and effective in its own terms.[16] It is no surprise, then, that devotion to God all over the world should have many of the same characteristics, but it remains a source of wonder that at least in this case (and the miraculous birth of the Buddha would often be included for comparison, as well) the details should be so strikingly similar. For those who hold such views, these parallels say nothing about historical influences one way or the other, but point to the coherence of the impulse propelling both narratives. And perhaps that is not far off the mark.

Yet it is worth noting that there is a significant disparity between the Vaiṣṇav notion of avatar and Christian ideas of incarnation.[17] The latter means quite literally taking on a body, and presupposes a fundamental distinction between flesh and spirit, body and soul. Indian analyses of human experience have rarely been cast in such dualistic terms. It is typical, rather, for psychological or spiritual factors to be understood on a continuum with aspects of reality that are most readily available to sensory perception. It is a question of subtler as against grosser; simpler and more fully integrated as against more diffuse and complex.[18] Hence when Viṣṇu/Krishna "descends" (that is what the term avatar literally means) into fleshly form, it does not imply that he is subject to the pollutions and limitations of the flesh in the same sense that at least some Christian theologies have thought was necessary as God became incarnate in Christ. Indeed, though his form is human, his divine powers are available to him whenever he needs them, and his divine beauty shines irresistibly through the medium of his earthly form. Furthermore, the inner radiance of his personality expands irrevocably, contagiously, and transforms the section of earth he has chosen as his own into something perfect, something more than earthly, at the same time that all its features remain the commonest: subtler and finer, while at the same time simple. Because the gross data of experience, including the flesh, are themselves permeated by the divine, all this is eminently possible. Original sin and the fall do not separate God from humankind with the same irrevocable force in India as they do in the Christian world—certainly until or in the absence of the coming Christ.

It is consistent with this that the theology of the avatar is usually conceived in dramatic terms rather than any other.[19] Drama is not foreign to Christian theology, but it is reserved for a description of the interrelations between the various faces or masks of Godhead, the persons of Trinity, rather than touching earth directly. The original meaning of the trinitarian "person" was in fact just that: mask. In Vaiṣṇavite thought, on the other hand, the whole world process is conceived as a drama. All the world is literally a stage and God (Viṣṇu/Krishna), in many forms, is the actor. He creates, if it can be called that, in play only (the word is *līlā*) and the form of what emerges is dramatic. Then, in a special role, he enters the drama himself: that is what happens when Krishna is born. Krishna is one in a succession of earlier avatars, but according to the Braj understanding he is the complete avatar.[20] Part of the reason is that he is completely human. Unlike any of the other avatars, which recapitulate the evolutionary process from aquatic to amphibian to animal and mammalian forms of life, Krishna is completely like us. There are other human avatars, too, but they are heroic and ideal, whereas Krishna is like us in every aspect; radiant he may be, but that radiance shines through a personality full of foibles and pranks. We need not decide whether this Krishna avatar seems complete to us because of our human perspective or whether it is objectively, cosmically, so: the Indian suspicion of an ultimate differentiation between ontology and epistemology means that the question is never addressed as fundamental. From what other perspective might we speak, after all?

Krishna's human birth, then, is a role within a play of his own devising. And he plays it playfully, with an ease and a sense of fun that are also part of the meaning of the term *līlā*. By a further extension of the same logic, the best way to make oneself aware of the nature of this divine action in the world is to represent it dramatically: hence the *rās līlās*. As one more aspect of the same conception, the players are by rights considered as the very forms (*svarūps*) of Viṣṇu/Krishna; and the closer to the center of the drama one comes, the more this is true, and it is essentially true of the roles of Krishna and Radha.[21] Thus it makes perfect sense in terms of the theology of avatars that these Brahmin boys who play Krishna and Radha should be understood as very incarnations of God. They become so completely the embodiment of the divine play making, and they transmit that play so fully to others, that within the confines of the dramatic setting into which they descend (to use the Vaiṣṇav term) they are indeed divine.

The *kṛṣṇa janma līlā* (The Birth of Krishna) focuses on the moment at which that cosmic descent takes place. Like all the Krishna *līlās*, it can be performed at any time of the year that seems right; its dramatic quality makes it accessible at all times. But because of its temporal precision, it is always performed in Braj on the occasion of the great festival that celebrates that same event, *śrīkṛṣṇajanmāṣṭamī*, the birthday of Krishna. All the *līlās* that have been performed during the previous twenty-two days culminate in this moment when the fullness of the divine descent is known; they end with their beginning.

Janmāṣṭamī, as the festival is familiarly known, is celebrated on the eighth day of the waning half of the lunar month of *bhādrapad* (Hindi *bhādra, bhādõ*: August–September.) The name implies as much, meaning literally "Krishna's birthday, the eighth." Or if one calculates the months from the new moons rather than from the full moons, as some calendars do, then it is near the end of the sacred month of *śrāvaṇ*, which precedes *bhādrapad*.[22]

However one reckons, the seasonal significance remains constant: *janmāṣṭamī* is the culmination of the rainy season with all its rich associations. The monsoon is a dark time, a time of clouds, and *janmāṣṭamī* celebrates a birth in darkness. The requirements of the festival begin to take effect at evening, and they delineate a fast, not a feast.[23] After nightfall on the evening following the seventh of the month, one should eat no more grain until night falls again on the eighth. Thus the day of Krishna's birth is set aside as holy from all the time that surrounds it, and there are some devotees who abstain from even a drop of water the entire time. On the whole, however, Vaiṣṇavs have been suspicious of any calculated mortification of the flesh, even over as limited a period as this; furthermore, the festival is one of great joy. So fasting means not that one stops eating, but rather that the entire basis of what one eats changes, setting this time apart from the eating patterns of ordinary life. Cereal grains such as rice and wheat, which form the staples of the diet of north India, are abjured on this day, and one does not prepare foods by placing them directly over the fire or on a dry griddle without any cooking medium.[24] Instead, one is treated to a most delicious array of foods all cooked in *ghī*, or in vegetable oil if that cannot be afforded. In place of the ordinary grains, special noncereal flours are used, derived from the pulp of various fruits such as waterchestnuts, the peculiarly Indian *kūṭū*, and the seed of the famous lotus *(makhānā)*. Milk and milk products, normally expensive even in Braj, are not proscribed. As in the case of *ghī* as against vegetable oil, the milk of the cow is preferred over the more readily affordable milk of the water buffalo, and since milk—again, especially cow's milk—is the basis of all the delicious sweets of the region, they too are appropriate for this fast. Fasting, then, becomes a wonderful way of feasting.

The admonition to fast is accompanied by another: to remain awake. This is one of the four occasions in the course of the year when this is strictly enjoined.[25] All through the night worshipers gather to please God and themselves with songs of praise; this makes it not only easier but better to stay awake. Then too, in typical Vaiṣṇavite fashion, there is no rigid insistence on the length of this vow of wakefulness. One may consider that the night is over at three in the morning, as the first hints of dawn appear, and retire for a little rest, or one may even settle for two or three hours earlier. Most important of all, however, there is the excitement associated with the nocturnal birth itself.

This is a feature not universally insisted upon in the ritual texts, but it is an important aspect of the celebration of *janmāṣṭamī* in Braj today. As the night deepens, one sees streams of pilgrims threading their way through the twisting alleys of Brindavan to gather at what is today the most popular temple in town, that of Bānke Bihārī. The midnight ceremony there is not open for the public to see, but shortly thereafter, at one A.M. or so, people begin to trickle into the temple precincts, and then to throng, in preparation for the great *darśan* that will come at three or four A.M. It is a very special occasion, for it is the only time of the year when the deity is visible at this especially holy hour of the day *(maṅgalāratī.)*[26] To the eyes of the faithful, Bānke Bihārī, the lithe, flute-playing Krishna, appears with a peculiar clarity at this early morning hour; but profane vision is sometimes impeded by the unprecedented size of the mob that mills around awaiting that vision.

When day dawns, preparations begin for what is in many ways the most spectacular event of the festival. From every path to Brindavan and by boat from across the Jumna the herders converge on the temple of Rādhā Ramaṇ, bearing huge cannisters of milk, while from the temple itself there issues a counterprocession of priests and devotees, similarly burdened with great pitchers. Several hale young *gosvāmīs* are at the core, and singers and drummers provide atmosphere as all proceed to the Jumna to fill the pitchers full of the holy water necessary for the ceremony to come. Today Rādhā Ramaṇ will be bathed not only in this water but in the five pure, ambrosial substances called *pañcāmṛt:* three of the sacred products of the cow — milk, curd, and *ghī* — plus honey and crystallized sugar. Much of the morning passes in the gathering and preparation of these, in addition to the scores of other juices and herbal extracts with which Rādhā Ramaṇ will be showered, and all the other delicacies of the great "fast." Everything must be absolutely fresh.

As midday approaches, the great temple bell begins a rapid peal. Everyone rushes inside to the din of another, interior gong placed near the corner of the audience hall. There on the dais before the inner sanctum one sees something that occurs only twice a year.[27] All the members of the priestly family that cares for Rādhā Ramaṇ who have been initiated in the rites of that service are gathered. They take turns showering the image with the five holy substances and all the others. Only two senior members are excepted: one sits at the side reading the ritual injunctions for the event as laid down in the Sanskrit *Haribhaktivilāsa* and its derivative the *Kṛṣṇajanmatithividhi,* and another acts as his assistant by correctly identifying the various elements that the texts mention. A third may sit directly behind the image, grasping its feet to make sure that it is not accidentally upset in the course of the great activity that is focused on it.

Rādhā Ramaṇ himself, a small, rhythmic, triply-bent image of Krishna whose petal-shaped white eyes present a brilliant contrast to the jet-black color of his skin, is dressed very simply for the occasion. Aside from the ever-present golden, jeweled crown that sits atilt his head and the jeweled golden bands that adorn his waist and ankles, he wears only the simplest white cloth. But for a sash thrown back from his neck, he is naked above the waist — dressed with an informality one never sees on a normal day before he relaxes at evening, and never at all, with one exception,[28] on festival days like this. The priests of the temple bend over him with vessels containing the pure and for the most part white substances that constitute the *pañcāmṛt,* and pour them just above and behind his head, so that the audience that mills about just in front and shouts its huzzahs is given the impression that the deity is being showered with a great liquid abundance. Stream after stream crests over the head of Rādhā Ramaṇ and drops to a rare righthanded conch held by another of the priests. From there it is directed to the feet of the Lord,

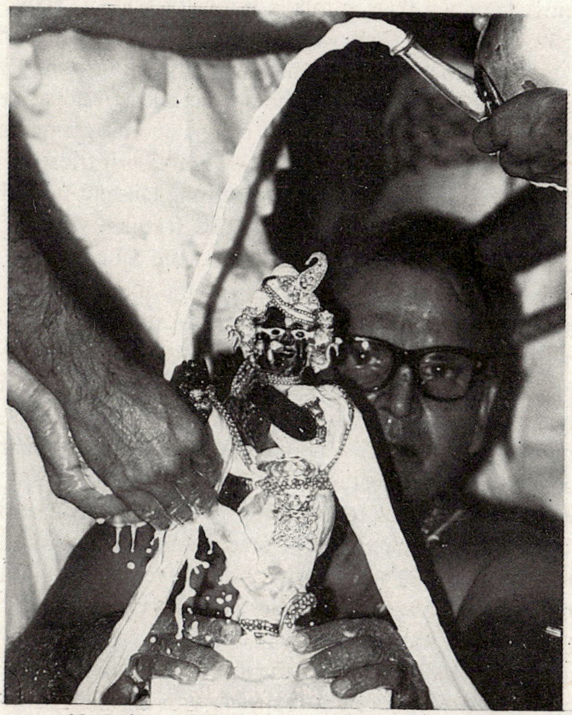

20. Bathing Rādhā Ramaṇ in milk on *janmāṣṭamī*

which are aswim in white, thence to flow off and be collected in huge basins that are set all around. There the various substances that go into the *pañcāmṛt* combine; they will later be offered to the worshipers as Rādhā Ramaṇ's grace *(prasād)*.

This regal shower continues for hours. When it is over, the deity retires to his private chambers for yet another bath, and to undergo a number of ceremonies that are performed daily. Some of the crowd wait in the vicinity of the temple for him to reappear, circumambulating it as they do. Others wander off for other *darśans* and return upon their completion. When they do, the temple bell is already ringing again, and Rādhā Ramaṇ's symbolic birth is complete. As these pilgrims cross the threshold into the inner precinct they see great silver-handled umbrellas and fringed circular flags, symbols of royalty, bobbing above the great crowd. And as they wedge their way toward the image itself, they see that Rādhā Ramaṇ wears his most stately garb for this ceremony of honoring the newborn king*(rājopacāra.)*

Thick red plumage decorates his crown, and his garments are of purest saffron and gold, overlaid with a vast, intricately brocaded mantle of silver and gold. Everything fans out in such an aura from his face that the distinctive features which commanded the spectator's attention before—the delicate arms that hold the flute transversely to his lips and the golden anklets that accentuate the graceful bend of his legs—are all but invisible. The whole of his front, as far down as his knees, is covered with a display of the most striking jewelry, anchored in ample circlets of silver and bordered with a double row of purest pearls. But this monarch is also a child, born today, recipient of the mantras and ceremonies of protection befitting any newborn infant, and we are reminded of his tender state by the solid silver animals that bedeck his complex, many-tiered throne. He is customarily attended by a few such shining beasts, for every Hindu divinity is thought of as possessing vehicles of this sort, but today there are a great many more: his toys.

It is a vision radiant enough to glow in the mind until a year hence, when it will once again appear with all the freshness of the divine descent; and the crowds linger before it, etching it on their memories as songs from the back of the room filter through the great din to spice the epiphany with word and pitch. For members of the Vallabh Sampradāy, the community that takes the sixteenth-century philosopher saint Vallabhācārya as its founder, the year begins and ends here. *Janmāṣṭamī* is its first day.

For many, however, the day is not yet complete. As night

21. Rādhā Ramaṇ dressed for the ceremony of honoring the newborn king *(rājopacāra)*

approaches, great numbers of pilgrims make their way seven miles down the muddy road to Mathura, where they join pilgrims from all over Braj and far beyond to worship in the great Vallabhite temple of Dvārakādhīś and in the monumental temple that has recently been built just behind the place where the birth itself is said to have occurred. This is an ancient site, as Mathura is an ancient pilgrimage city, and the zealous Moghul emperor Aurangzeb saw to it that the earlier temple was destroyed and replaced by a glorious mosque. Even that earlier temple had previously been sacked twice.[29] To the people of Braj the fortunes of Mathura in Muslim times do not seem very different from what it endured at the hands of Kans himself.

But as ways were found to circumvent the authority of Kans, here too ingenuity and persistence have been rewarded. In the early decades of this century Hindu leaders sponsored excavations at the back of the mound on which the mosque is built, and as they dug down they discovered a series of cells—evidently Kans's old jail! Most of them lay under the mosque itself, and there were bloody assaults on the Muslim precinct to try to claim the area once again as Hindu, but to no avail. Ultimately those had to be left as they were. One, however, lay outside the grounds of the mosque and that has become the focal grotto of the great Temple of Krishna's Birth that has been erected to honor it. On the night of *janmāṣṭamī*, legions of worshipers descend into greater darkness still, and crowd into the underground cell for a glimpse of the image that has been installed there. Elsewhere across north India this pilgrimage is repeated in miniature as the faithful worship at little creches they have prepared in their own homes to depict the same scene of humble birth. The mother and father surround the child in wonder in their cramped little cell, and often there is also a representation of Vasudev bearing his son across the river and of Yaśodā cradling the newborn baby.[30]

By the time the next day begins the special precincts of time that were guarded by fast and wakefulness have passed: the holy birth has occurred. But the very ordinariness of this second day makes it especially fit for another aspect of the birth festivities. By this time it is mythologically correct that the presence of Krishna in Braj should be celebrated: the night journey is accomplished, and Vasudev has safely removed the infant from all that threatens him in Mathura. Hence the scene shifts away from the city and back to Braj proper, the surrounding countryside, where Krishna is welcomed by the herdspeople of the land. The texts allow for the creches one sometimes sees the night before to be present on this day, too: temporary structures called *sutikāgṛhas*, sheds set apart for the mother and child after the delivery of a child, which Hindus regard as ritually polluting. Over the years, it seems, this particular feature of the celebration has become less visible in Braj, but its legacy remains. The second day of the *janmāṣṭamī* sequence is the day when all may come to share with the mother and father in their happiness at the birth of a son, and the mother and child are always set apart in some way from the father. Typically, as in the *līlā* appropriate for the day, Yaśodā will be shown gently rocking a cradle in which her son is placed, as Nanda looks on.[31] In the play, the cowherd friends of Nanda and Yaśodā all flock to their side to sing songs of congratulation *(badhāī.)* In real life everyone gathers at the temple—cowherds, pilgrims, everyone—to do the same. The feast is called *nandotsav*, Nanda's festival, because a boy has been born into his household. The fact that the focus has shifted somewhat from the divine birth to its effects in the human realm permits a kind of conviviality that would not have been strictly appropriate the day before.

And it is conviviality with a vengeance. Even in the decorous temple of Rādhā Ramaṇ there is an uproar. Little ruffians from the street pour in on this day because they know that the priests in charge will sit in the balconies of the great audience hall and throw down pennies for anyone who is there, as fathers of newborn babies distribute cigars. With each toss of a coin there is a mad scramble across the floor of the temple. This largesse does not stop with money, of course: there are sweets as well.

But the greatest riot is some distance away, in the temple across the river in the sleepy town of Gokul, which forms one of the seats of the Vallabh Sampradāy and is considered by them the spot where Krishna was received after the perils of his midnight escape. On this day Gokul springs to vivid life as pilgrims from far and wide stream in to join Nanda and Yaśodā in their happiness. Great rustic wooden doors form an appropriately pastoral background in this temple, which is properly termed a *havelī* because it is part of the house of one of the scions of the Sampradāy. In truth, it is a huge palace whose grandeur altogether dwarfs the town in which it is set, but on this day it has all the informality of a home.

Informality, indeed! Sureś Gosvāmī, the host, a lively, robust man in his twenties who has studied philosophy, breaks into the crowd that is waiting for him with huge leaps and shouts of gladness. He carries an enormous clay pot of yoghurt colored yellow with turmeric, and flings it about indiscriminately in a wild abandon of joy. Other pots mysteriously appear, and he himself is constantly going into the back rooms and coming out with more. The supply seems endless, and as more and more appear they are disposed of with greater and greater haste. Foreigners are not spared: I ended up with a huge one upside down over my head. As it crashed to my shoulders every spot of white on the clothes I was wearing was instantly dyed yellow, and my eyes were full of the stuff.

Snaking through the crowd a hasty circle of hands emerged, linking dancers who leapt into the air and sang,

Nanda's alive with joy today.
Praise God, a son is born!
Elephants, horses, and palanquins
he gives to his little Kānh.[32]

All about there was a rain of coins, sending the boys scurrying between our legs.

The front of the great courtyard-like room was the focus of it all. There sat the musicians of the *havelī* singing tender songs of congratulation before the image of Krishna, songs that were inaudible above the raucous crowd. They were joined by a member of the temple family who wore a long white beard for the occasion, impersonating Nanda. And all their eyes focused on the newborn baby, beautifully decorated for this day and placed in an ornate silver swing, his cradle. At his side sat his mother Yaśodā, impersonated by another male of the family, but fully made up to appear a woman and wearing the traditional skirt and overgarment of Braj. She smiled and rocked her child back and forth. The din of congratulation closed about them:

Nanda's alive with joy today.
Praise God, a son is born!

This, then, is the birth of Krishna. The play translated here forms but one aspect of the great festival, but it mirrors the whole, and each year sets it in its proper dramatic context. It was performed by the company of Svāmīs Natthī Lāl and Śrī Rām on the morning of *janmāṣṭamī* itself, August 18, 1976, just before the great ceremony down the lane at the temple of Rādhā Ramaṇ.

The stage of the Śrī Caitanya Prem Sansthān provides the set-

22. The court of Ugrasen

ting. Modeled after a Western stage,[33] it is far more elaborate than the simple theater-in-the-round in which the *rās līlā* is traditionally performed. One traditional element in staging the *rās līlā* remains prominent here, however; the throne at the back of the stage. By rights it is Krishna's and Radha's, but in the course of the play it can be occupied by others as well, and as the curtain opens we see that it has become the focus of a great court scene and enthrones another personality altogether. This is Ugrasen, presumptive father of Kans and king of Mathura.

Played by one of the adult members of the troupe, he is a majestic old man with a white beard whose richly decorated blue and gold robes billow over the throne. He bears the silver staff of royalty, and is attended by two courtiers dressed in saffron and gold. Their erect postures and the silver staffs they hold suggest formality and eloquence even before they begin to speak, as do the silver-patterned draperies that form the backdrop. The audience understands that this is Mathura as it was before the disruptions caused by Kans.

As in a traditional performance, the musicians *(samājī)* sit cross-legged at stage right. This is a rather large company, and there are some eight or ten musicians, including players of various stringed instruments, small cymbals, and sometimes a flute; Svāmī Natthī Lāl himself plays the drums *(tablā)*. The leader of the ensemble is Svāmī Śrī Rām, who stands at a lecturn upon which rests a small keyboard instrument called a harmonium. It was imported into India in the last century, and has since become standard in the *rās līlās* despite the fact that it cannot be tuned exactly, as stringed instruments can. Its sound is that of a small reed organ, but in the Indian fashion no chords are ever employed. With one hand the *svāmī* operates the bellows and with the other he runs his fingers melismatically over the keyboard as he sings the musical lines that frame the dramatic action. The other musicians, all members of one *rāsdhārī*'s family or the other, often sing along as well; sometimes individuals intone favorite passages alone. All of them know the lines from having been players themselves as children. When the drama calls for it they take the various roles that adults can play; otherwise they sit together as musicians, two or three generations in an ancient tradition.

The *rās* is already completed, and Svāmī Śrī Rām begins the *līlā*, the play itself, by leading the musicians in a song that is general enough to serve as a transition between these two sections but particular enough to introduce the *līlā* for Krishna's birth. It terminates in an invocation to Nārad, the divine messenger who intervenes in worldly affairs to make sure that heaven-made plots take their proper course. Nārad is the patron of all plots, and a musician as well—he carries a drone instrument (classically it should be the difficult *vīṇā*) and sings wherever he goes; so it is appropriate to invoke him as the play begins. But there is the more particular fact that Nārad will actually appear as the play proceeds: hearing this song, the audience will look forward to his arrival. For now the song introduces Ugrasen and his court in Mathura.

When Nārad finishes, the players take up their lines immediately and the colloquy between music and drama proceeds regularly from then until the end of the performance. In the text that follows the reader can follow this alternation of song and speech, poetry and prose, by noting that anything with verse and tone is indented, whether it is sung by the musicians—with Svāmī Śrī Rām normally acting as their representative—or by one of the players. Everything else is simple dialogue. This antiphonal relationship of drama and song is one of the secrets of the vibrancy of the *rās līlā*, and the reader should keep in mind, alas, that by reducing it to print half its appeal is removed.

The Birth of Krishna

MUSICIANS:

Tell us a story to capture and gladden
  the hearts of the saints, a ladder to heaven:
A tale of the Jumna, that joyous ocean
  that lies beside Mathura, flowing and splendid.
The blessings conferred by the sight of that river
  are known to the far distant ends of the earth.
Hurry then, Nārad, to the king of the region:
  Ugrasen, guardian of pious devotion.[34]

GUARD: [*in clipped, military cadence*] Bows at attention! The Great King—King above all kings! Give out the shout: hail to Great King Ugrasen!

CHAMBERLAIN: Hail great Maharaja Ugrasen! Hail Ugrasen, protector of cow and Brahmin!

UGRASEN: Tell me, Chamberlain . . .

CHAMBERLAIN: Yes sir . . .

UGRASEN: There's no obstacle to the practice of worship in our realm, is there?

CHAMBERLAIN: No My Lord, you are the very avatar of compassion. In your realm no one has any difficulties. All your subjects are blissfully happy.

UGRASEN: Good, that's the way it should be. No one in this kingdom should be beset by any problem.

CHAMBERLAIN: Right you are, Lordship.

UGRASEN: All who dwell in this realm of mine ought to be able to pursue the duties appropriate to their several stations, and so it will remain for as long as I reign on this throne. For it is said, "*dharmo rakṣati rakṣakaḥ*": righteousness protects him who protects righteousness.

Who stubbornly defends the right,
him the Creator defends.
For right is the basis of all that is;
without it the world dissolves.[35]

Anything in this realm that conduces to righteousness must be allowed to flourish.

CHAMBERLAIN: My Lord, in this kingdom of yours the reading of the *Bhāgavata Purāṇa*, the singing of hymns, and the worship of images proceed with great joy. Ascetics, Brahmins, and cows are well looked after. Everywhere one hears the singing of religious songs, and everyone is happy.

UGRASEN: Even so, there's one desire that nags at my heart.

CHAMBERLAIN: What's that, My Lord?

UGRASEN: Well . . . [*He ruminates a bit before he announces his concern.*] I'd like to sponsor a great, lavish ceremony of sacrifice to Viṣṇu.[36]

CHAMBERLAIN: [*jubilant*] All hail King Ugrasen, incarnation of righteousness! That's a wonderful idea, My Lord!

UGRASEN: Will you then summon some Brahmins? Tell them that the king wants to sponsor a great sacrifice to Viṣṇu on the banks of the Jumna.

CHAMBERLAIN: Yes, of course.

UGRASEN: You go call them. I'll retire for my prayers.

CHAMBERLAIN: Consider it done.

[*Exit* UGRASEN]

[*The* CHAMBERLAIN *raises his voice to summon the* BRAHMINS, *who come on stage presently, their parts being taken by some of the same boys who normally play the role of* GOPĪS. *A young man leads them.*]

O Brahmin-gods, O Pundit-kings, hail you Brahmin-divinities! Do come in, do make your entrance. I prostrate myself before you. [*This he does with symbolic bow. The leader of the* BRAHMINS *responds with a word of blessing.*]

BRAHMIN: May you be happy. Tell me, what's going on? What's happening?

CHAMBERLAIN: Listen, My Lord. Today our King Ugrasen has had a new wish come into his heart. He feels that a great sacrifice to Viṣṇu should take place, to assure the happiness of each one of his subjects. A wonderful plan, isn't it?

BRAHMIN: The Lord of Mathura wants this?

CHAMBERLAIN: Yes, of Mathura.

BRAHMIN: Well, and why not? As the incarnation of righteousness he is continually disposed to do good. It's a fine plan. [*Enter* UGRASEN, *who addresses the* BRAHMINS.]

UGRASEN: God has shown great kindness to me in that you have obliged me by coming here. I lay my request at the feet of all of you.

BRAHMINS: And what is it, King?

UGRASEN: I would like to sponsor a great sacrifice to Viṣṇu, and for that I must rely upon the good graces of all of you. If you will undertake this sacrifice, any substance you may need will be supplied to you by the court.

BRAHMINS: Well and good. Such a sacrifice must indeed take place.

UGRASEN: Chamberlain!

CHAMBERLAIN: My Lord.

UGRASEN: Go and see to the making of a great pavilion—a canopied place where the sacrifice can take place—and make sure that every convenience is made available in the preparing of the sacrifice.

CHAMBERLAIN: Yes, yes, My Lord, don't worry, it shall be done.

BRAHMIN: Where will it all take place?

CHAMBERLAIN: On the banks of the Jumna, sir. Since such a ceremony should be carried out in a secluded place, the gardens on the banks of the river should serve us well.

[*As the scene changes and* UGRASEN *and the* CHAMBERLAIN *go off, the* BRAHMINS *wander about the stage as if on their way to the Jumna.. As they go, the* MUSICIANS, *who are joined antiphonally by the* AUDIENCE, *anticipate the sacrifice in song.*]

MUSICIANS:

Hari Hari Hari Hari – remember his holy name.
At his lotus feet reveal your heart
and gently lay it down.[37]

AUDIENCE: [*Repeats the same.*]

MUSICIANS:

Wherever the tales of Hari continue to be sung,
that place becomes an ever-filling Ganges riverbed,
A riverbed where holy rivers rise and
race and course:
their names are Sarasvati, Indus, Jumna, Godavari.
Hari Hari Hari Hari – remember his holy name.
At his lotus feet reveal your heart
and gently lay it down.

[*As the* BRAHMINS *seat themselves in a circle on the stage—the canopy and all remain imaginary—the sounds of Sanskrit mantras begin to emanate from their midst.*]

BRAHMINS: OM, auspicious Lord Viṣṇu. Garuḍa, too, is auspicious. Auspiciousness pertains to the lotus-eyed one. Hari is the very repository of auspiciousness. OM, Lord of Mount Kailāśa, *svāhā*. OM, Earth. *Svāhā*. We meditate upon the glorious splendor of the Vivifier divine. May he himself illumine our minds! OM, treasure-bearing Earth. *Svāhā*.[38]

[*As the mantras continue,* KANS'*s threatening presence suddenly darkens the side of the stage. Clad in deep blue and garlanded with jewels of contrasting pearl color, he stands tall and wields a great trident. This suggests to the audience at once that he is devotee of Śiva, and the white ashen smear across his forehead confirms the impression. A huge tilak mark at the center of his forehead, of the most vivid vermilion and large enough to remind one of*

Śiva's third eye, completes the picture. He swaggers onstage and then stops abruptly, listening as the BRAHMINS *drone on.*]

OM, Prajāpati, Lord of Creatures, *svāhā.*

KANS: [*peremptorally*] Fang! [*This is* KANS'S *advisor: his name, appropriate to the ranks of demonic forces, means literally "diamond-hard tooth." His enormous, well-pillowed midriff, furry moustache, and supercilious expression indicate that he is the* vidūṣak, *the buffoon.*]

FANG: Sultan, your gracious command? [*His use of Urdu, India's Muslim tongue, signals to Hindu audiences a foreign presence. Kans's language is similarly sprinkled with Urdu.*]

KANS: Every day I come here to the Jumna to relax — but today! What's this hullabaloo we've got today?

BRAHMINS: [*droning on, unmindful*] *Svāhā, svāhā* . . .

KANS: Where's this blasted *svāhā svāhā* noise coming from?

FANG: Lord, at your father's command these Mathura Brahmins have come down here into your pleasure garden and raised a low altar on the ground. And they're tossing *ghī* and dried fruits and sweets and so forth into it as they chant *svāhā svāhā* over and over again.

BRAHMINS: *Svāhā, svāhā* . . .

KANS: [*reddening as his anger rises*] You mean these Brahmins . . .

FANG: Yes, Sultan . . .

KANS: . . . are making a great sacrifice to Viṣṇu?

FANG: Yes, a great sacrifice.

BRAHMINS: *Svāhā, svāhā* . . .

FANG: [*Sensing his master's imminent rage, he interrupts the chanting with great imperiousness.*] Hey, stop that! Come over here! Just what do you people think you're doing?

BRAHMINS: We're performing a great sacrifice to Viṣṇu, at the command of King Ugrasen.

FANG: And what's the point in that?

BRAHMINS: Well, it makes the gods happy. And if the gods are happy they send rain. And when there's rain, then trees can grow up to shade the animals, and grain can be planted to benefit human beings.

KANS: [*He can no longer keep his regal distance from this conversation and breaks into loud, scornful laughter.*] Ha, ha, ha! By throwing these various ingredients into the fire you think you're insuring the prosperity of the realm!

BRAHMINS: Yes, that's right.

FANG: [*the perfect sycophant*] Your Majesty, this doesn't lead to prosperity, it just damages the kingdom.

23. Kans threatening the Brahmins

KANS: You're so right. Just look at the way these fools throw all that good food and grain into the fire when we need it to make our warriors strong on the field of battle! My father's getting senile. He's got hardening of the head! He isn't fit to rule any longer. [*Menacingly, with flashing teeth*] Oh you Brahmins. . . . [*Turning to his aide*] Fang, get rid of these people.

FANG: Get out! Out! Scram!

[*The* BRAHMINS flee before the lumbering advances of FANG, leaving him and KANS to congratulate one another on the wisdom of their action.]

KANS: Yes, get rid of these bringers of bad luck. These people

24. Fang

have buffaloed my father until he doesn't know what he's doing.

FANG: Buffalo nothing! They've made a complete ass of him!

KANS: Right. Oh these Brahmins are a dime a dozen nowadays.

FANG: Right you are.

KANS: [*with a violent flail of his trident*] Off with their heads, all of them.

FANG: Absolutely, Sultan.

KANS: Throw the bastards in the Jumna, and all their hymn-singing, sacrifice-making paraphernalia with them! Get rid of all of it!

FANG: [*a bit timorous*] But they're going to go and complain to your father.

KANS: [*snidely, ominously*] Really? Well, we'll just see what happens to my father.

FANG: [*the purest echo*] Right, we'll just see what happens to him. Shall we go then?

KANS: [*menacingly*] Just suppose he does try to stop what I've done, then. . . . Let's go.

[*Exit* KANS *and his courtiers.*]

[*Curtain, When it rises again the scene has shifted to the court of* UGRASEN, *where the righteous king is seated on his throne. The* BRAHMINS *rush in at the side but stop short before entering the throne room.*]

BRAHMIN: [*with every formality*] An announcement for the incarnation of righteousness, for Ugrasen, Great King, King above kings. An announcement for the incarnation of righteousness.

UGRASEN: Guard! Go see who it is that's calling out with an announcement at the door.

GUARD: [*Going over to the* BRAHMINS] What is it, sir, some shortage of materials?

BRAHMIN: No. If the king will allow us to enter . . .

GUARD: Yes, yes, do come in. Well?

BRAHMIN: We were performing the sacrifice on the banks of the Jumna . . .

GUARD: [*impatiently*] Yes, yes . . .

BRAHMIN: . . .when the crown prince suddenly appeared on the scene, destroyed all the ingredients of the sacrifice, and tossed our ritual manuals into the river.

GUARD: [*leading them immediately in the direction of the throne*] Come in, come this way.

BRAHMIN: [*agitatedly, to Ugrasen*] You are the very incarnation of righteousness, O King. Consider, then, this atrocity. There we were on the bank of the Jumna conducting a great sacrifice to Viṣṇu, as you had commanded, when suddenly out of nowhere the crown prince appeared and devastated the entire sacrifice. He threw all our books into the river, tossed in our images too, and even our children, and gave all of us a good beating.

UGRASEN: What! Can this be true?

BRAHMIN: Yes Maharaja, it's all true.

UGRASEN: You mean Kans is capable of perpetrating such a horror?

BRAHMIN: Yes, Your Lordship.

UGRASEN: May God forgive him his sin – he's such a simpleton! And as for this particular offense, may you forgive him as well.

BRAHMIN: Oh well, Your Lordship, he's just a child.

UGRASEN: I'll call him into court right now and give him a lesson in proper behavior, and if he doesn't pay heed then I'll mete out the proper punishment.

BRAHMINS: Praised be Ugrasen, incarnation of righteousness, Great King.

UGRASEN: And as for you, sir, return to the sacrifice grounds, and whatever supplies you find you need for the ceremony, just ask and again they will be yours.

BRAHMIN: As you command, My Lord.

UGRASEN: Yes, do begin again. [*They depart.*] Chamberlain!

CHAMBERLAIN: What is it, My Lord?

UGRASEN: [*lost in his own resolution*] For as long as I sit on this throne protecting the right, no injustice, no excess, no misbehavior, and no criminality are to be tolerated. Chamberlain, go to the prince and call him before the throne.

KANS: [*appearing with his courtiers*] No need to call, Father, I'm already here. [*He announces his sectarian bias to the* AUDIENCE *in general.*] Hail Śiva! [*to* UGRASEN] Well, Father, what is it?

UGRASEN: Son, I've heard it from the very mouths of Brahmins that . . .

KANS: That what?

UGRASEN: At my bidding they were carrying out a great sacrifice to Viṣṇu and you went and destroyed it. And as if that weren't enough, you laid a hand on the Brahmins as well. Causing trouble . . .

KANS: Listen, Father, I had no idea what stupid sort of sacrifice that was supposed to be. And what's the point of it anyway? What is it but a bunch of Brahmins squandering good food and supplies by feeding them to the fire while they sit around making a huge noise? So yes, I roughed them up a little.

UGRASEN: No, no, my son, you don't know what you're saying. Don't you have any idea what benefits such a sacrifice brings to the country and its subjects? As it is said [*in Sanskrit*],

He thrives who does not harm the right.
He is powerful who does not harm the right.
He has no enemies who does not harm the right.
Righteousness forever spells victory.[39]

In the presence of righteousness there is no disease. Where there is righteousness no ruler is toppled from the throne. Righteousness indeed spells victory.

KANS: [*fuming*] Sermons like this I . . . listen, I know the whole story. [*Quoting his own verse of Sanskrit to counterbalance that of his father*]

I know the right, yet am not inclined to do it;
And know the wrong as well, yet never do avoid it.[40]

So, Father, I'll do whatever I think best, and I'm certainly not going to allow those Brahmins to go on ruining our kingdom.

UGRASEN: Oh son, give some thought to your actions.

If you don't uncover the root of the right
You'll never discover its meaning.

First attend to the protection of the right, then attend to any ambitions you may have for yourself. Never the latter before the former.

KANS: And just where was all this fine righteousness of yours when you told these Brahmins that you were ready to have

25. Battle of wills between Kans and Ugrasen

me tied up and banished—a formidable son like me?[41] [*He quotes a vernacular rendition of his earlier asseveration in Sanskrit*]

I know in every measure what is right,
but the right is hard to abide,
And I know in equal measure what is wrong,
but the wrong is hard to abandon.

There's some odd thing that takes over in my brain:

It drives me wherever it wants,
and that's the direction I go.
I know full well that it makes me
a helpless, powerless pawn.[42]

I may be destroyed myself in the process, but I can't shake my fate.

UGRASEN: Don't distort justice so—you'll be sorry. Listen,

When righteousness gets angry
it dispenses thousands of wounds;
It brings you to a certain end,
it grinds you down to bare bones.

Pay attention to your father, son. Follow my orders.

KANS: [*quoting yet another Hindi paraphrase of the sentiment he has voiced already*] Father,

I know, after all, what's right—
I wasn't born yesterday—
And know as well what's wrong,
but I can't seem to shake myself free.

So you can save your breath, Father, I'll do as I see fit.

UGRASEN: Be careful. As long as I reign on this throne, you had better abstain from wrongdoing. And if you don't, you'll have your reward.

At this point Kans breaks into derisive laughter, and a second later the coup d'état is accomplished. He trains a piercing glance on his father, reaches out for him with a great melodramatic gesture, pulls him off the throne and puts him in the charge of his guards. The old man is shuffled off the stage. He is shaken, but retains every ounce of his dignity.

Once seated on the throne, Kans launches into a blustering

monologue in which he offers a unifying interpretation of Hindu scripture that implicitly justifies the action he has just taken. In one breath he solves all the puzzles that have attended their sometimes arcane expressions. Very simply, he announces that they all refer to him. "*I* am the subject of the Vedas and Puranas!" he shouts, flinging his forefinger into the air and bouncing it off his chest in a grandiloquent expression of self-affirmation.[43] And with this made clear he settles into the throne with complete confidence, ready to do business.

26. The obsequious Kālīcaran

His first action is to call for Kālīcaran, hereditary priest to the court. A messenger shouts out for him from the back corner of the stage, announcing that he is wanted in the throne room. Soon Kālīcaran appears. He is wearing the forehead markings appropriate to a devotee of Śiva, but as he shuffles along he mumbles one of the names of Viṣṇu, as Vaiṣṇavites customarily do when setting out on any journey or new task: "Nārāyaṇ, Nārāyaṇ, Nārāyaṇ." Hearing this, the messenger stops him short with a warning. "Don't you know who's on the throne these days?" Kālīcaran comes to his senses and readjusts this inveterate habit of his as best he can. "Oh, yes, hail Śiva, hail Śiva!" he nervously stammers.

In Indian history it is not a thing unknown that the religious orientation of one ruler differed from that of his predecessor, though this was normally the case when whole dynasties changed rather than individual rulers in the same succession, and was usually attended with little acrimony. Kālīcaran, however, is justly apprehensive, and in his abstracted priestly way tries to accommodate himself to change by coming before Kans with blessings befitting the new rule. The mantra he manufactures on the spot rhymes but contains precious little meaning, and the audience is suitably amused at its senselessness. Moments like this and others in which players in the *rās līlā* attempt a little pidgin Sanskrit give people a chance to laugh at the pretensions of the Brahmins and to give expression, through laughter, to what everyone suspects of many Brahmins: that their abracadabra is really little more than gibberish. When Kans breaks in to ask what in the world is the import of this string of meaningless syllables, then, he is not the only one who wonders.

Kālīcaran embarks skittishly on a letter-by-letter analysis of his formula of blessing, rescuing it from nonsense by showing how each consonant has meaning: the vowels only provide the sound. The pattern he follows, however, soon gets him into trouble. He is very careful to change his Vaiṣṇavite frame of reference, but he does so by thinking in terms of the threefold expression of divinity that encompasses Brahmā, Śiva, and Viṣṇu. He knows, of course, that every reference to Śiva will be pleasing to Kans, yet he is unable to improvise with enough success to avoid the inevitable reference to Viṣṇu that follows directly afterward. His mantra has begun with the word *varanā*, an oddly Sanskritized form of a common Urdu word meaning "otherwise," and he atomizes the term to display its inner meaning. "V" is for Brahmā," he explains, already confusing two initial consonants that are often equivalent in Hindi but not in Sanskrit. "R is for Rudra." So far so good: the first is the Creator, the second a Vedic deity associated with Śiva. But as he proceeds to the third letter he loses his concentration. "N is for

Nārad," he says, and everyone knows that Nārad, as the messenger of the gods, ruminates continually on the name of Viṣṇu: he more than anyone else is always saying "Nārāyaṇ, Nārāyaṇ" as he travels about.

The association is not lost on the court. The guard starts: "Watch out!" But it is too late. Kans has noticed and is about to fly into a rage. Menacingly he demands, "Whose name was that?" If you so much as breathe that name again, why. . . ." Kālīcaran begins again: "V is for Brahmā" and so forth. The audience waits for him to repeat his slip, and of course he does, many times. At the end of a long sequence in which the pundit walks a tightrope of words, quite unsuccessfully, they are satisfied with laughter. Fun has been poked at Brahmins, and Kans has had to pay a price as well.

As it turns out, all Kālīcaran's efforts were for naught. In his anxiety he has assumed that he was called to court to sanctify this coup d'état, but in reality Kans is too sure of his own authority to require any such legitimation. He requires Kālīcaran's services in regard to another matter altogether, and makes it known through the services of old Fang, who has now been elevated to the rank of chamberlain.

KANS: Chamberlain!

FANG: Your Highness?

KANS: Tell this pundit why I've summoned him.

FANG: Well, Pundit, do you know why you've been called before the court?

KĀLĪCARAN: [*sheepishly*] Uh . . . uh . . . to perform a sacrifice?

FANG: [*disgusted at the thought of it, on behalf of his lord, and a little dismayed at* KĀLĪCARAN'S *evident lack of perception*] No, not for any sacrifice, Brahmin. It's that His Highness's sister is old enough to be married and we've got to find a groom for her. That's why you've been sent for.

KĀLĪCARAN: [*He misunderstands, hearing* vaḍ, *"banyan," instead of* var, *"groom."*] So you need a banyan, eh? Well, if you don't find one, perhaps it would be a good idea to worship the *pīpal* tree. People do that a lot.

FANG: Not banyan—*groom!* We're trying to find a bridegroom for the king's sister.

KĀLĪCARAN: Oh, oh, oh, a bridegroom. [*Still trying to rearrange his foggy consciousness*] A groom is what you need. Hmmm. Well, Your Lordship, how stout should he be? How old? I don't even know how old your sister Devakī is.

KANS: She's sixteen.

KĀLĪCARAN: Uh-huh. Well, if she's sixteen, the bridegroom should be eighteen, according to the rules established in the sacred texts.

KANS: Oh shut up and listen for a minute. For my sister Devakī we need a groom who's wealthy, self-confident, good-looking, masterful, and strong. And if he's not strong already, don't worry, I'll make him strong.

KĀLĪCARAN: [*taking out a notebook and beginning to thumb through it*] Whatever you say, Your Highness. Let's see now, Bombay, Calcutta, Madras, Lucknow . . .

FANG: [*cutting this pleasant anachronism short*] Hey pundit, what's that you're looking at?

KĀLĪCARAN: It's my directory, Mr. Chamberlain, sir. I'm looking in it for a nice groom for His Highness. [*He ponders over each page, looks off into space, then turns to the next.*] But it's not so easy. Whenever I find one that's self-confident it turns out he's not handsome, and so forth. There just isn't anyone!

KANS: So what does that mean? That my sister is going to have to stay single?

KĀLĪCARAN: [*vaguely reflective*] Yes, it could mean that. Oh wait, Your Highness! I just remembered! Right nearby, near Mathura, there's a young man by the name of Vasudev, son of Surasen. He meets every qualification, and furthermore he's a distant relative of yours.

KANS: Well hurry up and go get him.

KĀLĪCARAN: At your command.

KANS: Look, if he's willing, then fine: let him come willingly. And if he's not, then bring him by force. One way or the other be sure you come back with a marriage procession that has this Vasudev in it.

KĀLĪCARAN: Yes, sir. [*Exit* KĀLĪCARAN]

[*Curtain. When the curtain opens, the scene has changed, and* KĀLĪCARAN is in the presence of a tall, reserved young man.]

KĀLĪCARAN: Greetings, Vasudev.

VASUDEV: Come in, do sit down.

KĀLĪCARAN: Forgive me, Vasudev. I've come on necessary business that has to do with you.

VASUDEV: And what is the pressing business?

KĀLĪCARAN: [*a bit fidgety*] Well, here's what it is . . .[*He stops himself in the middle of his sentence and launches hurriedly into another.*] Yes, but first of all, tell me this. Are you going to get married or not?

VASUDEV: [*surprised at this query, coming out of the blue*] Huh, what's that, Pundit?

KĀLĪCARAN: [*hesitantly, in jerks and starts*] Um, listen, this has nothing to do with the matter at hand. Just tell me if you're going to get married or not.

VASUDEV: You mean your business *does* have to do with marriage.

KĀLĪCARAN: [*a bit chagrined that his artful approach has had no effect*] Yes.

VASUDEV: Well then, better tell me what it's all about first of all.

KĀLĪCARAN: All right, here it is. Listen carefully. I've got to be quick with this. There isn't much time because over there everything. . . . [*Again he decides to give up any attempt to disguise the matter. Whatever guilt he may feel for having gotten* VASUDEV *involved in this affair, he is incapable of the artifice required to hide the fact.*] Look, over in Mathura King Ugrasen has been deposed by his own son and clamped in jail. The prince has made himself king and sits on the throne himself.

VASUDEV: [*taken aback*] Really?

KĀLĪCARAN: Yes, and here's the thing. He has a sister—actually his first cousin—and he wants you to marry her. So he's sent me to get you.

VASUDEV: Oh come on, Pundit. You must be making fun of me.

Do you mean to tell me that the king of the great realm of Mathura wants some little princeling like me to marry his sister? Where's the sense in it?

KĀLĪCARAN: [*as inattentive to* VASUDEV'S *question as he had been unconcerned before to discover the reason for* KANS'S *summons*] Look, either you come willingly or we'll have to take you by force, because that Kans is the sort of person that once his anger starts bubbling, there's no stopping it. Satisfied one moment, livid the next. So you'd better come along with me right away. We'll make a marriage procession of it. Come on.

[VASUDEV *is still quite overwhelmed with the suddenness of all this, not knowing whether he should be overjoyed or apprehensive. But he tags along behind* KĀLĪCARAN, *who offers him a little advice as they proceed.*]

Look Vasudev, when Kans gets it in his head to do something it's best just to put your fingers in your ears and keep your peace and go along with it.

[*At that the curtain rises, revealing the royal court and the figure about whom* KĀLĪCARAN *is so concerned.*]

Hail, Your Highness. Here's Vasudev.

KANS: [*affecting with some difficulty the air of politeness and respect one expects on the part of a member of the family of the bride when addressing a member of the family of the groom, and particularly the groom himself*] Yes, yes, welcome, Vasudev. Come right in.

VASUDEV: [*also the soul of decorum*] Well, sir, I hope everything is going smoothly for you.

KANS: Oh, but do tell me about yourself, Vasudev. Has any inconvenience befallen you on your journey, I hope not?

VASUDEV: No, nothing at all.

KANS: [*bellowing*] Chamberlain! Pundit!

KĀLĪCARAN AND FANG: [*hurrying forward*] Yes, yes, Your Majesty.

KANS: Take Vasudev here and get him a bath and dress him up like a groom.

KĀLĪCARAN: But not just like that! What about the wedding pavilion?

KANS: Oh forget about it![44]

KĀLĪCARAN: Come on, Vasudev. [*He motions* VASUDEV *in his direction as Kans adopts an attitude of royal indifference. Then after a gesture or two with* VASUDEV, *he turns to address the king.*] Well, the marriage is complete, Your Highness, and such a happy . . .

KANS: [*a little surprised*] What? It's already over?

KĀLĪCARAN: Yes indeed, Your Majesty, and what a happy occasion it was. Never before was there a marriage like this, and never will there be one again.

KANS: [*At a loss to know what to say on an occasion that calls for expressions of joy, he grumbles on with a gruff, artificial politeness.*] Well then, Vasudev, is there any other way I can be of service to you? If there's any difficulty . . . ?

VASUDEV: No, no, everything's just fine. There are no problems whatever.

KANS: Nothing at all that troubles your mind, nothing?

VASUDEV: No, no, everything's just dandy. [*He hesitates a moment and begins slowly*] Well, yes, there is one request I'd like to make: I really must be getting back.

KANS: Oh heavens no, Vasudev! You must stay three or four months!

FANG: [*to* KANS] Not three or four months, Your Majesty, three or four years!

VASUDEV: But Your Majesty is aware what is involved in administering a kingdom, and I shall have been away . . .

FANG: Never mind about that. [*To* KANS] You can let him go now, but when he comes back in a week, he'll have to stay for at least four or six months.[45]

KANS: Yes, you're right. Now tell me, what should we offer for a dowry?

FANG: You should give twice as much as you received yourself.

KANS: Oh no! Four times as much!

[*He insists on this with great pride, since the size of the dowry is a measure of his wealth and position.*]

FANG: Excellent. That means ten thousand elephants . . .

KANS: Ten thousand elephants . . .

FANG: And ten thousand horses . . .

KANS: Ten thousand horses . . .

FANG: And ten thousand cars and ten thousand servant-girls.

KANS: Ten thousand cars and ten thousand servant girls?

FANG: Yes, Your Majesty.

KANS: What else?

FANG: And, munificent King, fifty thousand asses.

[*The* AUDIENCE *loves this impertinent addition to the list.*]

KANS: Asses! What for?

FANG: Now, now, is it going to be your responsibility to gather all this together or mine?

KANS: Yes, yes, quite right. But that brings up another point. We're going to be giving him a contingent of slaves and servants along with the rest of his treasure, and there will be expenses in looking after them. So we'd better provide for them with even further resources.

FANG: Yes, Maharaja, you are right.

KANS: Well then, sign over to him the revenue from five towns. Put them in his name.

FANG: Done. Yes, Your Majesty, no one could possibly give more than you will be giving.

KANS: Good. And I myself want to serve as my sister's carriage driver.

FANG: Oh excellent, Your Majesty, nothing could be finer.

[KANS *refers to the moment when the married couple drive away to their quarters to spend their first night together, and this is the next scene that materializes on the stage. The wedding ceremony itself is left to the imagination. We first see the newlyweds—and, indeed,* DEVAKĪ *for the first time—as the curtain rises midstage to reveal another curtain at the back, on which a Moghul-style horse and carriage have been painted in brightest blue, red, and gold. Holes cut in the curtain make windows for the carriage, and through them we see* VASUDEV *riding in the front seat and the demure* DEVAKĪ *behind him, her face entirely covered by the veil of her traditional red wedding sari.* KANS *stands before the curtain as if he were ready to mount the carriage and drive it away when his attention is distracted by a verse that wafts across the stage from the musicians' quarters.*]

MUSICIANS:

He lifted Devakī into the carriage,
  himself to serve as the driver,
And bursting with pride he mounted the carriage,
  intending to take her away;

27. Kans ready to drive off Devakī and Vasudev in the nuptial carriage

Mounted the carriage, bursting with pride,
  until a voice from heaven cried:
"This will be the death of Kans—
  Devakī's eighth-born son"[46]

VOICE: [*Loud but unseen, it addresses* KANS *from the rafters, so that he cranes his neck backward, starting in horror and amazement.*] Well, King Kans, what's making you so puffed up with pride at the marriage of your sister Devakī? Devakī's eighth child is going to be the death of you — your death!

KANS: [*struck with terror*] Can this be true?

VOICE: [*in ominous repetition*] Listen, King Kans, what's making you so puffed up with pride at the marriage of your sister Devakī? Devakī's eighth child is going to be the death of you — your death!

KANS: Can it be true that my sister's eighth child will be my death? [*Dumbly*] Death!

MUSICIANS:

Hearing this voice he stepped down from the carriage,
and downward fell his pride.

KANS: [*Turning on his heels and dragging Devakī out from behind the carriage-curtain, he brings her to her knees with a great threatening gesture.*] Sister Devakī, how happily I arranged for your marriage! How happily I prepared to bid you farewell! And now I learn that the very one whose marriage I so joyfully prepared is to be the mother of my own death! Now I have no choice but to kill you — I'll never breathe a sigh of relief until I do.

DEVAKĪ: [*pathetically*] Oh brother, brother!

KANS: Yes . . .

DEVAKĪ: [*raising her joined hands to him in a piteous gesture of petition*] I beg of you . . .

KANS: [*fighting off the fraternal sentiments that are genuinely his*] Oh no, no tears for me. I'm keeping my eyes wide open until I've turned you to ash.[47]

DEVAKĪ: [*with helpless weeping*] Brother!

KANS: [*steeling himself*] Oh, I can be a cruel lion if I have to be.

DEVAKĪ: [*her upraised hands still pleading*] But none of the fault is mine!

KANS: None?

DEVAKĪ: No. I've done no crime. [*Even so,* KANS *begins to unsheathe his great scimitar.* DEVAKĪ *reacts with astonishment.*] How can you take a sword to a member of the weaker sex? [*Desperate, she raises her tearful petition beyond her brother to the gods.*] How can all this be?

28. Kans threatening to kill Devakī

Where is the Creator dozing? How can it be that I am to perish with the sword of my own brother laid to my neck? [*Turning her gesture to the* AUDIENCE] You citizens of the world, close your eyes today! For a bride, snatched away from the most auspicious moment of her life, from the very wedding pavilion, to have all her hopes burned up in an instant! [*And again to heaven, now addressing Viṣṇu specifically*] O bearer of the discus, once I am burned, then take me to yourself. Discus-bearer, my sole trust is in you.

KANS: [*grasping* DEVAKĪ'*s neck and raising his sword above it*] Prepare the soul that is your own executioner to meet its death!

VASUDEV: [*authoritatively, having emerged from the carriage*] Stop, King!

MUSICIANS:

Then Vasudev, wretched, spoke . . .[48]

VASUDEV: Rash! It's rash of you, King, to take the sword to a woman! The whole thing sheds no glory on you.

KANS: Vasudev, are you against me too?

VASUDEV: Against you? No, it's you yourself who have started down this evil road.

KANS: How so?

VASUDEV: Because after giving a girl in marriage she no longer has anything to do with you. You have lost your authority here. It is altogether mine.

KANS: Listen, Vasudev, if you're so enamored after just a moment's time spent with this girl, don't worry. I'll scour the world from the snakes beneath to the gods above and come up with the most beautiful bride in all creation and lay her at your feet. But this one — this mother of death — I've got to put her behind me.

VASUDEV: Look, I have just one request. Hear me out.

KANS: Speak on.

VASUDEV: First of all, there's the fact that Devakī is your sister. Second, she wears the bangles of a married woman. And third, it was you yourself who arranged the wedding. All that being the case, would you contemplate such a thing? Don't forget: everything that is born must by the same token die. So how is it that someone as strong as you is afraid of death? On this earth many heroes have come and gone, you know. Let me remind you of eminent figures such as Dilīp, your own progenitor, or Bali, who was so strong on earth that his fame resounded to the heavens; yet he too had to leave the earth when his time came. And then there was Droṇ, master in the art of archery, who was nonetheless relieved of his earthly burden by Karṇa; and Rāvaṇ, renowned for his wickedness, who nonetheless joined the ranks of the gods when he died. So you see, even a hero whom the texts describe as being powerful as the sun has to meet his end sometime.[49]

KANS: But you know what people say, Vasudev: no iron, no sword. Well it's the same thing here. No Devakī, no son.

MUSICIANS:

Then Vasudev asked the king
 to listen to his petition:
"Why should you butcher poor
 Devakī
 when the enemy here is her son?"[50]

VASUDEV: What I can't see, King, is why you want to harm poor Devakī. It's her eighth child that is to bring your death, not she.

KANS: Well, who's he going to get born from? Logic dictates that if there's a tree bearing poisonous fruit, you have to cut it out by the roots; otherwise who knows how many other trees can come from it? If I kill Devakī there simply won't be a son to deal with.

VASUDEV: Oh, don't worry about that:

Take away any son she may have,
 but give us back her life.[51]

King, I swear that I will turn over to you every child she has.

KANS: Oh Vasudev, I can't believe that. There's not a father in the world who would throw his own beloved children before a cruel lion.

VASUDEV: [*reaching heavenward in a gesture of ultimate solemnity*] Let the sun and moon by my witnesses. Every single child that shall ever come to Devakī I will give you, I will give you, I will give you.[52]

KANS: All right, but until Devakī has had her eighth child the two of you will have to remain in my jail. Is that agreed?

VASUDEV: Agreed.

KANS: [*to the* CHAMBERLAIN] Take them off to prison. See to it that their hands are put in handcuffs and their feet in fetters and make sure that a constant watch is kept over them.

FANG: Very well, Your Majesty.

[*He takes them off at the back and once again, when the mid-stage curtain rises, we see a painted curtain at the back of the stage. But circumstances have changed. This time it is no nuptial carriage, but a prison. The curtain is painted entirely black, but between four narrow vertical strips rectangular squares representing bars are cut away to show the cell itself. And there we see the languishing couple,* VASUDEV *and* DEVAKĪ. *As* KANS *had displayed himself before the earlier curtain, legs spread wide in pride, so he does now, but this time it is a pride of defiance more than self-congratulation.*]

KANS: And if there should be any slip-up . . .

[*Having thundered out this last imprecation,* KANS *relaxes his vigilance for a moment as the* MUSICIANS *break in to sing a verse that will inform the* AUDIENCE *that some months have passed before the dialogue resumes.*]

MUSICIANS:

The moment his very first son was born,
Vasudev brought it to Kans.[53]

VASUDEV: [*holding a soft, white bundle of cloth intended to suggest an infant*] Chamberlain! [FANG *appears from the wings.*] Here. Take this, our first son, and hand it over to the king. [*He does so.*]

KANS: [*soliloquizing as he holds the little bundle*] It's Devakī's eighth son that spells death for me. Why am I concerned with this child? Why should I kill it? And what harm could it possibly do to me? Look, the poor thing's so fragile. All I have to do is blow on it and it'll fly heavenward.

In this crucial moment of indecision Nārad appears — messenger of the gods, troublemaker, arranger of plots. His presence on the scene here is dictated by the fact that for the right to be totally vindicated, Kans must be fully deserving of the punishment that awaits him, and Kans — half-human after all — is wavering. Nārad therefore appeals to his demonic nature. Playing devil's advocate, he assures Kans that he has done well thus far, right down to the moment when he drove some of the sacrificers into the river, thus committing the practically unpardonable offense of killing a Brahmin. He urges Kans to continue in his bloodthirsty course, assuring him that the only way in which he can be sure of policing Devakī's progeny is to kill every one of them. After all, argues Nārad, the gods do not add the way humans do. They are clever. They talk of Devakī's eighth child, but who knows where they start numbering this series of eight? Thus any one of her offspring could be the eighth, the one to kill him. If he is to defend himself he will have to kill them all. Kans is very squeamish about doing so, but eventually he comes around, and in one swift, violent gesture he flings the little white bundle up into the rafters and out of sight.

Doubly squeamish the second time that Vasudev presents him with an infant to massacre, he insists that Fang perform the deed for him. In a fury of pusilanimous repulsion, however, Fang shrinks from the task, and Kans must again throw the child to the winds himself. Nārad has gone off by this point, but his intervention has performed the necessary function of maintaining Kans in a path of villainy that will fully justify the retribution that looms over him. He may not be responsible for the fact that his nature was determined when a demon raped his mother, but for these acts of vengeance that would not be required by his fate he can clearly be held to account. Thus Nārad makes sure that Krishna's victory over the king of Mathura will be the vindication of justice over the most despicable of tyrannies.

The demise of the third through sixth sons of Devakī is left to the imaginative recall of the audience. Nor is an attempt made to incorporate in this *līlā* the story of the miraculous circumstances surrounding the birth of the seventh. In any case, everyone knows the story well: how the transfer of the fetus Balarām from the womb of Devakī to that of Rohiṇī made it appear that Devakī had aborted, and thus the child was saved from the wrath of Kans.

The *līlā* jumps to the eighth pregnancy. Devakī, having seen the destruction of all her progeny, is by this time frantic. We witness a scene in which she calls out to heaven from her prison cell, attempting to enlist the pity of the gods. First she appeals to Śiva, who appears as she crouches before him, head bowed to the ground. He, however, refers her to a higher authority: he tells her to pray to Viṣṇu. That she does, and once again the divine figure materializes on stage. The curtain at the rear rises to reveal a tableau of Viṣṇu reclining on the great serpent Śeṣ, as he did at the beginning of creation. A cardboard structure represents the hood of the serpent and a cloth painted blue and decorated with lotuses suggests the primeval ocean on which it swims. Viṣṇu himself is portrayed by the boy who will represent Krishna, and he is quick to assure his mother-to-be, who is prostrated low before him, that all the terror she has endured is in the cause of good. He urges patience upon her, and describes her role as one in a great drama of salvation.

As the curtain falls and a calmed Devakī goes off, divine conversation continues in the wings. We hear Viṣṇu explaining to Yogamāyā, the goddess who personifies supernal sleight-of-hand, what her role is to be in the plot that is about to unfold. She will abandon her divine status and take birth in the womb of Yaśodā, Nanda's simple wife, across the river in Braj. Her pregnancy will proceed simultaneously with his own time in Devakī's womb, and at the moment of birth there will be a transfer even more dramatic than that attending the birth of Balarām. She departs for Braj.

Soon we are in the presence of Kans and his courtiers once again. The birth is at hand, and Kans is making sure that nothing allows the situation to slip out of his control. He doubles the guard on the prison by making even such exalted personages as Fang take their turn at the vigil. As night approaches and it seems the delivery must come before the morning dawns, he charges them all sternly not to submit to sleep. All vow that they will not let their eyelids fall. But no sooner does he walk offstage than we see every courtier drop into weary slumber—again through the mysterious power of Yogamāyā, as the story goes. Fang falls asleep with a particular lack of ceremony: the moment Kans leaves he crumbles to the stage, making a great thud. All the audience can see of him are his large feet and the holes in his socks, and over that his great mound of a stomach.

Once the guards have lain about the stage for a moment, snoring vociferously, the curtain rises to reveal once again the prison at the back of the stage. And there one sees the great event. For a second time Viṣṇu reveals himself, but this time he stands erect, Krishna with four arms. Two cardboard arms are raised with the characteristic discus and conch; the forearms are alive and rest akimbo on the hips. First the audience gasps at this vision and then, since all the tension of Kans's threats seems relieved and salvation at hand, it breaks out in applause. Devakī and Vasudev bow low in prayer, and as they do so this remarkable child directs his father as to how he should transport him to safety.

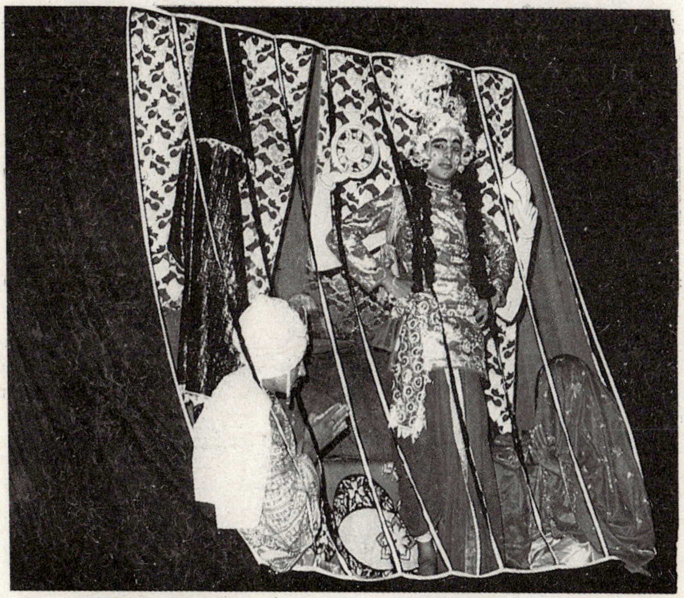

29. The birth of Krishna

And so it all takes place. A curtain drops in front of the city of Kans—palace, prison, sleeping guards, and all—and we see the upper half of Vasudev's torso as he wades through a tank sunk at the front of the stage. His son sits in a basket atop his turban, head shielded, as was Viṣṇu's, by the cardboard hood of the holy serpent Śeṣ. The Puranas relate how Vasudev, afraid that this most special of sons should be easily detected in his four-armed form, had requested him to take the form of a simple baby, and indeed that has been done here. Krishna is played by a different member of the company now, the *svāmī*'s little seven-year-old son who usually acts the part of the child Krishna. The audience watches with delight as the concerned father sways under the burden of his newborn son while he fords the monsoon-swollen waters of the Jumna, and this tiny

30. Vasudev carrying Krishna across the Jumna to safety

Krishna enjoys his ride as much as he relishes all his childish roles.

Once the pair has crossed the tank, the miraculous escape to Braj has been performed, and the curtain lifts again to direct our attention to the aftermath in Mathura. We do not see Vasudev return to prison bearing the girl child that Yogamāyā has become, but we know that it has happened because once again he comes before the court with the ancient tidings: "It's a girl!" This time, however, he has to rouse the guards from their slumbers, and there are many yawns and sleepy clearings of the throat before they suddenly snap to consciousness and realize what has happened. Fang catapults belatedly into action and calls for Kans, relaying the birth announcement as soon as the latter makes his menacing appearance. Kans stalks toward the prison and beckons Devakī, who emerges from behind the bars cradling in her arms the familiar little white bundle. With a defiant shout Kans lunges forth and grabs the baby, flinging it into the rafters one last time.

But this time the rafters answer back. It is Yogamāyā risen from the dead, standing triumphant in a balcony just above the stage and bearing in her four arms not only the energies of Viṣṇu as symbolized by the discus and conch, but also the capabilities of Śiva, as represented by the trident. Full of power, she directs an untamed, derisive laugh down at Kans—a laugh we have not heard since Kans directed it at his father and deposed him—for all his wicked efforts have been no match for the machinations of fate. Kans is stunned and terrified. He falls to his knees before his sister, whom he has just robbed of her last motherhood, and implores her forgiveness. And indeed, her female energy remains as kind as Yogamāyā's has been implacable. As her brother beseeches her with the tremulousness and humility she had once brought before him, she forgives him immediately, assuring him that all this has not been strictly speaking a fault of his, but rather the outworking of providence itself.

Yogamāyā watches over this scene of family reconciliation, scattering the seeds of forgetfulness. For both Kans and Devakī must lose sight of this shaft of divine light that illuminates the circumstances of Krishna's birth on the day of the incarnation itself. Otherwise the great drama could not proceed, generating its *līlās* from this day of Krishna's full epiphany until the next, a year later, when the birth will be enacted again. Already the invisible curtain of oblivion begins to fall in the very next action we observe, for Kans's act of piety and insight is overlaid with a parallel gesture on the part of Fang. Just as Kans had made his supplications to Devakī, so now the bloated, supercilious chamberlain bows before Kans. This time, however, it is not penance for an offence against godliness, but rather in regret that the cause of evil has not been more perfectly served. Fang has not seen the face of Yogamāyā. He only acts reflexively, caught in her swirling garments. As he does so he draws Kans back into the role he must play, as the tale goes, until the time of his own simultaneous defeat and release years hence, when Krishna will vanquish him in tournament, David against Goliath.

But that is long ahead, and in fact that final heroic confrontation is no longer as essential to the telling of Krishna's story as it once was. It is possible to see whole cycles of *rās līlās* without witnessing the battle that was once the culmination of the entire saga, the great wrestling scene in which Krishna and his brother defeat the most powerful wrestlers in the realm — not to mention wild elephants — and Krishna drags the evil king down from his royal box by the hair until he lies bruised and dead at his feet. All that is no longer quite necessary. Today's *rās līlās* celebrate play and epiphany more than heroism. They elicit feelings rather than recording events. Their purpose is to invite the audience's participation in the play more than it is to document a victory to which they, with the rest of humanity, are heir.

Hence it is more than chronologically appropriate that the day after the curtain falls on the *līlā* of Krishna's birth, as now it does, it rises to welcome all who have come to Braj to join with those who live there in celebrating the birth of Krishna into this very commonplace realm of cows and cowherds. As in temples on that day, so in the *līlās* all is frivolity and joy as the people of Braj gather at Nanda's house to congratulate him and

Yaśodā on the birth of their son. The men roughhouse and joke, and all present join with the women in the songs of congratulation they bring to Krishna's parents, as they would to any mother fortunate enough to have a son. These simple, ebullient songs of blessing and congratulation envelop the divine child in the humble world where his worshipers live, and there he will stay, mysteriously, even after he responds to the call from Mathura and departs again.

Year by year, as the day rolls around, Yaśodā joins the chorus herself. In well-known words drawn from the most famous collection of poetry in Braj, the *Sūr Sāgar* attributed to the great sixteenth-century poet Sūr Dās, she invites the world to share her happiness:

"Hey friend, it's my little boy's birthday today:
call all the womenfolk, let them flock
to sing their birthday blessings.
Smear sandalpaste on the courtyard floor
and there make an altar and all together
blow the horns with joy.
Summon the Brahmins and have them set
an auspicious time, go dress little Syām,
clothe him with ornaments.
Bring the finest saris from the five basic colors
for all women to wear, both older and young:
let them join in joyous dance."
Thus she called the cowherd women
and it went this way, "Quick! Hasten!
why do you delay?"
She cradled Krishna and showed him to Nanda,
but he hurried her on, "The moment is coming,
so bathe the little one."
Sūr sees the beautiful charm of Syām,
how body and spirit the young women share it,
blessing the birthday boy.[54]

Chapter III

The Theft of the Flute

Introduction

THERE ARE no fixed conventions governing the order in which the *rās līlās* should be presented, besides the obvious fact that in a monsoon sequence the play depicting Kirshna's birth will fall at *janmāṣṭamī*, the festival celebrating the event. In addition, it is likely that the *mahārās līlā*, the Great Circle Dance, will be performed on or about the full moon, since it was a full moon that inspired it; and it is also likely that among the last of the *līlās* to be performed will be some version of the *dān līlā*, the *līlā* of the gift (Krishna's to the *gopīs*, theirs to him, or both). This is intended to elicit generosity on the part of the audience that has been attending the *līlās* throughout the cycle; it reminds them of the gift they have been receiving, and asks them to return it in the measure they can with monetary offerings. If a *rās līlā* troupe accepts an engagement at some other time than during the monsoon, it is sometimes thought desirable that the plays follow a rough sequence describing Krishna's development from child to adolescent, especially if the engagement lasts a full month, as is preferred. But in no case are there fixed rules.

Some *rāsdhārīs* insist, in fact, that the spontaneity that is so important to the message of these plays would be compromised if an order were laid out in advance. Since one of the aims of the *līlās* is to encourage the audience to participate in whatever mood *(ras)* they depict, the mood of the boy who plays Krishna is cardinally important at the time of any given performance. The repertory is so well known that he can make his choice just before the play begins, and some *rāsdhārīs* feel strongly that this is the way it should be. Everything depends, they say, on what he feels at the moment the *līlā* begins. Other *rāsdhārīs* are not reluctant to announce the subject of the *līlā* next to be presented at the end of a performance, in the hopes of drawing the audience back for more. But no one will be surprised or offended to find upon returning that the *līlā* for the day is entirely different from what had been predicted. Perhaps some special personage has appeared and is to be honored with a favorite *līlā*; perhaps a donor has offered to underwrite the costs of another; perhaps a player crucial to a given *līlā* has laryngitis or is sick; perhaps the players just changed their minds. I know of only one company that prints a schedule of the *līlās* they will perform in a given rainy season, and even that is often honored in the breach.

Given this absence of prescribed schedule—even a positive suspicion of schedule—it is significant that one *līlā* seems to be performed more often at the beginning of a series of *līlās* than any other. It is the *banśī corī līlā*, "The Theft of the Flute." This *līlā* has an innate charm, and that is important; it sets the right tone for the sequence of *līlās* that will follow. Like the flute itself, it issues a sweet summons for all around to join in the play that is to come. In addition, it gives the audience a useful introduction to the most central personages of the *līlās* and to some of their most characteristic themes.

The dramatis personae are sharply reduced in number from

the array we observed in the play depicting Kirshna's birth. Here there are no parents, no great antagonistic presences like Kans, not even a crew of unruly cowherds. Aside from Krishna, there is only one other male figure, his faithful but bumbling friend Mansukhā, who fulfills the function of the buffoon or jester *(vidūṣak)*. All the rest are *gopīs*, and Radha is their chief. With the exception of Mansukhā, whose position is theologically though not theatrically marginal, these are the most central players in the *rās līlā*. It is the *gopīs* who dance in the *rās*, that mandala which expresses the quintessence of love; only they join the charmed circle in which all participants have the sensation that they are in direct and full contact with Krishna. The flute *līlā* draws attention to this fact by showing how Mansukhā thinks he has access to this magical circle, but in fact does not. Dizzy and deluded, unready for love, he falls to the floor unconscious, a failure.

Nonetheless, Mansukhā's presence in the cast is important. Not only does this dull-witted eight-year-old entertain the audience marvellously, but he serves as a needed foil for the more serious implications of the drama. By his incomprehension of the ties of love that bind the Braj girls to Krishna, he illustrates the *gopīs'* unique exaltation. If he were not outside the circle of the *rās*, we would not be able so clearly to sense the power it has for those whom it comprehends. And there is the fact that Krishna needs a friend, someone to share confidences with in the battle of the sexes, that most familiar topic of all the *līlās*.

In this play, the battle of the sexes is given an interesting twist. It is true that Krishna is pitted against Radha and the other girls as they try to steal his flute. Indeed, Krishna must appear before a feminine tribunal before he can get it back. But in another sense this is not male versus female, but a squabble among the women involved. For the flute itself is pictured as a woman, as is frequently the case in the literature of Krishna, and the *gopīs* are jealous of her hold over him. She is with him always and in the most intimate of contacts, as the songs at the beginning of the *līlā* make clear.

The girls respond to her music, yes. She announces the *rās* itself; her music beckons them into the circle and creates the motion that animates the dance. She enunciates the grammar in terms of which the sexes meet, Krishna and his women, as subject and predicate, predicate and subject. But by the same token they resent her, for she controls them altogether too much, not only creating the conditions for their participation in love, but also preventing them from doing anything else. At the first note from the flute they look up from their work, and as she plays on they lose all concentration and are torn away from their homes and families to follow where she leads. She robs them of their independence. So they, to regain it, will steal her, making Krishna at least in that one moment clearly dependent upon them; for without her he has lost his language, lost that music by which he animates the world. She is his grammarian, and without her he is speechless.[1]

The issue of dependence is fundamental in the theology and mythology of Krishna, for Krishna is love, love spells dependence, and the human soul resists it. From the most ancient times the poets and philosophers of India have dared to ask which was stronger, God's dependence on humankind or ours upon the divine.[2] In the plays of Krishna this debate is constantly waged: is Krishna (the summation of everything divine) more dependent upon Radha (who in large measure symbolizes the heights to which human devotion can rise), or is she more dependent upon him? In one scene we will see her miserable without him because of some misunderstanding or lover's quarrel, and in the next we will see him sunk in a depression no less deep. In one scene we see him asserting his control over her, and in the next we find that she is in command. Thus proceeds the tug of war between the two parts of the human-divine relation, which the theologians of Braj insist is an inseparable totality.

Nobody wins or loses in *līlās* such as these. It is all just a play in which one role or another asserts itself, and the resolution brings the reemergence of harmony rather than a measurable gain for either side. In this respect the play is like music, generating dissonance between its constituent chords only to resolve it, and it is no wonder that music itself, Krishna's bamboo flute, is the subject of this first play in many *rās līlā* sequences.

Similarly, the resolution of the play is quite specifically

musical. As the play moves into its final moments we find that Krishna is unable to regain his flute on juridical grounds. No argument can be brought that will persuade the court that he has a legitimate charge against the *gopīs*. They are innocent until proven guilty, and he cannot produce sufficient evidence. What then will avail? The matter is crucial, for he is bereft without his flute. If its music is not returned to him, the whole of his *līlā* will come to a silent halt, its animation lost.

There is an Indian tradition, ancient and as modern as Gandhi, to the effect that the ultimate weapon in the hands of the victim of overwhelming circumstance or adversity is truth. By an "act of truth," it is said, the predicament can be unraveled. The person need but confess publicly his or her own position as it truly is, and the power of that revelation will be enough to turn the tide.[3] Krishna performs an act of truth at the end of the flute *līlā*, but Krishna being who he is, it cannot be a merely verbal proclamation: it is musical. He sings his plight, making a simple musical statement of the fact that without his flute he is lost. That confession cuts to the heart of the matter, and the judge, who is Radha, is immediate in her response. The flute is returned, simply and without justification. Music and sentiment are the victors.[4]

There is more to say about Radha's position of supremacy in the *līlā*—how she takes on the role of arbitrating the passions of Krishna and the *gopīs*—but it is well first to notice some of the particular themes that come to the fore in this *līlā*, since they are all expressive of the quality of ultimate musicality or actionlessness that we have been describing. These are themes that appear in many *līlās*.

First, there is jealousy, and in the plays of Krishna it is always an unfounded jealousy. In this *līlā*, the *gopīs* have no cause to be concerned that Krishna's attachment to the flute can ever stand in the way of his love for them. Quite the contrary, the flute is the vehicle by means of which he spreads that attachment abroad in the land. There is no genuine conflict, only an imagined one in which the ends become jealous of the means. The *gopīs'* sentiments are touching and amusing, and Krishna's response at least equally so, but the whole thing is a tempest in a teapot, a comedy. There is nothing serious here but the emotions, and those, to be sure, are of great importance. There is no real issue, only a misunderstanding fanned by feeling. Ultimately it is all just play. And because the *rās līlā*s are plays about play, such jealousies as these are a common subject.[5]

A second representative theme in the *banśī corī līlā* is that of cross-dressing. One plot after another in the *rās līlā*s turns on this motif, in which a boy dresses as a girl or a girl as a boy. Sex roles, symbolized by dress, are clearly, almost rigidly, defined in India, so their abrogation is always a matter of amusement. The *līlā*s take advantage of this fact time and again. Often Radha disguises herself as a cowherd and goes off to test Krishna's love for her,[6] or she may slip into Krishna's presence under her friend Lalitā's billowing shawl.[7] Krishna can play this game too, of course: he eludes the careful guard kept by Radha's mother-in-law, and tries to fool Radha as well by dressing up as a woman selling mynah birds, or as a dyer woman or some other female.[8] Ultimately they may even take each other's roles, as they do in the *paraspar mān līlā*, or, with complete exchanges of dress, in the *rājdān līlā*.[9] The transferability of all sex roles between Radha and Krishna illustrates the extent to which they are themselves interchangeable, two aspects of a single reality. Each time such a change takes place the spectators contemplate that fact, one whose implications are far-reaching enough to suggest that even humanity and divinity are but different costumes for an undifferentiable nondual reality.[10]

The flute *līlā* only hints at this, for the change of clothes takes place not between the central personalities, Radha and Krishna, but rather among their attendants. It is Mansukhā who would change clothes and adopt all the marks of womanhood in order to gain access to the circle of the *rās* dance. That is quite impossible for him, and in fact neither Krishna nor Radha is even present to hallow the dance: the whole thing is a trick and a joke. But there is a serious precedent, for legend says this was just the transformation required of Śiva when he sought access to the intimacy of Krishna's presence. He had to become a woman, a *gopī*. This scene figures importantly in the *mahārās līlā*, and we will discuss it soon. For now it is sufficient merely to note that the *bansī corī līlā* announces it and provides a general introduction to the motif of changing dress that is so prominent thoughout the *līlā*s. Like the motif of jealousy, it defines a realm of action that has to do with changes of appearance rather than substance.

Finally, the flute *līlā* incorporates the theme of thievery, which is at least as critical and familiar in the *rās līlā*s as the other two. Once again the motif is distinctly playful. Nothing is lost or gained, nothing is produced or destroyed; no work is done. It is merely that something changes place; there is a temporary change of possession, hide and seek. Here the object in question is the flute, and the *gopī*s are the thieves, but this is an inversion of the most familiar form of this theme. More than an inversion, in fact, this act of thievery on the *gopī*s' part is a gesture of retaliation, for Krishna is a great thief, and a number of *līlā*s present him so. In one play he steals Radha's ring, but most frequently the object of his desire is what the *gopī*s have in such abundance to give: their milk products. He exacts a toll of curd and butter from them on the banks of the Jumna, preventing them from marketing the goods in Mathura until they pay up.[11] He pretends to be a boatman, and agrees to ferry a band of *gopī*s across the river on their way to the city, only to hold them up in midstream and demand a share of the goods they bear.[12] Most familiarly, we see him creating havoc in his own and various *gopī*s' houses in his search for butter.[13] No wonder, then, that Krishna surmises toward the end of the flute *līlā* that the *gopī*s have just been taking their revenge. And no wonder that the sermonlike materials that introduce the *līlā* to the audience focus almost entirely, as they often do, on Krishna in the role of butter thief.

It is charming to see the tables turned in the *bansī corī līlā*, and interesting that the object the *gopī*s choose to steal from Krishna has as much to do with his love for them as butter has to do with theirs for him. The flute is the medium through which he expresses his love, calling the girls to him. It concentrates into musical form his every loving wish. Similarly, the butter the *gopī*s produce is the symbolic essence of their love for Krishna, the concentrated form of milk, the liquid of love that flows naturally in the female species and whose abundance in Braj is stimulated by the presence of Krishna.[14] Both these acts of thievery, of butter and of the flute, are thefts of love. Thus the *rās līlās* are constantly showing us how love stimulates mischief, and underlining the point that the greatest lover of them all, Krishna, is the greatest mischief-maker. For love is play, not work.

But *is* Krishna the greatest lover of them all? There is a dimension of this flute *līlā* that addresses just that question. The songs at the beginning of the *līlā* describe the unquestionable supremacy of the flute, the central symbol of Krishna's love-making. We learn how its powers and attributes exceed even those of Brahmā, God conceived as creator, and how it transcends the world altogether. As the *gopīs* sing this message, they are at once praising the flute in the highest terms and describing the monumental proportions of their opponent in love. What have they to match it? one begins to ask.

At the end of the play it becomes clear what they have to equal and even exceed the supremacy of the flute. They have Radha. She is their captain, and she becomes the arbitrator of the destiny of the flute. This is a significant fact; for if the inner logic involved in comparing Brahmā unfavorably with the flute is the desire to demonstrate that the transformations caused by love are even more earthshaking than those involved in making manifest the universe, then Radha, into whose power that of the flute is entrusted, must be possessed of a power in love that exceeds even that of the flute. In other words, we are asked to consider the possibility that Radha, by virtue of her love for Krishna, attains an order of supremacy superior to his own.

This is an important theological question in Braj, and has led to the formation of a separate community, the Rādhāvallabhīs, who hold quite firmly that this is so.[15] Other communities, like the Caitanyites, are reluctant to rank the two divine personages in this way, since the relation between them is inconceivable in mortal terms.[16] But insofar as it is Radha's love that exalts her and nothing else—no heritage of divinity such as Krishna bears—the *rās līlās*, including those composed by Caitanyites, raise the question as to whether by virtue of the purity and intensity of that love she deserves to be seen as supreme.

In Hindu society it as almost always a surprise for a woman

to be ranked higher than a man (especially when the man is God), so there is a special power in the representation of Radha and Krishna that was selected to serve as the tableau preceding the *bansī corī līlā*. One saw Radha reclining on the throne and Krishna seated at her feet, massaging them; it was the inversion of the classical pose according to which Lakṣmī massages the feet of Viṣṇu as her intimate service to the Lord of the Universe.[17] The *gopīs* remind us of this inversion when they describe how Krishna has become subservient to his flute (they imagine her a woman), but we know this is only the hyperbole jealousy breeds. The real shock of recognition comes when we see Krishna in a position of clear subservience, standing in supplication at Radha's throne. By virtue of the purity of her love, it seems, she among all the *gopīs* has earned her exalted position as the arbiter of Krishna's passions, and Krishna must come to her feet for a verdict. At last one sees that Radha's sweet silence through the drama has always concealed a presiding presence.

The *bansī corī līlā* is not alone in affirming or at least raising the question of the superiority of Radha over Krishna and thus pointing to the supremacy it symbolizes, the victory of love over all else. Time and again the *līlās* show how Krishna's power is limited by Radha's. In one play, the *gopīs* come picking flowers and Krishna stops them with the claim that he owns the garden, but they are able to come back with arguments to the effect that all of Braj belongs to Radha.[18] But the most memorable testimony to Radha's supremacy, one that elicits a great hush of excitement in the audience, is the moment when Krishna takes on the humble role of washing her feet and then goes further and drinks the water he has used in the process.[19] A more abject gesture of submission is hard to conceive.[20]

The primacy of Radha in Braj was part of what made it such a special occasion when the *bansī corī līlā* was performed by Svāmīs Śrī Rām and Natthī Lāl on August 14, 1976. The performance drew its sweetness from the fact that the company revolved around a young and winning Krishna, and that the other players were also young, not straining the limits of puberty, as in some cases. And this *līlā* has a peculiar combination of musicality and plot, of sweetness and mischief. During the entire *līlā* there was a special quality of affection and attentiveness in the audience. Even at the end, when people normally rise noisily to press toward Radha and Krishna in their living form and go their way, there was an unusual sense of calm and reverence, as if the whole audience had been transfixed by the music of the flute.

But this quality of affectionate absorption, which I have never witnessed in quite this measure, was generated even before the *līlā* proper began. One sensed it already when the *rās*, the dance sequence, culminated in the unusual vision of Krishna in attendance upon Radha. Even when the audience had returned to their places after having made their offerings and taken a close look, the musicians sang on, their eyes fixed on the divine couple. In contrast to normal practice, they were joined at that point by Puruṣottam Gosvāmī, the sponsor of the *līlā*s at the Caitanya Prem Sansthān. Covering his head to signify his connection with the *gopī*s, his own femininity as a lover of Krishna, he took a place behind the musicians, hidden from the public view. And there, inspired by the vision of the supremacy of Radha, the supremacy of love, he poured out songs of his own composition so heartfelt that they cast a unique spell over this *līlā*. Audience and players both were drawn into a special mood of indulgence, affection, and peace.

The Theft of the Flute

Enter four SAKHĪS *as the* MUSICIANS *set the stage in song*

MUSICIANS:

A flute, a tuneful bamboo flute
  —or is it a fisherman's pole?—
The name is the same and so is the goal:
  to tangle, lure, and snare.
Hari's little bamboo flute
  makes mountain ranges shatter
And drives me to such madness
  I could twist and shatter it!
Hari's captivating reed
  plays deep as it plays strong,

And on the banks of the Kālindī
Krishna Dās is startled by its sound.[21]

SAKHĪ 1: Hey friend, where's that flute that's playing?

SAKHĪ 2: I don't know, friend. Where do you suppose?

SAKHĪ 3: I don't know, but it's playing so sweetly that it's driving me to distraction.

SAKHĪ 4: Do you think you're the only one who's going crazy? Not at all. That flute's unsettling the hearts and minds of all of us. And it's no wonder. That flute is more powerful than Brahmā, you know.

SAKHĪ 2: Oh come on. Do you mean to tell me that slip of a stick is greater than Brahmā?

SAKHĪ 4: That's right, friend.

SAKHĪ 2: But Brahmā's responsible for creating the whole world! And what, I'd like to know, has this flute created?

SAKHĪ 4: Just listen, my friend [*as she begins to quote a* pad *of Gadādhar*]

It's cleverer by far than all of Braj,
it rules the universe—
our dear one's little flute.

You see, all Brahmā did was get the world going, but this flute has managed to turn the whole thing inside out!

SAKHĪ 2: How's that, friend?

SAKHĪ 4: Well, on the one hand it takes dumb matter and breathes life into it, and on the other it takes what has consciousness and renders it still as a stone. See what I mean? It turns the whole creation inside out.[22]

SAKHĪ 3: That's true enough, friend, true enough. [*Then she continues the* pad]

Brahmā, Creator Lord, proclaims
four Vedas with four mouths:
Half of what this proud one has
to thunder forth her calls—
our dear one's little flute.[23]

SAKHĪ 4: What's that, friend? I know Brahmā has four faces, four mouths, but how many did you say this flute has?

SAKHĪ 3: Brahmā just has four, but this flute has eight.

SAKHĪ 4: How's that?

SAKHĪ 3: Look, she has eight openings through which she thunders day and night—in other words, eight mouths. And,

The four-faced one pervades
this brilliant, potent world he's made.
But she commands the lotus hands
of Hari—see her pride!—
our dear one's little flute.[24]

SAKHĪ 4: Brahmā has lotus throne, friend, I know that, but what's this about the flute?

SAKHĪ 3: Well, Brahmā may have one lotus throne, but she has two of them. You know how soft Syām Sundar's hands are, soft as lotuses. And that's where she sits day and night, enthroned in splendor—not on one lotus throne but two!

SAKHĪ 4: Yes, I guess you're right about that, but . . .

SAKHĪ 3: [*interrupting to continue her presentation of the evidence*]

One lone celestial goose
is enough for the Master of Fate.
But she rides all the milkmaids,
each one her spiritual bird—
our dear one's little flute.[25]

SAKHĪ 4: I know that Brahmā travels on a celestial goose, but what does this flute have to travel on?

SAKHĪ 3: Brahmā only has one such goose, but she has droves of them, males and females both, to bear her around where she will. It's the truth: all she has to do is play a note and we Braj *gopīs* just get up and go off where she wants. One note and it's as if she had innumerable great geese at her command—us! And friend, she's greater than Lakṣmī, too.

SAKHĪ 4: Oh come now. First this brittle little twig is greater than Brahmā, and now she's supposed to outshine Lakṣmī, too?

SAKHĪ 3: That's right. [*Continuing the same* pad]

Śrī may dwell with the Lord of Vaikuṇṭha,
but she serves him at night as masseuse;
While *this* one takes his mouth as her throne,
her luxuriant couch, his hand.

SAKHĪ 4: Lakṣmī is in charge of the service of the feet of God, Nārāyaṇ himself. Night after night she has the privilege of massaging them. And what service is this flute in charge of?

SAKHĪ 3: You're right that Lakṣmī is in charge of all that for Nārāyaṇ, for God himself, but look what this flute does: she turns the tables and makes Syām Sundar serve *her!*

SAKHĪ 4: Just how does she do that?

SAKHĪ 3:

She pillows her head on the swell of his lips
  and spreads out her bed on his flowerlike hands.
A delicate beauty, she's fanned by his breezes
  and loosening strands in the length of his hair.
His fingers massage at the flesh of her feet
  but nothing persuades her to yield to delight;
Anyone else would have slumbered with joy
  but sleep doesn't touch her, this vigilant flute.

[*These verses having been introduced from another poem, we return to the longer* pad *to which it was relevant, both generally and in its mention of the motif of massaging the feet.*]

SAKHĪ 4: Well my friend, you've explained a lot about Brahmā so far, but tell me, what about the sacred thread he wears and his Brahmin's braid?[26] What does the flute have that can match that?

SAKHĪ 3: Listen friend,

The deathless drink of his lips has dissolved
  her familial braid and thread.
Even at that, Gadādhar says,
  she's won Nandanandan's love.

You see, this flute has drunk the ambrosial liquid of Syām Sundar's lips, his kiss of deathlessness, and in doing so has abandoned every tie and rule of the householder's life. In a manner of speaking she's taken the vows of asceticism. And do you know any ascetics who keep their brahminical braids and their sacred threads?

SAKHĪ 4: No, I guess not. But tell me, what sort of renunciate is she?

SAKHĪ 3: Oh, she's gone through a very strict regimen of self-mortification.

SAKHĪ 4: She has? What kind of self-mortification?

SAKHĪ 3: Just listen [*adducing a* pad *attributed to Sūr Dās*]:

Through pains austere she has endured,[27]

Through snow and rain and scorching sun,
borne with silent courage,
Cut and pierced with seven holes,
breaking apart her tortured heart,
And through all she proclaimed it was for his love,
to have his lips upon her,
So when he holds her in his hands
she'll have him in her grasp as well.
And Sūr Śrī says that's why it all was dared,
each austerity.

SAKHĪ 4: [*adding another* pad *from the great treasury about* KRISHNA*'s flute, this one a* savaiyā *of anonymous composition, and emphasizing quite a different side of the suffering associated with* KRISHNA*'s flute*]

A fire burst forth from the bamboo groves
when they gave the world this bamboo flute.
She sounds at evening, midnight, dawn
and singes us, this bamboo flute.
Manmohan's[28] become addicted to her:
he's always playing his bamboo flute.
The sound has sent us from our homes in Braj
now that you've conquered here, bamboo flute.

SAKHĪ 3: [*singing still another anonymous* savaiyā *in which the power of the flute is described*]

A jug half full at the side of the well,
the earth untouched, untilled today—
all she can do is sit and sigh.
One girl hears and trips and falls,
another falls unconscious all,
others can't restrain their eyes
from pouring forth the tears inside.
Captain of emotions, you

who've captivated the women of Braj,
why is it you hunt us down
and make us figures of ridicule?
Friends, the time to act is now:
it's time to cut the bamboo down,
for if the bamboo cannot grow,
the bamboo flute will never sound.

SAKHĪ 3: [*continuing this testimony to the power of the flute by introducing yet another song*] Let me tell you what happened to one poor soul.

SAKHĪ 4: What's that?

SAKHĪ 3: [*reciting a* pad *of Raskhān*]

Some poor girl has gone mad today, my friend;
she's unable even to dress herself.
Her mother can do nothing but pray to the gods,
and her mother-in-law has summoned the exorcists.
That, says Raskhān, is what all Braj is doing,
searching their minds to think what might avail,
But nobody thinks to root out the cause
of this dread constellation:[29] the flute.

SAKHĪ 4: [*answering with another* pad *of Raskhān, in which a mother bemoans her daughter's fate*]

Who's enchanted this wandering cow[30]
by playing his beautiful bamboo flute?
Whenever her ear encounters the sound
she bids all propriety farewell,
Wending her way to Nanda's door.
What's to be done with this newlywed girl?
Where, says Raskhān, is a woman in Braj
that Krishna's not whirled and spun like a top?

SAKHĪ 3: [*getting down to business*] Well then, my friend, how are we going to steal away this flute?

SAKHĪ 4: I'll tell you how you can steal it away, but first we've got to make sure that no one's listening.

SAKHĪ 3: Why, who's going to hear out here? We're in the jungle!

SAKHĪ 4: True enough. It does seem that when there's something to be overheard the very walls have ears, but here we are out in the jungle. We'll be safe.

[*Alas, the trees have ears, too, and we witness* MANSUKHĀ, *the comic character who accompanies* KRISHNA *more than any of his other friends, at the side of the stage. The boy who plays* MANSUKHĀ *is a charming, chubby little character about eight years old.*]

MANSUKHĀ: [*to the* GOPĪS] Ha, ha, ha, girls, that's what you think! I've been listening to the whole thing, this little conference you're having.

SAKHĪS: [*goodnaturedly*] Well, then, come right over, Mansukhā.

MANSUKHĀ: [*holding back, a little wary of their graciousness since he has evidently intruded upon them and heard something he shouldn't have*] Well, what is it? Is some festival going on today? I assume I'll be the first to be invited, right?

SAKHĪS: [*beckoning him over and trying to conceal their sarcasm*] Come on over here, Mansukhā. When it comes to you there's no question of invitations. Why, our doors are always open to you.

MANSUKHĀ: [*wagging his head back and forth in denial. His relations with the* GOPĪS *have not, in fact, always been so cordial; there's always a scuffle of some sort.*] Uh uh. This doesn't look too auspicious. Something's fishy here. Listen, you girls, I understand what's going on in your little klatsch.

SAKHĪS: [*in mock surprise*] Oh well! I believe we must have an astrologer with us, a mindreader. Yes sir, do give us the benefit of your expertise.

MANSHUKĀ: Listen, there's no need for astrology here. It's written all over your faces.

SAKHĪS: Really?

MANSUKHĀ: [*rather grandly*] Yes, the face is the mirror of the mind: it registers whatever's going on. So I've seen everything.

SAKHĪS: Just what did you see? You wouldn't mind telling us, would you?

MANSUKHĀ: Look, when I came up, there you were rubbing your hands together and your eyes were glancing about in all directions to make sure no one was looking. And when

31. Mansukhā overhears the *gopīs'* conversation

I descended in the midst of this little harem your faces turned bright red and your hearts started thumping and then you started talking real slow, under your breath. Never mind all your questions. It doesn't take much to add two and two and get four. I know what you were talking about.

SAKHĪS: [*perhaps justly suspicious of* MANSUKHĀ'*s mathematical capabilities, as we shall presently see*] Well, tell us then, what were we talking about?

MANSUKHĀ: You don't think I heard, do you?

SAKHĪS: Well . . .

MANSUKHĀ: You girls are planning to steal away brother Kanhaiyā's flute![31] Right or wrong?

SAKHĪS: [*with exasperation*] You're right, Mansukhā. That flute plays at night, it plays in the daytime—it's *always* playing and we can't get a stitch of work done.

MANSUKHĀ: Well stuff a little cotton in your ears! That's easy.

SAKHĪS: Listen, if we go stuffing cotton in our ears, how are our mothers-in-law and our in-law aunts going to shout their orders at us? They'll start saying we're deaf. No, you just tell us how we're going to get ourselves out of the cage this flute, our co-wife, has built.

MANSUKHĀ: Oh that's no problem at all. You just shut up and go down and jump in the Jumna! That way the cage itself disappears.

SAKHĪS: Why should we go jump in the Jumna? Much better to break that flute in two and offer *it* to the Jumna!

MANSUKHĀ: [*Having taken his potshots, he is now ready to adopt his most elevated tone.*] Now girls, what's all this ranting and raving against the flute? Don't be so jealous: just take yourselves as her equals. Look, praise pertains to the great and holiness to the holy.[32] You're not going to advance your own position by being revengeful and trying to strip her of hers. Instead, you should be more like her: you should change yourselves. And by raising your own status in that way, hers will seem less by comparison. What you need to do is learn to love as well as the flute does, and then Syām Sundar will love you too. [MANSUKHĀ *backs away a little as their contempt for what he has said becomes evident.*]

SAKHĪ 3: Why you little Brahmin boy, you fool, you greedy little character! Have you gotten so fat on our gifts and offerings,[33] have you gotten so big for your britches, that now you're giving *us* instructions on how to love? Listen, that flute's just a dumb stick of wood and you're a complete ass!

MANSUKHĀ: Well I may be a complete ass, *sakhī*, but what makes you think you're such a clever pundit? Huh, pundit?[34] You know what they say [*and he quotes a* dohā *of Premānand*]:

With ear, eye, mouth, and nostril
  assembled in a single place,
Everyone manages to speak, see, and hear—
  but the wise have something more.

SAKHĪ 3: Scram! Get out of here! No more sermons on pundithood, thanks. And if you don't, I'll give you a nice swat and will your face get red!

MANSUKHĀ: Listen *sakhī*, all that would happen if you tried to give me a swat is that your hand would get red.

SAKHĪ 3: [*her hand raised in a threatening gesture*] Out! Out! Get out of here!

MANSUKHĀ: All right, I'll go, but I'm going to tell Krishna.

SAKHĪ 3: Well then, go tell him, see if I care. But scram!

[*With that she chases him offstage. The curtain falls midstage, and* MANSUKHĀ *reappears in front of it. He takes a moment to think things over.*]

MANSUKHĀ: So, the *gopīs* are plotting to steal away Kanhaiyā's flute. Let's think, what should I do about that?

[*In a little scene intended to demonstrate that he lacks something in intellectual faculties, he begins slowly to count on his fingers, as if that would give him the key to what action ought to be taken. As he counts them down one by one, he recites the names of signs of the zodiac, an apparently arbitrary association. As with anything that has the flavor of a mantra or sacred utterance, this is versified, but since it is* MANSUKHĀ *who is composing, the verse is rough indeed and the rhyming a bit crude.*]

Pisces, Aries, Capricorn,
  and Leo's down with the flu.
The girls have adopted a line of attack,
  but they'll all be left spinsters when
        the results are back.

[*Even he feels his formula has been rather inelegant and unhelpful. He scratches his head.*] No, that's not right. [*He makes another attempt.*]

Pisces, Aries, Capricorn,
the fear of a beating makes you shrink forlorn.
But if that means you get hit on the head,
it's not worth it because it just splits open.

[*Again he feels unsatisfied with his efforts at both poetry and insight: somehow his own banal concerns always intrude.* MANSUKHĀ *is forever thinking either about how he can get something to eat or about how he can avoid a beating; here the latter theme has crept into his poetic utterance. He continues undaunted, nonetheless—much to the* AUDIENCE*'s delight. He is still trying to count out the meter on the fingers of one hand.*]

Seven, five, and thirteen,
and old Ghansyām herds lots of donkeys . . .

[*Already the verse seems to have gone astray as* MANSUKHĀ*'s mind wanders onto an idea for some new mischief, and* KRISHNA *appears on stage at this point to save it from the certainty of an even more inglorious conclusion than its predecessors.*]

KRIṢHNA: Hey pal!

MANSUKHĀ: [*looking up from his concentrations*] Oh, hello.

KRISHNA: Hey stupid, what are you thinking about so hard?

MANSUKHĀ: I don't know. I was trying to think, but nothing seemed to come to mind. And it was all for your benefit: I was trying to think something out.

KRISHNA: [*somewhat surprised at* MANSUKHĀ'S *altruism and not sure he wants to benefit from it*] For *my* benefit? Why, what's going on?

MANSUKHĀ: [*proud to have* KRISHNA *at this moment dependent on him for news, and not anxious to come to the point too quickly and relinquish his position*] Well, you lazy Kanhaiyā . . .

KRISHNA: [*sensing already that this is going to be a tiresome affair and anxious to prod him on*] Yes . . .

MANSUKHĀ: [*reeling off a series of participles that will delay his coming to the point*] . . . Oh you Kanhaiyā, always boring people, always complaining, always showing off, always drinking milk, always giving someone else something to drink. . . . [*Suddenly his mind is dry: no further epithets come readily to mind. He stammers on, waiting for further inspiration.*] And . . . and . . . and . . .

32. Mansukhā reports the news to Krishna

KRISHNA: And . . . and . . . and . . . what? Tell me something, will you?

MANSUKHĀ: [*dragging his moment of glory out as long as it will last*] You mean you thought I wasn't going to tell you what's happening?

KRISHNA: Oh come on, idiot.

MANSUKHĀ: [*affecting great hurt at this impatience on the part of his friend*] Now there you go ridiculing me, calling me a fool and a glutton. Always laughing at me!

KRISHNA: Listen buddy, have it your way. You're a clever pundit, you are.

MANSUKHĀ: [*still hurt*] That's right. When there's something you want from me, then I'm a clever pundit. Otherwise a fool.

KRISHNA: Listen, aren't you going to tell me?

MANSUKHĀ: [*still not willing to relinquish his control over the conversation*] Well, tell me this. Which do you love, the flute *sakhī* or the milkmaid *sakhī*s?

KRISHNA: I love them both, of course.

MANSUKHĀ: Yes, but which one more?

KRISHNA: But I love them both: I love the flute and I love the Braj girls.

MANSUKHĀ: Well then watch out, stupid, because your flute's about to be stolen!

KRISHNA: What's that, pal? That would be disastrous!

MANSUKHĀ: Oh don't act so grief-stricken. If they steal one flute *sakhī* there are always other *sakhī*s. If some *sakhī* takes your flute today, you can always make another. What about it, buddy, will you teach me how to play too? We'll take some nice tall *sakhī* and turn her into a nice two-piped flute.[35]

KRISHNA: Listen, you tell me the truth about all this.

MANSUKHĀ: I just did. Today your flute's going to get stolen. You've got bad feeling to deal with among your wives, pal. One side's burning with jealousy for the other.[36] You'd better watch out: those *gopī*s are getting ready to take revenge on your flute.

KRISHNA: Well what's our strategy?

MANSUKHĀ: Strategy, strategy, I'm a regular treasure house of strategies!

[*One remembers the array of clever strategems* MANSUKHĀ *was able to produce just before* KRISHNA *came on stage.*]

Shall I tell you one? Two? Three? Four? Five? Ten? [*And*

then, realizing he skipped some numbers once he got beyond the one hand he has been relying upon to figure things out since we first saw him, he doubles back.] Shall I tell you eight? Nine shall I tell you?

KRISHNA: Let's settle for just one.

MANSUKHĀ: Here it is: give me the flute. Where is it?

KRISHNA: [*dismissing the idea out of hand*] Never mind, idiot.

MANSUKHĀ: Yes, give the flute to me.

KRISHNA: But the girls will just take it from you.

MANSUKHĀ: [*incredulous, offended*] From me?

[*He launches into a meaningless verse that sounds like Sanskrit but is not and greatly amuses his audience. One hears the pieces in jagged array: Sanskrit particles, words, and conventions that have come into such common usage that they are within the range of even rustics like* MANSUKHĀ. *The grammar is all askew.*]

My Brahmin a thousand influences, so dance the most, cut up the most, all peace love hail.[37]

[*This gives many in the audience a chance not only to laugh at their own ignorance of Sanskrit—most Sanskrit recited at ceremonies would have just about that much meaning for them—but also at the competence in Sanskrit of many of the Brahmins who do the chanting.* MANSUKHĀ *graciously interprets, for* KRISHNA *and the* AUDIENCE *as well, what he has just pronounced in the language north Indians revere as the mother of all tongues. Given the fact that the exercise in Sanskrit was entirely bogus, the content of his translation also becomes laughable, an occasion for people to make light of Brahmin pretensions in regard to the canons of relative purity that are supposed to govern the caste system. Here is what he says:*]

Yes, before this Brahmin body of mine none dare set foot. Much less should anyone conceive of laying a hand on it!

[*Thus our* MANSUKHĀ *again: everything is reduced to its most vulgar. For him even brahminhood is a matter of the body.*]

KRISHNA: Pardon me for interrupting, but how do you manage to bellow out after the cows all day long and then come around here feeding us all this pundithood fodder?

MANSUKHĀ: Why, I learned it all from being around you!

KRISHNA: You what?

MANSUKHĀ: I learned it all from being with you: anything you can do I can do too. I wander around shouting after the cows like you, I eat the other cowherds' leftovers like you[38] — it all comes from being around you.

KRISHNA: [*responding to this attempt by* MANSUKHĀ *to puff himself up to* KRISHNA*'s stature*] But listen here, pal, what about when I lifted up the mountain and tamed the snake Kāliya? And what about when I killed Pūtanā? What were you doing then?

MANSUKHĀ: Well, all that was due to the power of my mantras.

KRISHNA: [*Even he, who knows* MANSUKHĀ *well, is taken aback by the audacity of this claim.*] Huh? How's that?

MANSUKHĀ: Do you want to know what my clever contribution was when you lifted up Mount Govardhan? I came running to help hold it up with my cowherd's stick. [*Somehow the level of* MANSUKHĀ*'s intelligence and concern never gets beyond flesh or force, no matter how he tries: here it's his stick that makes him so clever!*] And what was so clever about the way you killed Pūtanā?[39] Why, once she was dead it was I that was left with the task of whacking at her and cutting her in pieces and throwing her piece by piece into the Jumna. Where would you have been without me? And as for Kāliya, why do you think he was so docile, a regular plaything in your hands? It's because before you ever got to him I nailed him with a spell.[40] If it hadn't been for that, with your first thrust at that black snake the whole scene would have been black as coal. Then where would the dashing brilliance of the whole affair have been? So the very fact that all Braj worships you is really due to the effects of my mantras. Now what do you think about that? Do you still suppose I'm not going to be able to protect one puny little flute?

KRISHNA: [*unwilling to carry the discussion any further for fear of diatribes yet unheard*] All right, friend, enough. You win, I lose.

MANSUKHĀ: Lost! You didn't lose: I *defeated* you! [*He struts about the stage a bit.*]

KRISHNA: [*getting down to brass tacks*] All right then, I'll give you the flute. But what am I going to call the cows with?

MANSUKHĀ: With your throat, of course. Use your voice to call them. That's what I do, and it's louder than your flute any day.

KRISHNA: Yes indeed, blowhard! Hats off to you, king of *gandharvas*![41]

MANSUKHĀ: Now there you go ridiculing me again. Ridicule, ridicule, that's all I get. All right, let's test it out: you play and I'll sing and we'll see which is louder.

KRISHNA: Fine.

[*They begin a little duet,* KRISHNA *playing his flute in the transverse style one is accustomed to see in modern depictions of his musicianship. He produces a haunting, high-pitched tone that contrasts in every way with the low, bellowing sounds that issue from* MANSUKHĀ'S *mouth. Their duet epitomizes the contrast between their two personalities, the one clever and even suave when the occasion demands it, the other entirely rough-hewn. The* AUDIENCE *receives the performance with great enthusiasm. After a few bars* MANSUKHĀ *is too excited to go any further.*]

MANSUKHĀ: Victory, victory, victory! I've won!

KRISHNA: What do you mean you've won?

MANSUKHĀ: Well can't you see? The sound of my voice is so irresistible that hearing it not a single bird can resist. Look, in a flash they all have fallen to the ground. [*He spreads his arms in front of him to indicate the fallen birds to which he is referring. They comprise the* AUDIENCE *seated on the ground in front of him, and some among them are perhaps quite devastated indeed by the sonorities he has produced.*] Just look at them all! [*With gestures pointing to various parts of the hall, all the way to the back*] Fallen here! Fallen there! Fallen way back there!

KRISHNA: Listen blowhard, you've been bellowing like an elephant.

MANSUKHĀ: Bellowing! [*The debate has come to turn not merely on the question of volume, but on quality as well.*] Well, as for you, you're just a little cuckoo. [*Imitating its call*] Cuckoo, cuckoo.

KRISHNA: [*ready to take up the debate in those terms*] A cuckoo does sing on the sol, after all.[42]

MANSUKHĀ: That may be, but an elephant roars with a deep sound. So I win.

KRISHNA: [*again feeling it is pointless to continue such a debate*] All right, never mind. Here, you take the flute, and whatever you do, don't lose it.

MANSUKHĀ: Listen brother, this flute doesn't have any more chance of getting lost than I myself do.

[KRISHNA'S *face registers the fact that this is not necessarily a very comforting thought and he charges* MANSUKHĀ *with the seriousness of his task again.*]

KRISHNA: Look, hold onto my little flute very carefully, will you? You won't lose it now?

[*Having said this, he hesitantly gives* MANSUKHĀ *his beloved flute. Immediately upon taking the instrument in his hands,* MANSUKHĀ *becomes completely absorbed, fascinated to find out how it works, how it is possible to make such unearthly sounds with it. He reassures* KRISHNA *absentmindedly.*]

MANSUKHĀ: No, no, of course not. [*Dumbly, as if he has never really looked at it before, a definite possibility*] Say, what are these holes, anyway?

KRISHNA: The seven notes of the scale.

MANSUKHĀ: You mean they're *in* there? [*He puts the end of the tube to his eye and looks to see if it is true. He shouts into the flute to encourage or intimidate the notes into coming out.*] Come on out of there!

Mansukhā's approach to musicianship having failed, Krishna gives him a little instruction in these matters, introducing him to the seven notes of the scale as sung—a teacher of Indian instrumental music always begins with the voice—and then trying to get him to produce the sounds on the flute itself. The results are disastrous, of course. He is unable even to retain the notes of a single octave: he twists his do re mi's around so that they come out meaning "Go drink some water, you miserable ass."[43] After the audience has been diverted by the spectacle of the prodigious Mansukhā as music student, the plot recommences. Krishna exits, going his way after having tried one last time to urge on Mansukhā the importance of not letting go of the flute. As Krishna goes off, the curtain that provided the backdrop for their little colloquy is raised, revealing the familiar throne at the back of the stage. Radha is seated upon it, and her friends, the other *gopīs*, hover nearby. Mansukhā, however, delighted at last to be in possession of the little flute all by himself, does not notice. He breaks out in a clumsy little dance of sheer delight, waltzing around the front of the stage with something less than the grace of a *gandharva*. At the back of the stage the *sakhīs* observe that they are once again in the company of Mansukhā, and that this time he has the flute. Radha remains silent throughout the scene, reigning serene from her regal position, but the rest of the girls soon cluster in a little caucus to discuss this development. The eldest among them speaks.

SAKHĪ 3: Hey girls, look at this! We're not going to have to steal the flute from Syām Sundar after all. Somehow she's gotten into Mansukhā's hands, and you all know what a gluttonous crazy fool he is.[44] All we have to do is offer him a little food and the flute will be ours. Let's go. [*She leads her little troup downstage and they all announce their presence to* MANSUKHĀ.]

SAKHĪS: Hello friend Mansukhā! All honor and reverence.[45] [MANSUKHĀ *finds nothing untoward in the deference the* GOPĪS *accord him, and responds by summoning all his brahminhood for the dispensing of blessings on them all. As each one in her turn comes forward to bow before him in reverence, he lifts his hand in a vaguely pontifical gesture.*]

MANSUKHĀ: May your life be long and your husband's as well.[46] [*And to another, and another*] May your life be long, and your husband's as well. [*But the decorum required by this role is ultimately too much for him, and as the last of them comes forward he cannot restrain himself from offering a slightly different blessing.*] May your husband leave home and become an ascetic.[47] [*The blessings over, he addresses them as a group.*] Well *sakhīs*, tell me, why have you come?

SAKHĪS: Because we want you to perform the rite of worship to the sun on our behalf.

MANSUKHĀ: I'll be glad to do it, girls, but just now I'm sunk in concentration upon Sarasvatī.[48]

SAKHĪS: Oh what a shame, because we've prepared offerings of carrot halvah and pastry with cream.[49]

MANSUKHĀ: [*his meditative state abruptly at an end*] What? What's that again?

SAKHĪS: Pastry with cream.

MANSUKHĀ: [*eagerly*] Yes, yes, and do tell, what else?

SAKHĪS: And halvah made with carrots.

MANSUKHĀ: [*Now lost in a different sort of meditation, he licks his lips and speaks slowly, relishing the thought of it all.*] Oh *sakhī*, that makes my mouth water.

SAKHĪ 3: Well then, come quickly.

MANSUKHĀ: [*catching himself and returning to his former elevation*] No *sakhī*, I don't like sweets; I just like music.

SAKHĪ 3: Well then, maestro, would you care to sing a poem celebrating the life of nonattachment? If that's the sort of thing you like, perhaps you have some love for Syām Sundar's circle dance.

MANSUKHĀ: [*Bursting with excitement at the sudden prospect of taking part in the exclusive* rās līlā, *which her remark implies*] Oh *sakhī*, why didn't you say so in the first place? I have nothing but the greatest love for Syām Sundar's circle dance.

SAKHĪ 3: Well if I didn't mention it then, I'm mentioning it now.

MANSUKHĀ: But how are you going to perform it?

SAKHĪ 3: Well, that's a problem. You'll have to become a girl, of course.

MANSUKHĀ: Oh *sakhī*, never mind these little quibbles. You can show me the circle dance just as I am.

SAKHĪ 3: [*pretending to be horrified*] What! Why, Śiva himself had to become a *sakhī* in order to witness the circle dance!

MANSUKHĀ: All right then, if Śiva became a girl in order to see it, I will too. [*Then, with a moment's puzzlement*] But how am I going to do that?

SAKHĪ 3: Don't worry. I'll deck you with the sixteen decorations that befit a married woman.

MANSUKHĀ: Think of it, not one, not two, not three [*and then, familiarly, his arithmetic becomes a little fuzzy and he terminates the sequence abruptly*], but sixteen! Sixteen! Do tell, what are they?

SAKHĪ 3: Well, I'll apply mascara.

MANSUKHĀ: [*carefully numbering them as they are mentioned*] That's one.

SAKHĪ 3: And then I'll put a beauty mark in the middle of your forehead.

MANSUKHĀ: That's two.

SAKHĪ 3: Then I'll hang a pearl from your nostril and set a stud in your nose.

MANSUKHĀ: That's four.

SAKHĪ 3: And I'll put anklets on you and dress you in a skirt and a shawl and a sari.

MANSUKHĀ: That's eight.

SAKHĪ 3: [*not wanting to put his mathematical abilities to too severe a test*] And so on until you have all sixteen womanly decorations.

MANSUKHĀ: [*Now that some of the details of this sex change operation have been laid out, he is having second thoughts.*] Look, if you put a beauty mark on, then never mind about the mascara. And the pearl in the nostrils is all right, but leave off the nose stud. I'll take the shawl, but never mind the skirt. And if you dress me in a sari, then let's forget about the shawl. That way I'll still be half a boy.

SAKHĪ 3: Well, whatever you want.

MANSUKHĀ: Whatever I want?

SAKHĪ 3: Yes, we'll count those as the sixteen decorations.

[*At that they set about dressing him as a girl, a process that turns out to be much abbreviated, in any case. They simply cover him with a shawl and let it go at that, anxious to execute their plan. Already the music has started in the background, and soon the girls are singing a* rasiyā *appropriate to the occasion and dancing around. They draw* MANSUKHĀ *into the center of their circle as they do so, whirling around him time and again.*]

SAKHĪS:

I heard the sound of the bamboo flute,
  I turned around, and I saw
That it was Kanhaiyā playing her,
  Nanda's darling boy.
Look under the fluting banyan tree,
  see him and his girls in a circling dance,
And somehow between each two of them
  one of him takes his place.
A peacock-feathered crown he sports
  and golden yellow garments;
His neck is gilt with a victory garland
  woven of forest flowers.
And it was Kanhaiyā playing her,
  Nanda's darling boy.

[*They sing these lines over and over, and as they do their pace quickens.* MANSUKHĀ *is no match for them: soon he is dizzy and exhausted, visibly drooping. Presently we hear a thud and see nothing left in the center of the circle but a little heap on the floor. The music ends abruptly, and all the* GOPĪS *rush over to where he has fallen, searching his clothes for the flute. In no time at all the oldest of them has found it and holds it up triumphantly for* RADHA *to see.*]

SAKHĪ 3: Here it is, Kiśorī, Syām Sundar's bamboo flute!

RADHA: Bring it over here.

[*This is done immediately, and in a flash the flute is invisible. With a swift, effective gesture* RADHA *slips it under her garments. Part of the fun of this for the audience is to see how remarkably efficient the* GOPĪS *are—*RADHA *included—in their handling of the flute, by utter contrast to* MANSUKHĀ'S *verbose but ineffectual protestations of competency. Knowing smiles and chuckles spread through the gathered crowd: the deed they have been waiting for is now accomplished. The* GOPĪS *cluster around* RADHA *at the back of the stage, as they did when they first appeared in this scene. This time, however, they are fully in control* *of the situation and there is no need to placate* MANSUKHĀ *with false reverence. Now the roles have changed altogether and their solicitousness rings entirely false as they call out to him with singsong sweetness.*]

SAKHĪS: Oh Mansukhā! [*The eldest among the girls goes over and gives him a little slap to awaken him.*] Oh friend Mansukhā! [*He senses some disturbance in his sound sleep and thinks the sweet, buzzing sound he has heard—her voice—and more particularly the little cuff he has just*

33. The theft of the flute

received must come from a fly circling round his head. He retaliates with an aimless swat and mumbles sleepily.]

MANSUKHĀ: Ooh! Those flies are really biting!

SAKHĪS: Mansukhā! Oh Mansukhā! It's morning. Time to get up.

MANSUKHĀ: [*drowsily, rubbing his eyes*] Huh? "Scorning?"[50]

SAKHĪ 3: [*bending over him with great condescension and speaking with the clearest elocution*] Morning, not scorning. The sun, Sūrya Nārāyaṇ, has risen.[51]

MANSUKHĀ: Eh? Sūrya Nārāyaṇ? Where?

SAKHĪ 3: [*pointing over the heads of the* AUDIENCE] Look, over there. [*He shuffles to a more or less upright position in order to greet the sun with some morsel of that enthusiasm and respect incumbent upon every Brahmin.*]

MANSUKHĀ: Hail, hail the sun, hail Sūrya Nārāyaṇ. [*That perfunctory greeting having been uttered—not even the brief* gāyatrī mantra *universally pronounced by Brahmins at sunrise—he awakes to more immediate concerns as he recalls what has happened and that his cowherding was interrupted at midday.*] Gee, I'd better get going. What happened to my cows? They must have wandered far and wide. I should have tied some cloth on their horns so I could tell them from other peoples'. [*Then all of a sudden he realizes what really is missing.*] Hey! [*He places his hand on his chest where there is an inner pocket in his shirt, and feeling nothing, reaches inside, again without result. Now suddenly he is fully awake.*] Hey, where'd the flute go? What happened to the flute? [*Then recalling fully*] Oh yes, the *rās līlā*, the circle dance! What kind of *rās līlā* was that anyway? I entered into it with nothing but love and even so those *sakhīs* did their daily dirt. I'd better go see what I can do. [*He crosses downstage to where the girls are gathered, and greets them one by one, thus adopting the manner in which they initially had greeted him when the flute was not yet theirs. In fact, his deference is extreme: he prostrates himself at their feet.*] Greetings, *sakhī*, respectful greetings.

SAKHĪ 1: [*repeating the blessing that formerly had been* MANSUKHĀ'*s prerogative to dispense*] *Cirjīv!* May you live long.

MANSUKHĀ: Let's have it. [*He stretches out his hand.*]

SAKHĪ 1: Have what?

[*She has reason to play dumb, of course, since she can only assume that he is referring to the flute. That, however, is not the case:* MANSUKHĀ'*s stomach is always the concern of greatest priority for him, and he believes he has heard the mention of something to eat. Instead of her blessing of longevity,* cirjīv, *he has understood her to have mentioned the seed of the* piyāl *tree,* cirõjī. *It is often included in halvah,* khīr, *and tasty mixtures of dried fruits, and it stirs his appetite.*]

MANSUKHĀ: But you said I could have some *cirõjī.*

SAKHĪ 1: No, no, I was just giving you a blessing.

MANSUKHĀ: Well then if you won't give me that, let me have a look at your sixteen marks of womanliness.

SAKHĪ 1: [*bristling at his impertinence*] Get out of here!

MANSUKHĀ: [*changing tone as he recalls the matter at hand, whispering secretively*] Hey, come over here. [*He beckons her closer for a private word.*] Have you got it?

SAKHĪ 1: Got what?

MANSUKHĀ: You know, this.

[*He raises his hands as if he were holding the flute and hisses out some vaguely flutelike sounds. Custom forbids that he should directly say the name of the object he seeks, thus by implication not only falsely accusing the person he is talking to but also tipping his hand to the real thief, if it should not be she. It would be best if he actually knew who the thief was, but in the absence of that knowledge, all he can hope is that as he describes it some look of guilt will come across the face of the* GOPĪ *he is addressing, and that sign of recognition will enable him to confront her with her crime point-blank and demand the flute back. She, however, will give him no such satisfaction. She looks entirely mystified by his display, totally innocent.*]

SAKHĪ 1: What in the world is it? It must have some name.

[*But* MANSUKHĀ *is unwilling to yield on that point, and passes on to the next* GOPĪ, *producing in the audience the delighted anticipation that the whole charade will be repeated, as indeed it is. He gestures to the next girl.*]

MANSUKHĀ: Hey, come over here a minute. Tell me . . .

SAKHĪ 2: What?

MANSUKHĀ: Have you seen it? [*He repeats his clumsy imitation of playing the flute.*]

SAKHĪ 2: I don't understand these gestures you're making.

MANSUKHĀ: Come on. This. Have you got it?

SAKHĪ 2: What?

MANSUKHĀ: *It!*

SAKHĪ 2: [*impatiently*] Oh Mansukhā, I just don't see what you're getting at.

MANSUKHĀ: [*flustered, beckoning to a third* GOPĪ] Hey you, come over here. Have you got it?

SAKHĪ 3: [*as dumb as the others*] What?

MANSUKHĀ: You know, this. [*Again he poses as a flutist and whistles out his woodwind sound.*]

SAKHĪ 3: Huh? Come on, it must have a name, whatever it is.

MANSUKHĀ: [*Utterly exasperated, he gives up the hope that any of these potential thieves is going to tip her hand all by herself.*] Your rival, your co-wife, the flute!

SAKHĪ 3: [*still apparently quite uncomprehending*] Huh? Who gave you a flute?

MANSUKHĀ: Syām Sundar did.

SAKHĪ 3: Oh come on, how could dear Syām Sundar give his flute to someone as stupid as you?

MANSUKHĀ: Oh so you're going to browbeat me, eh?

SAKHĪ 3: Well listen to you! We invite you to take part in the *rās līlā* and then you turn around and accuse us of being thieves!

MANSUKHĀ: And you! First you go stealing things and then you turn around and start insulting me on top of it!

SAKHĪ 3: Get out of here!

MANSUKHĀ: Oh yeah?

SAKHĪ 3: You mean you'll only go if I give you a good swat? [*She jumps forward and chases him offstage, leveling a couple of good blows on his neck and back in the process. As he flees, he hunches over in an attempt at self-protection. The curtain drops.* MANSUKHĀ'*s shouts of pain offstage yield to sobs as he reappears in front of the curtain. Soon* KRISHNA *joins him.*]

MANSUKHĀ: Waah! Waah!

KRISHNA: Hey stupid, what happened? What are you crying like that for?

MANSUKHĀ: [*rather encouraged by this show of concern*] Waaaaaaaah!

KRISHNA: Oh come on, quiet down.

MANSUKHĀ: Only if you'll coax me out of it. Come on, wipe away my tears.

KRISHNA: [*obliging this altogether direct request for solace*] All right now, why are you crying, brother? What happened?

MANSUKHĀ: Oh something very bad happened to me.

KRISHNA: Well tell me, what?

MANSUKHĀ: Promise you won't hit me if I tell you?

KRISHNA: Listen pal, I'll only hit you if you won't tell me. Now come on, what is it?

MANSUKHĀ: No, first tell me that you won't hit me.

KRISHNA: All right, I won't hit you. There.

MANSUKHĀ: [*Struggling to words. but at the fear of being beaten up yet again he retreats hastily.*] No, no, I can't tell you.

KRISHNA: Now look. . . .

MANSUKHĀ: [*regaining a modicum of courage*] Yes, now look, listen very carefully, look. [*Once these introductory expressions can be repeated no longer, the words come very slowly.*] Uh . . . your . . . flute . . .

KRISHNA: [*surmising what has happened and rushing in to complete the great, damning sentence*] . . . got lost.

[MANSUKHĀ *cringes immediately at the divulging of this awful truth, sure of being pummeled again.*]

KRISHNA: Listen idiot, just tell me. You're not telling me the whole thing.

MANSUKHĀ: [*still cringing*] You won't listen anyway. What's the point in telling you?

KRISHNA: Oh I will, too. Come on.

MANSUKHĀ: Look, see these fingers of mine?

KRISHNA: Yes . . .

MANSUKHĀ: [*Again his speech slows as he has to return to the main point, from his hands to what they once held.*] Well, today . . . uh . . . your . . . flute . . .

KRISHNA: [*again rushing in to save him the agony of finishing his sentence*] . . . got lost. [*The* AUDIENCE *laughs loudly at the deliberate pace of* MANSUKHĀ*'s repeated squirmings and the alacrity of* KRISHNA*'s response.*] Come on, let's hear it. Out with the truth.

MANSUKHĀ: [*criticizing his companion for not giving him a*

chance even to finish his sentences] Look stupid, you're not even listening. How can I go on?

[*Again they wrestle over this point. Again* MANSUKHĀ *begins to explain what happened with painful hesitancy, and again* KRISHNA *jumps in to finish his thought for him. This time* MANSUKHĀ *is jarred loose from his fearfulness by aggravation at the way* KRISHNA *is always butting in. He mimics* KRISHNA.]

MANSUKHĀ: "Got lost," "got lost." Why keep making such a big fuss? Yes, it got lost. It got lost, that's all. It just got lost.

KRISHNA: [*resigned*] Well, isn't that just what I told you, that if I gave the flute to you, you'd lose it?

MANSUKHĀ: Listen, I was the one who told you that I'm just eight pounds' worth of fool, but you insisted that I take it. So what could I do? I took it, and now it's lost.

KRISHNA: Well, how?

MANSUKHĀ: [*Having attempted to shift the blame away from himself this once, he does so again.*] I made an offering of it in that *rās līlā* of yours.

KRISHNA: But friend, how can there be a *rās līlā* without me?

MANSUKHĀ: Oh. [*Realizing there was indeed something amiss about the whole thing from the start*] Well, I took your place. It was just like your *rās līlā* except I was there. Listen brother, the flute's stored away in the *gopīs*' treasure-room. All you have to do is go and make application for it, and it'll be yours again.

KRISHNA: Oh fine! You lose it and I go retrieve it!

MANSUKHĀ: [*again exercising his expertise at shifting the onus of responsibility onto others*] Some friend you are! You can't stand the thought of enduring some slight inconvenience for the sake of a friend. Some friend you are!

KRISHNA: [*trying to reach some helpful compromise and realizing that* MANSUKHĀ *is afraid of any confrontation with the* GOPĪS] All right. You come along and point out which one of the girls has it—from a distance, of course.

[*At this the curtain rises, revealing the* GOPĪS *in the accustomed position around* RADHA'*s throne at the back of the stage.* KRISHNA *advances downstage, but* MANSUKHĀ *remains somewhat behind. As* KRISHNA *approaches the row of* GOPĪS *he turns to* MANSUKHĀ, *waiting for some indication of which one he should confront.* MANSUKHĀ *points to the whole group with the vaguest gesture possible.* KRISHNA'*s expression reveals the fact that he finds this of no help at all, though he does not want to say anything that would destroy the secrecy of their signal system.* MANSUKHĀ, *however, feeling guilty, bursts out with an accusation to his friend.*]

MANSUKHĀ: What's the matter? Can't you read my gestures? [*Then, in a more explicit attempt to justify the vagueness of his indication*] Right, brother, that's right. It's Kiśorī's whole pack of thieves. So you might as well ask each one of them.

KRISHNA: Well which one shall I start with?

MANSUKHĀ: Why not the one sitting over there?

[KRISHNA *beckons her forward.*]

KRISHNA: *Sakhī*, have you got my flute?

SAKHĪ 1: Who says I do, Syām Sundar?

KRISHNA: [*with a nod of his head in* MANSUKHĀ'*s direction*] Mansukhā over there, he said so.

SAKHĪ 1: [*shouting menacingly at* MANSUKHĀ] Ah ha, Mansukhā! So I have the flute, do I?

MANSUKHĀ: [*uncertainly, but forced to bluff*] Yes, you do. So come on, give it over.

SAKHĪ 1: Why'd you lie and say I did it?

MANSUKHĀ: Who says I said so?

SAKHĪ 1: Our dear Syām Sundar.

MANSUKHĀ: Well, then, ask him.

[*At this impertinence the* GOPĪ *goes after* MANSUKHĀ, *hand held high to give him a good cuffing. He rushes away as fast as he can, shielding his neck from her blows, but she is too fast for him. The* AUDIENCE *has the fun of seeing* MANSUKHĀ *pummeled yet once more. When she has had a satisfactory physical revenge, she concludes with a verbal triumph, too.*]

SAKHĪ 1: Listen, don't go lying about me, all right?

MANSUKHĀ: [*Regaining his composure and forced to proceed*

further with the inquisition, he offers another suggestion to KRISHNA.] See that one sitting over there? [*He indicates the next* GOPĪ *in the line.*]

KRISHNA: Which one? Oh I see. [*To the* GOPĪ] Come over here, will you *sakhī*? [*She does, and smiles up at him with glowing innocence.*] Have you got my flute?

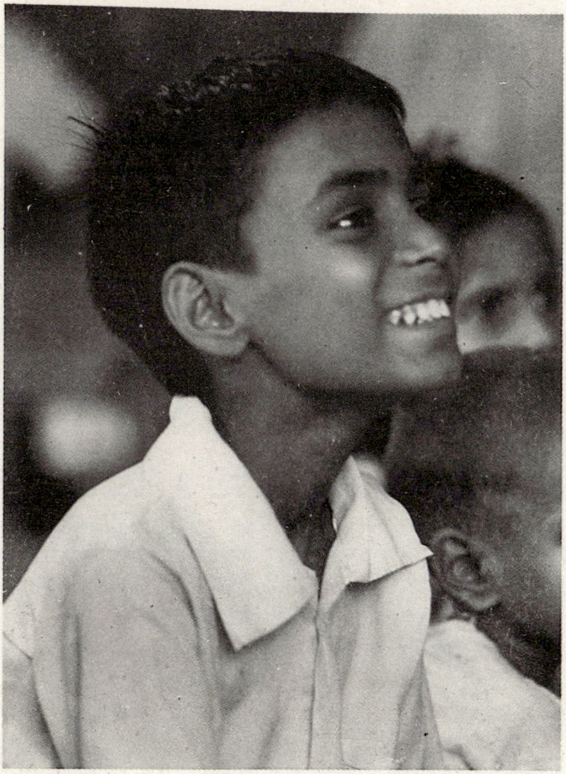

34. A young spectator

SAKHĪ 2: Why, who says I do?

KRISHNA: Mansukhā says so.

SAKHĪ 2: [*directing her attention to* MANSUKHĀ, *as had the* GOPĪ *before her*] What's that, Mansukhā? I have the flute, do I?

MANSUKHĀ: Right, so give it over.

SAKHĪ 2: [*returning the challenge*] Why did you lie about me, Mansukhā?

MANSUKHĀ: Why, who says I mentioned your name?

SAKHĪ 2: Syām Sundar.

MANSUKHĀ: Then better ask Syām Sundar.

[*At this point exactly the same chase ensues, and with the same results.* MANSUKHĀ *gets his deserts and the* GOPĪ *triumphs easily.*]

SAKHĪ 2: So listen, just don't go throwing my name around like that. Hear?

[*This time* MANSUKHĀ *reacts to his defeat by repeating, ironically, just what the* GOPĪS *have been saying to him, but directing his remark to* KRISHNA.]

MANSUKHĀ: Listen brother, don't go mentioning my name like that. When they ask you just say that some Braj *gopī* told you.

KRISHNA: Oh, I see. [*This time he doesn't even wait for further directions from* MANSUKHĀ, *and just moves on to the next girl in line, beckoning her forward.*] Come over here, *sakhī*. Do you have my flute?

SAKHĪ 3: Why dear, who says I have it? Who told you I have your flute?

[KRISHNA, *unwilling to go through all this again, points a slow, silent finger in* MANSUKHĀ'*s direction. This time, in anticipation of what is to come,* MANSUKHĀ *jumps in and tries to interrogate this most formidable of the* GOPĪS *before the whole process turns into another rout for him. Anxiously, from what he now knows is not such a safe distance, he takes the offensive.*]

MANSUKHĀ: Come on, you have it. Give it over.

SAKHĪ 3: What are you doing accusing me? Why have you mentioned my name?

MANSUKHĀ: [*His impetuousness having put him in the same bind he has always been in, he has but one response.*] Who says I mentioned your name?

SAKHĪ 3: Syām Sundar says so.

MANSUKHĀ: Well then ask him.

[*Now the* AUDIENCE *is treated for a third time to the chase they have come to expect at this point in the dialogue. They—and especially the children among them—have been giggling in anticipation of this, and now it is on, with* MANSUKHĀ *suffering predictably his most resounding defeat yet. He arches his back as he flees before the* GOPĪ'*s advancing fist, but to no avail. A shower of blows rains down on his neck and he cringes beneath them ignominiously, much to the* AUDIENCE'*s satisfaction. The* GOPĪ *concludes the episode with the same threatening command we have already heard twice before.*]

SAKHĪ 3: Just don't go mentioning my name like that.

MANSUKHĀ: [*defiant from his safe distance*] Oh yeah?

SAKHĪ 3: Yeah.

MANSUKHĀ: [*Bleeding from this confrontation, he turns the accusing finger to* KRISHNA.] You told her, didn't you?

KRISHNA: Told her what?

MANSUKHĀ: Why, she saw it in a dream, I suppose?

[*Increasingly as the play moves on,* KRISHNA *sees the pointlessness of getting embroiled in arguments with* MANSUKHĀ, *and simply proceeds with the matter at hand. Seeing that* MANSUKHĀ'*s approach to the whole affair has gotten him nowhere, he addresses the entire company of* SAKHĪs *in song. Thus begins an anonymous poem in four stanzas, composed in the form of a dialogue.*]

KRISHNA:

Now give me back my flute, I ask:
  why are you waging such a war?
Why should you want to make people laugh
  and suspect a lover's quarrel?
What if rumors begin to spread?—
  that's something you should consider—
This flute has been known to turn people's heads,
  so don't be foolish: return it instead.[52]

SAKHĪS: *(collectively)*

Fools you call us, you
  who have made so much of yourself:
Watch your tongue, we'll slap you down,
  for we are headmen's daughters.

Not long ago you'd come to our doors
  bundled in a torn and tattered blanket,
Begging for simple buttermilk—
  now you'd give us a lecturing!

KRISHNA:

Girls, do you think you understand
  the meaning of this flute?
She lures beyond the Three-World Realm,[53]
  she who's captured my heart.
The one whom Śiva and all the sages
  have always wanted to win
But never could attain, my friends:
  is that who you'd try to subdue?

SAKHĪS:

At least we know exactly who you are:
  Yaśodā's little boy—what more?
So if you've forgotten your flute and it's lost,
  then don't give us the blame.
You whose mouth plays Muralī—
  Bamboo Flute she's called[54]—
Pity the village into which you were born,
  for soon you will cause it to fall.

KRISHNA: Oh my god, what a thing to say! What a thing to say!

SAKHĪS: That's right, you'll be the death of us all.

KRISHNA: [*responding in kind with a final stanza*]

If everything is lost and destroyed,
  then what about yourselves?
This village of cowdung gatherers[55] teems
  with four hundred thousand strong:
A quarter of you hover around me,
  another quarter comes and goes,
A third quarter stands there staring at me
  and the rest are lost in desire.

[*Feeling he's stated his case conclusively,* KRISHNA *turns to his old friend* MANSUKHĀ.] Just look at that, Mansukhā, how they try to shrug off all responsibility. Come on, now, let's get down to business. Who has the flute?

MANSUKHĀ: See the one who's just been sitting there so far? [*He indicates* RADHA, *who has remained passive, elevated above all this wrangling on her royal seat.*] She's got it herself.

KRISHNA: What? You mean Śrī Syāmā Jū?[56]

MANSUKHĀ: Who else?

SAKHĪ 3: [*speaking for the whole company of* GOPĪS *and taking immediate offense that* RADHA *should be dragged into this*] You blabberer! What nonsense, you Brahmin's boy. Are you insinuating that our Śrī Kiśorī Jū[57] is responsible for stealing that little slip of a flute?

[*In a flash she is chasing after him again, her hand raised in a threatening gesture, and the other* GOPĪS, *though a little smaller and less vicious, are close behind.* RADHA, *of course, is too elevated to take part in this renewed attack on* MANSUKHĀ. *The cringing* MANSUKHĀ *emits breathless and piteous appeals to the* GOPĪS.]

MANSUKHĀ: Mercy! Have a little mercy! I beg you, have a little mercy! I'm about dead! Listen, did I make any charges about stealing? Did I? [*In fact,* MANSUKHĀ *has been careful not to say this outright, always trying to shift the dangerous onus of accusation onto* KRISHNA. *He attempts further to conciliate his captors as the vehemence of their attack abates.*] No, listen, if you should happen to find the flute, then fine: do give it back. And if not, well, just sit there. Now please go have a seat.

SAKHĪS: [*in singsong chorus*] We didn't find anthing. We don't have your flute.

MANSUKHĀ: Fine then, just have a seat. [*They release him, and once he regains a second's composure he is back in the fray with a little speech calculated to salve his own hurt pride.*] All right then, it's time for me to stop waging this battle with mere words. The time has come for action!

[*And with that, hoping to find where the flute is hidden, he ventures little explorations in the clothing of the* GOPĪS, *who had been returning to their place at the back of the stage. This elicits an immediate response from the girls, and they swat at* MANSUKHĀ'*s indecorous hand.*]

SAKHĪS: Hey, get out of there, you lecher! Just watch your step.

You stick to moving your mouth and forget about your hands. [*Having repelled* MANSUKHĀ, they continue downstage to rejoin RADHA.]

KRISHNA: [*addressing the* GOPĪS *as a group*] Well, girls, who's the king of this place?

SAKHĪS: [*with a single voice*] Śrī Kiśorī Jū.

KRISHNA: Well then, I guess our flute has been found.

SAKHĪS: Oh ho, found is it? What do you mean it's been found?

KRISHNA: But it's perfectly clear. In any kingdom if something is lost and found, it becomes the king's responsibility to bestow it upon someone.

SAKHĪS: And who does the king give such a thing to?

KRISHNA: To me, Why not?

SAKHĪS: If that's what you want, you'd better join your hands in petition and go to our Śrī Kiśorī Jū with your request. If your flute is anywhere to be found in the realm, then she'll have a search made and give it back to you.

KRISHNA: [*plaintively, with* MANSUKHĀ *and the* MUSICIANS]

Radha, Śrī Bṛṣabhānu's daughter,
  dear one, return it, return my flute—
The flute without which my happiness fades,
That gave me the power to lift a mountain,
And how without it could I herd the cows?
Radha, Śrī Bṛṣabhānu's daughter,
  dear one, return it, return my flute.

SAKHĪS: [*The* MUSICIANS *continue to provide vocal and instrumental support.*]

What is it like, this flute of yours?
  We've never cast our eyes upon it.
We are rustics, not clever like you,
Kanhaiyā; to blame us is wrong:
It must have been lost in the woods.
Radha, Śrī Bṛṣabhānu's daughter,
  dear one, return it, return my flute.[58]

KRISHNA: [*with* MANSUKHĀ *and* MUSICIANS]

You're the clever ones here, you girls,
You're the ones who stole my flute.
How can I treat you as simple rustics,

You who've managed over the years
To nurse a grudge for a little curd,
Converting it into a wealth of curses.[59]
Radha, Śrī Bṛṣabhānu's daughter,
dear one, return it, return my flute.

SAKHĪS: [*with* MUSICIANS]

A thief can hardly complain of curses!
We're not your docile pupils, you know:
Remember when you fearfully fled
To us at midnight from Mathura?
Where were your fine pretensions then?
Radha, Śrī Bṛṣabhānu's daughter,
dear one, return it, return my flute.

SAKHĪ 3: Hey Syām Sundar, I have an idea. Would you ever submit your case to anyone else to decide for you?

KRISHNA: Well, who?

SAKHĪ: Would you accept Śrī Kiśorī Jū's judgment?

KRISHNA: Yes, I would. [*Then he paraphrases from the song of which he is about to sing a few bars, bending the meaning a little to suit his ends by substituting a few words that do not occur in the lyrics themselves.*]

. . . If it goes well for the boy involved. . . .

SAKHĪ: Well good then.

KRISHNA: Right. [*He sings as if he were addressing* RADHA, *but does not do so directly since the matter must be conveyed to her through her courtier, the* GOPĪ *with whom he has been speaking.*]

Make a just decision now,
Good or ill for the boy involved.
My fate is in your hands.[60]

Well then, *sakhī*, I submit the matter to Śrī Kiśorī Jū and I will certainly abide by her decision.

SAKHĪ: [*carrying the matter to the throne, to* RADHA] Syāmā Jū, there's a legal matter before you.

RADHA: [*Her first words in the drama are sung: she responds to* KRISHNA *with a high, clear, dispassionate voice.*]

Let each side present its views.
Let each one speak only truth.

I will balance and weigh the two,
waiving every other thought.

MUSICIANS: [*supplying* RADHA*'s line*]

The girls of Braj have stolen your flute?
Giridhārī, can you show us solid proof?[61]

KRISHNA: [*to* RADHA] Look, your friends have stolen away my flute.

RADHA: Well tell me, what's your proof of that?

35. Krishna appears before Radha's tribunal

KRISHNA:

It's in your hand – what more could I prove?
Those clever girls have stolen my flute.

[*Sure enough, as he sings, one sees that the flute which has heretofore rested invisibly on the throne beside* RADHA*, hidden under her garments as she sat immobile, has become visible as she leaned forward to enter into the dramatic action.*] Look, there's my flute in your very own hands.

RADHA: Ah yes, but that certainly doesn't prove that my friends were responsible for stealing it. Where's the evidence for that?

MANSUKHĀ: [*jumping in, as is his wont, and continuing the* caupāī *sequence*] I'll answer that.

They showed me the *rās* to make me forget it,
and once I was senseless they stole it away.

Your friends danced the *rās līlā* for me to the point that I fell unconscious. They they went and stole the flute.

SAKHĪS: [*uniting in self-defense*]

If you were unconscious, then where
was your memory?
How do you know how the flute got lost?

What about it, Mansukhā? If your faculties were so completely gone, then how did you manage to know we took the flute?

MANSUKHĀ: [*ever quick*] I kept one eye open.

SAKHĪ: Then why didn't you grab the girl that was stealing the flute?

MANSUKHĀ: Well, my second eye was asleep.

RADHA: [*continuing in* caupāī *and taking on the voice of a magistrate passing judgment on a case*]

Listen Krishna Murārī,[62]
the theft has not been proven;
You've lost the case as you lost the flute:
that is the court's decision.

Syām Sundar dear, the theft you allege has not been proven. But there is one thing: it's clear that the object in question is yours.

MANSUKHĀ: What sort of doubletalk is this? Not enough evidence to prove the theft, but plenty of evidence that the flute is ours? What is this?

[MANSUKHĀ, *always anxious to press a point beyond its proper bounds, is not satisfied with the shape of things. But buffoon that he is, he is left at the side as the action continues, for at this point comes the great moment when* RADHA, *out of her own volition and not from any juridical constraint, prepares to return to* KRISHNA'*s possession the flute she holds at her side.*]

RADHA: Here, take it, Syām Sundar. [*Extending her hand toward him with the flute*].

KRISHNA: Yes, Syāmā Jū, do give it to me.

[*But just as their hands are about to meet and the exchange take place, her friend interrupts.*]

SAKHĪ 3: Wait a minute, Kiśorī Jū! First extract a promise from him.

KRISHNA: What's wrong *sakhī*? What is it you want?

SAKHĪ 3: [*to* KRISHNA] Promise you won't play the flute while we're working in the kitchen.

KRISHNA: What! No, friend, I'm going to play my flute. I can't agree to a thing like that.

SAKHĪ 3: Well then, you won't get your flute back.

KRISHNA: And why not? *(More emphatically)* Why not? Look, *sakhī*, it's not just you who's in the kitchen, and not just two or three others like you, but thousands, hundreds of thousands! From sunrise until sunset you're busy blowing on the coals of the stove you cook on. It never stops, this housework of yours. Do you think I'm just going to stop playing my flute all that time? No, that just can't be.

SAKHĪ 3: *(with singsong superiority)* Well then, you won't get your flute back.

KRISHNA: I won't eh? The flute's in Syāmā's hands, not yours, and it's a matter of justice. And . . .

SAKHĪ 3: There's no injustice in that. It's just the other way around: you're the one who's been causing all of us endless trouble by playing your flute. That's where the crime is.

MANSUKHĀ: [*Having been temporarily bypassed by the action, he fastens onto this particle of dialogue to inject himself into the fray once again. He speaks with the greatest agitation and irony he can muster.*] Crime! Oh yes, a great crime!

KRISHNA: What's that, brother? Where's my crime in all this?

MANSUKHĀ: Well just look at the way you go thoo, thoo into your flute! [*He refers to the action of spitting, which, connected as it is with highly polluted saliva, has dirty connotations and is synonymous with bad behavior in general, so* KRISHNA *immediately corrects him. This little stand-off amuses the audience greatly.*]

KRISHNA: Not thoo, thoo. Poo, poo.

MANSUKHĀ: Oh thoo thoo, poo poo: it's all that same thing. [*Then continuing the burlesque, he extends the salivary metaphor.*] When it reaches these *gopīs'* ears it sinks into their hearts and comes to their eyes as tears. And once the tears start flowing, the fires they're standing over go out. And then they get all that smoke in their eyes. And with all that smoke billowing up, how can their eyes possibly retain their lotus-like form? And when they get dried out from all that smoke and crying, why, the poor things become skinny as elephants! Now I ask you, is that not a crime?

KRISHNA: [*not quite following the intricacies of* MANSUKHĀ'*s reasoning*] Eh? Crime?

[*Before this private little trial staged by* MANSUKHĀ *can go further, however,* RADHA *returns the play to its proper course. Once again, of her own free will—even against that of her friends, who have pleaded against it—she offers* KRISHNA *his flute. Once again she stretches out her hand.*]

RADHA: Here, Syām Sundar, take it.

KRISHNA: Yes, Kiśorī Jū, do let me have it.

[*This time the transaction is complete:* KRISHNA *has his flute back and the play is at an end. The* AUDIENCE *relaxes and some begin to rise up to go forward for the closer vision they know will soon be afforded them. But the supporting players have not yet quite had their final say.*]

SAKHĪ 3: Wait, Kiśorī Jū, I have a request!

[*But* MANSUKHĀ *interrupts.*]

MANSUKHĀ: [*maintaining his enmity with this* GOPĪ *to the bitter end.*] Oh no. You've already had your say. We've heard all this before. No indeed, it's *my* voice that will be heard from here on out. [*He puffs up his chest and points to himself with a grandiloquent gesture. Then he appeals to the* AUDIENCE *to join him in his great shout of self-adulation.*] Let us make our thought known with the force of the Vedas! Shout it out with the force you would a great mantra! Hail to Mansukhā!

AUDIENCE: Hail!

MANSUKHĀ: Louder! Hail Mansukhā!

AUDIENCE: Hail!

[*While this display is proceeding at the front of the stage, quite a different mood is struck at the back.* RADHA *invites* KRISHNA *to join her on her throne, which he does, sitting directly beside her and lifting the flute to his lips. Thus positioned, the two of them, flanked by* GOPĪS *on either side, become the tableau that the audience is invited to come forward and witness. Soon the stage is crowded with worshipers lifting their small offerings before the holy couple, bowing their heads before them, pressing their feet, and often stopping for a long moment just to gaze at the two of them and their disputed flute before others push them on.*]

Chapter IV

The Great Circle Dance

Introduction

THE GREATEST SYMBOLS are the simplest, and for that reason they are the most difficult. Their simplicity makes them accessible to all and makes it possible for them to magnetize great chunks of meaning. But the breadth they acquire in the process makes them difficult, and the communities who hold them dear find ways to make sure that some of that complexity and subtlety and depth is transmitted along with the symbol itself. The symbol may seem simple, and at bottom it is: no one wants to obscure its communicative power. Yet the community knows that what a novice learns in a first impression is very different from what one feels after one has returned to a symbol time and again and learned many generations' language for interpreting it.

The *rās*, the dance Krishna shares with the *gopīs*, is such a symbol. It could not be simpler. In visual terms it is a circle, and nothing on its periphery anchors it to any fixed point, so it rotates freely. In narrative terms, too, the *rās* is consummately simple. Out in the woods in the middle of the night Krishna flutes to the women of Braj and calls them away from their homes and families, their loyalties and occupations. He pulls them from the attachments that fix each in a particular social location, and integrates them into a single dance of which he is the sole focus, satisfying them with his presence. None of the women has a position preferential to or distinguishable from that of any of the others, and Krishna himself is equally distributed around the ring, multiplying himself in such a way that each of the *gopīs* feels his presence as intimate and encompassing. A true circle, it is purposeless: it points nowhere but to itself, it produces nothing; it is a dance of pure pleasure; love, and nothing else.

The *mahārās līlā*, the "Great Rās Līlā" or "Play of the Great Circle Dance," tells the story of how the *gopīs* were attracted to Krishna, and portrays the dance as it originally occurred. Paradoxically, for all the simplicity of the dance itself, it is the lengthiest and most difficult of all the *līlās*, the most heavily theological. The reason is that there is something special to protect here, a centrality that should not be misunderstood, and a simplicity that should not be left vulnerable to the winds of pollution. It is a teaching *līlā*: there is a great deal of talk and some explicit sermonizing, and much of the action is contrived with a didactic interest in mind. Sometimes it is frankly allegorical.

Take, for instance, the great battle that the *mahārās līlā* portrays. It would seem to be one of a large group, for the classical texts are full of Krishna's battles: how he subdues the snake, fights off the horse, and does away with demons of all descriptions. Perhaps the most celebrated involves a confrontation with Indra, king of the gods. As a mere child, Krishna proposes that the people of Braj stop worshiping this distant, volatile figure and venerate what is near at hand, Mount Govardhan, the symbolic center of their homeland. Indra, furious, pellets Braj with a storm that lasts a week, but Krishna rescues everyone by lifting Mount Govardhan on a single finger as a massive umbrella for cowherd and cattle. The battle that the *mahārās līlā* describes, however, is not reported in the traditional narratives,[1] and the reason is that it is not, strictly speaking, narrative. It tells its story to teach a lesson.

Krishna's opponent here, like Indra, has a place in the ancient Vedic pantheon, but he and the figures that surround him are less personalities in their own right than personifications. He is

36. Krishna lifting Mount Govardhan

Kāmdev, and he is just what his name says: the god (*dev*) of love (*kām*). He is Cupid, but with the important difference that there is nothing cherubic or infantile about him. He is never younger than an adolescent, for the sort of love he personifies is lust, the love that is motivated by the desire to satisfy its own pleasure, hence, broadly, desire. His constant companion is Vasant (Springtime), and he is wedded to Passion, his wife Rati.

As Kāmdev and Indra are different, the sorts of battle they wage are different, as well. Indra was a true adversary for Krishna. Krishna antagonized him knowingly, Indra responded aggressively, and Krishna raised his mountainous shield of defense until his enemy was defeated. But with Kāmdev, for all the talk of battle, the combat is never quite joined. Krishna never so much as lifts a finger: that, at least, he did in fighting Indra, even if a finger was sufficient to lift a mountain. Here he does nothing, and the fact is significant. For just as Kāmdev is allegorical, so is his enemy. It is not strictly speaking Krishna who is challenged, but rather what he stands for, love in a different sense from *kām*, a love that is called in Hindi *prem*. And the conflict between these two sorts of love does not have the attack and counterattack one normally expects in a battle, because what is involved is not struggle but incompatability. Where one is, the other cannot be.

For this other love, *prem*, is a world unto itself: it is pure. Unlike *kām*, it satisfies no desires of any who partake of it, and by the same token, it has no results in the natural world. *Kām* bears children, *prem* does not. *Kām* supplies much of the motivating force that brings the world of family and social obligation into being; *prem* builds nothing. And if *kām* can build, it can also exhaust itself, but *prem* cannot. It has only the most mystical relation to time; it is eternal.[2]

The *līlā* acts all of this out. Kāmdev does indeed exhaust himself in the fight, while Krishna is untouched by any effort. The woman do indeed have to leave behind the entire world that *kām* creates — their elders and husbands and children — in order to bridge the gap to Krishna's world of *prem*. And they have to prove at length to Krishna's satisfaction and, more important, for the edification of the onlookers, that they have done so. They reel off the arguments to show that the ethical world they have abandoned is simply not contiguous with the higher world they have entered. This fact is already suggested by the timing of the action: night obscures boundaries. But it is made entirely explicit in the role of Yogamāyā, who, we learn, has taken elaborate measures to distance the charmed circle of the *rās* from the mundane world in both time and space. She sees to it that there is no possible connection between the two by creating copies of all the participants in the *rās* so that no one at home misses them and can follow their tracks from one realm to the other. The two become entirely distinct, as eternity is from time. And the nature of Kāmdev's defeat illustrates the point yet again: he is unable to attack because the vision of what he is opposing transfixes him, and he loses consciousness. The consciousness of *kām* and the consciousness of *prem* simply do not mix.

Kāmdev is not the only one to storm the gates of the *rās*, however. There is another visitor, Śiva, and his presence is important. Śiva is an ambivalent divinity; some would say he represents contradiction itself. He is the consummate lover, and he is paradigmatic ascetic.[3] But in the *līlās* of Brindavan, he is always represented in the latter role,[4] and he appears in the *mahārās līlā* with all the paraphernalia of a confirmed yogi. As such he is Kām's natural enemy: whereas Kām propels the social organism, Śiva withdraws from it in disgust.

Once they actually came to blows; and this famous encounter is very much in the background of Kām's confrontation with Krishna as related in the *mahārās līlā*. Śiva had withdrawn into eons of meditation on his isolated Himalayan mountaintop. At first no one had minded: he was antisocial in any case, and sometimes downright unpleasant, never properly adjusted to the society of the gods. But he was powerful, and when the demons waxed strong and the gods could no longer control them, the gods had no one to turn to but Śiva. If he would beget a son, that son would be powerful enough to deal with the forces of disruption. The gods deputed Kāmdev to the mountains in the hopes of seducing this ascetic into a marriage with Pārvatī, the beautiful daughter of Father Himalaya. When his feet touched ground, Spring bloomed, but when he drew his bow of flowers and aimed his fragrant arrow at Śiva, the god grew incensed and cast a piercing glance at him from the third eye at the center of his forehead, where the fruit of all his ascetic regimen was concentrated as heat. The intruder was instantly reduced to ash.

The ultimate outcome of the battle, however, is uncertain. The elusive Kām was harder to deal with without his body than if he had retained it, and ultimately Śiva and Pārvatī did wed, produce a son, and through him restore order to the cosmos. Was Kām responsible, or was it the asceticism Pārvatī herself had undertaken in order to win her man? Tradition gives no univocal answer, but Kāmdev always claimed the victory as his, and does so in this *līlā*.

The *mahārās līlā* does not settle the debate as to which is the more powerful, Śiva or Kāmdev. Instead it pits them both against a third force, *prem*, as personified in the relation between Krishna and the *gopīs*, and there the outcome is clear: both desire and renunciation are bested. Kām falls away unconscious and finally dies. Śiva's fate is not quite so severe, nor is his confrontation with *rās* so brutal. Because all that he represents is understood as a withdrawal from life, in fact, there is no occasion for him actually to meet Krishna. He wants to, but he must turn about-face to do so, and that brings him into the company of the *gopīs*, who tell him quite simply that if this is the path he would choose, he must abandon his old personality and become one of them. Otherwise he is an anomaly and cannot enter the circle of the *rās*. Since he has already implicitly abandoned his ascetic identity even to take an interest in the *rās* (as the *līlā* says, he cannot accommodate it into his field of yogic concentration) he does so readily, and makes an entry into the realm of love that is, unlike Kāmdev's, both peaceful and successful. Once again there is no real connection between this world and the world from which he had come: he must alter totally to make the transition.

In the battle at Govardhan, Krishna ultimately replaces Indra. As it turns out, the mountain is an expression of Krishna himself, and to worship it, life's proximate center, is to worship Krishna, god of familiarity. It is no longer the chief end of religion to propitiate capricious Indra and his distant, vaguely understood heavenly host. In a similar way, Krishna replaces Śiva here as victor in the struggles of the gods. It was Śiva who did battle with Kāmdev before and was capable of reducing him to ash. Now it is Krishna who deals Kāmdev the deathblow; and that to the tune of a great deal of speculation as to whether his former antagonist had ever really defeated him. And, just as Krishna's victory over Indra signified the demise of one version of the meaning of religion in favor of another, Krishna's taking the place of Śiva does the same.

In the former case, it was a movement in the direction of a more natural, interior understanding of religion, as against practices of appeasement and sacrifice directed to the far reaches of the cosmos. The immediacy and stability of Govardhan supplant Indra's distance and unpredictability. Now that movement is further intensified. The form of piety that is here understood as arrayed under Śiva's banner—the religion that took ascetic practice as its standard—was also an interiorizing religion. It too purported to replace external sacrifice, Indra's food, with an interior one. But here the efficacy of all that is called into question. Śiva's followers, ascetics of every stripe, are called cowards by Kāmdev. He claims they are unwilling to meet life on its own terms: they have run from him, from *kām* with all its pleasures and demands. The clear implication is that this is no natural, interior religion at all. It is contrived and oblique, as bizarre and unhelpful in its practices as was the sacrificial piety it had been intended to displace, and every bit as wedded to the externals of life. Kāmdev points to the obvious ones, the various conceits and flagellations that surround the life of the yogi. But other voices, including that of Krishna himself, make the more fundamental criticism that all yogic techniques, even those that involve manipulations of only the mind, are unnatural, and in that sense external to the life process. They deflect life, they do not meet it, and so they cannot express what is truly endemic to human experience, truly interior.

This makes sense of what we see in the *līlā* itself. It explains why Kām is indeed Krishna's ultimate adversary. Kām and Krishna agree that theirs is a battle out in the open, on the field of life. Śiva, by contrast, does not even fight. In one sense this simply reflects the fact that he is not so formidable an opponent. But in another it shows that Krishna and Śiva, though fundamentally different, are not fundamentally opponents. Broadly understood, they both represent not life in the raw but religious responses to it, or better, access to the religious reality that undergirds it. Hence it is not that one defeats the other, but rather that each absorbs, and by absorbing supplants, the other.

Krishna's realm of love has room even for Śiva, though it transforms him fundamentally. When the great ascetic joins the circle of the *rās*, the final step has been taken in the interiorization and naturalization of religion.

What, then, separates Krishna's realm from Kāmdev's? What makes them opposite? It is nothing external; indeed, the terms remain the same, many of them. Krishna's is no flight from the life of the body: he insists quite pointedly that he too is fully sensual. He even describes himself (in a point that is not entirely consistent with the rest of the doctrine he preaches) as incorporating a version of *kām*. The *gopīs*, for their part, make it very clear (and Krishna tests it tirelessly) that so far as they are concerned he is directly analogous to the husbands they have left behind to be with him; he claims them completely, as a more marginal figure, some guru perhaps, could not. But the point is—and they say this too—that he is their true husband, the husband who makes their former marriages seem false and perfunctory. In other words, the realm that Krishna animates involves a total transformation of social life. It does not cancel anything, it confirms everything. Because natural life is supported by Krishna's eternal circle dance, it can be lived in a new way: for *prem*, not *kām*, in selfless love rather than selfishly. In a similar way, Christians have affirmed that the presence of the second Adam, Christ, redeems the life of the first Adam, fallen humanity, in this world rather than canceling or ignoring it.

And this realm of the *rās* has much to compare with the world before the fall. Certainly its setting is idyllic as Eden. But by contrast with the Christian view, this realm is not irretrievably gone. Indeed it is eternally available. Nothing has ever poisoned it: the poison of *kām* pollutes only itself, but the original liquid of love remains pure. It is called just that, liquid *(ras)* or the liquid of love *(prem ras)*; but the word has manifold associations (flavor, taste, aesthetic sensitivity, emotion itself), and at some point in the growth of the tradition, it was supposed that the name of dance itself, *rās*, is but a permutation of this more encompassing term. Grammatically this is possible. One word can be derived from another by a process called "increase" *(vṛddhi)*, and *rās* (with a long *a*) is grammatically the "increase" of *ras*, its concentrated form.

Thanks to Krishna in his relation to Radha, and by extension to the rest of the girls of Braj, *ras* flows eternal in this world. The problem is merely to refine one's gross sensibilities so that one may sense the movement of that flow, or to use the language of the *rās līlā*, hear the call of the flute. Then one is set adrift from the sedimentation and pollution that inevitably attend the ever-recurrent process of procreation and death; one can take the responsibilities required to keep the system going without congealing into a hardened mass under their pressure.

Eternally flowing, this stream has no real season. Hence it is quite appropriate that although everyone knows the *rās* was danced primordially on the night of the autumn full moon in the month of *kārttik* (October-November), one is encouraged to become aware of the constant presence of the great dance.[5] Time and again I have been assured in Braj that if one but had eyes to see, one would find it going on all the time.

Yet it is hard to remove the scales of *kām* from one's perception. It is not easy to recover the clearer vision beneath, to put away one's hardness of heart and recover one's true liquidity. The daily performance of the *rās līlā*—for it always includes the *rās* sequence as its first element, and without it no *līlā* would be complete or even possible—helps the process along. And the *mahārās līlā* does so in a special way. Here one has not one Krishna but many. He multiplies himself to be in the presence of each of the girls with whom he dances, just as he multiplies himself to be present in the heart of every devotee. The *mahārās līlā* represents this universally recognized divine miracle in a vivid way, showing how Krishna is both unitary and in that respect distant from the complex contrivances of socialized life (he haunts the untamed forest), and yet at the same time capable of making himself intimately present to all who seek a relation with him.

It is Radha who holds the key to this mystery, so she is understood as the teacher of the *rās*, its guru. It is she who has the idea in the first place, and she who makes it possible. For she is the link between the singular Krishna and the many *gopīs*. Eternally with him, his feminine half, she is also one of the company of girls that follow him and pine after him. If one understands Krishna as the divine Self and the *gopīs* as its human counterpart, as has often been done, then it is Radha who brings them together.

As Natthī Lāl and Śrī Rām's *mahārās līlā* is cast, however, this would be too simple an interpretation, for the *gopīs*, too, are quite special and represent various degrees of attainment along the spectrum that joins humanity with the divine. Radha's role remains the same, however: she is the one in whom all the *gopīs* unite. They are ultimately expressions, emanations, of her; their variety is caused by her selfless desire to satisfy her lover completely, in many ways. They are, thus, the field and expression of her love.[6]

At the beginning of the *līlā*, she challenges Krishna to satisfy all of them and her too, and at length he accomplishes the feat, by keeping the others in a state of waiting until she finally appears. Then he can embrace her without arousing their jealousy because at the same moment he grants them access to the *rās*. Once she is present he accepts them, too. From a theological point of view this says that only as expressions of her do they relate to him, but there is a deeper meaning, as well, and it has to do with relationships as such.

Radha symbolizes relation. She is constant, unswerving love. Krishna may have fun, he may even desert her for another, but her constant thought is of him. Indeed, since all the *gopīs* are in the final analysis but emanations of her, she meets Krishna even in his waywardness: even in the person of her archrival Candrāvalī, she expresses her constant attentiveness. He may have a divine history that makes him independent, but everything she is she owes to him. She has no other avatar; with her everything relates to him. Even when she is far from him, in anger, it is only because she is so near. He may do battle on several fronts, but the only demon she has to defeat is the one that sends the tortures of love, for love is all she is.

This is why there can be no *rās* without Radha; for the circle dance is no spectacular coupling between Krishna and his countless women, it is a testament of love itself. This is its singular meaning, and Radha must be there—Krishna's singular love—to make it possible. Her unity, the unity of the process of love, makes possible the multiple relations of subject and object, of lover and beloved, that the *rās* represents. She is the circumference of the circle in its totality, but at the same time her shape (love, the circular emotion) is what comprehends the infinite number of radii: indeed, her shape demands that these point-to-point relations be infinite. Love comprehends all. The most natural thing in the world, it is also the most exalted. Hence, as the *mahārās līlā* makes clear, it is the standard of religion itself.

Where Radha is present, then, religion must transcend the worship of objects, however great. It cannot be a linear affair. Awe, the Great Other, petitions and transactions of every kind with the Power that rules the universe—these cannot be the last word: the disparity between subject and object is too great. Hence Krishna abandons his lordliness to come to Braj. And the ultimate statement of his self-abandonment is his union with Radha, for only through her, paradoxically, can he taste himself.

In Braj it is considered a great fault to presume to worship Krishna in the absence of Radha. She is always there, for she is worship itself; she is love. No image of Krishna should stand by itself, so frequently one sees dual images of Radha and Krishna. But even if one cannot see Radha, her secret presence is felt. We have seen that more than one altar in Brindavan symbolizes this eloquently by including a throne for her invisible presence alongside his; it is tended with equal care, and is shaded like his with the umbrella of royalty. As Krishna insists in explaining why he is dancing the *rās*, then, hers is a pervasive and sovereign secrecy. The whole dance is an expression of his relation to her. So is his presence in the temples of Brindavan, where, as in the case of Rādhā Ramaṇ and Rādhā Vallabh, he even bears her name; and so is life itself.

In Brindavan one worships ultimately not Krishna but Krishna-and-Radha. One worships love itself, and the only true worship is love. One worships not an object but a relation, and one worships relationally; one worships by loving. This is what the great circle dance teaches, and as a circle it teaches by encompassing. In the *mahārās*, the circle expands incalculably to a giant mandala, and the only question is whether the devotee will find that he or she is already inside, and join the dance.

37. Rādhā Vallabh and the seemingly empty throne of Radha (credit: Dixit Studio, Brindavan)

The following is the standard form of the *mahārās līlā* as now performed in Brindavan. Unlike the other plays translated here, it owes its composition entirely to a single man, the leading figure in the reshaping of the *rās līlā* today, Premānand. The practice of performing the *mahārās* with several companies goes back no farther than half a century: it dates to the time a great number of companies began to gather in Brindavan. Initially it was a simple affair involving plenty of dancing, and woven primarily around a dozen or so passages from the *Rāspañcādhyāyī* of Nanda Dās, but making allowance for the traditional confrontation between Krishna and Kāmdev. Simple companies still render it in this form. Premānand felt the *līlā* deserved a more exacting text, and composed one based, like Nanda Dās's, on the five chapters of the *Bhāgavata Purāṇa* in which the story of the *rās* is recounted. It was intended to be performed over a period of five days, a chapter a day. The *rāsdhārīs* to whose companies Premānand taught the *līlā*, however, found that it placed demands on the memory that their child actors could not meet, and feared that their audiences could not tolerate such sustained dissertations. They selected certain passages and omitted others, producing a *līlā* that lasts no longer than three nights, and is in most cases performed in two nights or, as in the present case, on a single evening in one long sitting. Premānand is disappointed that the full version has never been staged, but concedes that it would have stretched the patience of the common people who make up the bulk of any *līlā* audience. And he takes great satisfaction that, as in this performance, a boy only nine or ten years old can recall Krishna's lines with almost complete accuracy.[7] It was performed by Ṣvāmīs Śrī Rām and Natthī Lāl, with the help of *rāsdhārīs* and *svarūps* from various other companies on the evening of the full moon of the month of *śrāvaṇ*, August 13, 1976.

The Great Circle Dance

Part I. Preparation

MUSICIANS: We honor the lotus feet of our teachers. We bow before our most gracious teachers. [*Having acknowledged the mercies of the gurus, without whom the knowledge of the* rās līlā *would not have been passed down from generation to generation, the* MUSICIANS *pay their homage to their gurus' gurus, the divine pair themselves, beginning with Sanskrit verses from the* Mahāvāṇī *of Hari Vyās Dev.*]

Our praise we raise to Lord Krishna,
  limitless, vast in intellect,
Who ever explores the immortal sea
  that flows from the lips of Radha.
Homage to Radha, Krishna's essence,
  and Krishna, the essence of Radha,
Whose beauty graces Brindavan's groves;
  to them and the guru give praise.[8]

[*Then follows the vernacular invocation, a poem attributed to Sūr Dās that is sung at the beginning of every* rās līlā.]

To Hari's lotus feet I bind my praise,

Whose mercy enables the lame to leap mountains,
  brings the blind to vivid sight,
Makes deaf ears hear, the dumb find speech,
  poor people sport the umbrella of kings—
Mercy on mercy, says Sūr, is my lord.
  Those feet, his feet, I ceaselessly praise.

[*Once these verses establish the properly auspicious context for what is to come, there is time for the recitation of several verses of praise, some directed to* RADHA, *some to* KRISHNA, *some to them both, and some to the place in which they rendezvous. Most are in the vernacular, but a few are rendered in elementary Sanskrit.*]

(1)

Sing the name of Radha, sing
  until that name invades your dreams,
The name that so compelled our dark Syām
  he drew it closely to his side.

(2)

Dark as a thundercloud threatens,
  noble and ample his manner,
He holds a mountain in the palm of his hand
  with the selfsame ease his tongue bears the flute;
Equally guardian of every Braj clan
  and darling of all of their daughters in love,

A basilwood necklace garlands this youngster,
this herdsman, this boy I worship.

(3)

Brindavan provides the finery
and the buzzing of bees the echoing tune
That decorate Rādhikā, the bride,
and celebrate Nanda's son, the groom.
Sing his praise, best prince of Braj,
sing his praise, high treasure of pleasure;
His is the heart in each devotee's heart
and the love of his lover: sing his praise!

(4)

To those in need every grace proceeds
from Bṛṣabhānu's princess daughter:
Even Gopāl will seek without ceasing
her merciful, mischievous, sidelong glance.

(5)

Beguiling Krishna, the shape of your eyes
suggests a ferryman's ferry,
And whoever is carried off, taken for a ride,
casts off to the shore on life's other side.[9]

(6)

If Braj is the sea, if Mathura the lotus,
and the lotus-seed is the pollen, Brindavan,
The women of Braj are all fertile flowers,
and shimmering Krishna the sole fleeting bee.

[*One of the* SAKHĪs *takes up a shiny platter strewn with flower petals on which several small lamps of* ghī *have been lit. She moves toward the divine couple, who are seated on the throne, and waves the tray in front of them with a circular motion that approximately traces the written shape of the syllable OM. This offering of light is an indispensible part of the worship of* RADHA *and* KRISHNA *as they make themselves present in the temple images: it both honors the objects of worship and makes them visible to the devotees in attendance. Here the temple rite is given a setting in life as the* GOPĪS, *representing all the inhabitants of Braj, perform this* ārati *ceremony. All the girls sing as one of their number waves the tray of lights.*]

SAKHIS:

Sing, friend, and lift the lamps
to the beloved and her lover,
To Bṛṣabhānu's beauty, that darling girl,
and him who moves the mountain.

And lift the cow-tail fan and spread
the camphor that decks the golden plate;
Offer up yourself as well
to him who plays in the jungle grove.
Sing, friend, and lift the lamps . . .

A peacock-feathered crown he has,
earrings, and a garland on his breast;
Muralī reclines on his sensuous lips,
my friend: it's Nanda's wondrous son.
Look at his eyes, his winsome charm;
a lithe and playful lad he is.
Sing, friend, and lift the lamps . . .

Radha's exquisite face, like the moon,
rises above her lovely yellow sari,
And Lalit Kiśorī sings her serenades;
she's the pride of Barsana
and the joy of her lover.
Sing, friend, and lift the lamps. . . .

There they sit, the pair, enthroned:
lightly he curls his arm around her,
And so they dwell on and on and on
forever in the hearts of the devoted.[10]
They are the wealth that enriches Braj,
the life that enlivens the circle dance.
Sing, friend, and lift the lamps. . . .

[*This* āratī *song has focused more on* KRISHNA *than on* RADHA, *and now the* SAKHĪS, *joined by the* MUSICIANS, *repair the imbalance with a* savaiyā *that associates her with the other most powerful female figure in Braj—Yamunā, the River Jumna, whose banks will play host to the circle dance. Here the seniority of the Jumna over* RADHA *in the house of Braj, correct from an historical point of view, is acknowledged without diminishing the sway of* RADHA*'s scepter.*][11]

There are blessings to reap when Brindavan's your home,
  where Yamunā's enthroned as the reigning queen:
Those who attentively bathe where she flows
  are known to reach Vaikuṇṭha and find heavenly home.
Just as the Vedas and Puranas have said,
  and just as the saints and sages have seen,
Yamunā fends off the minions of Death,
  as life's tides are channeled by Radha the Queen.[12]

[*With this the preliminary songs conclude, and* KRISHNA *bounces up from his position on the throne, then turns to address* RADHA, *who is still seated. He extends his arm as he speaks.*]

KRISHNA: Oh look, sweetheart! Look how the beams from tonight's full moon strike the sands of the Jumna and splinter into so many more reflected moonbeams.[13]

MUSICIANS:

"Look, my dear, how second by second
  new beams form—look, new! how pretty! . . ."
He faltered and found he could not say more,
  dazzled and silenced by the vast display.[14]

KRISHNA: Oh sweetheart, what a brilliant show on the banks of the Jumna! Look how the sand glitters!

The sandy shore—a spray of camphor dust,
  powder sent in showers by the moon,
An autumn pool left full by the rains—
  is now a lunar nectar in a shining bowl.

Oh look, dear, the sand doesn't look like sand at all. It looks like moondust scattered all over the ground. And the banks of the river look like a tank filled to the brim with nectar of immortality spilt down from the moon. No, it's more than that. That nectar seems divine.

RADHA: You're so right, dearest. How very sweet and soft the sand is, and what a matchless sheen it gives off. [*bending down as if to pick up a few grains*]

Gentle beyond gentle,
soft as a baby's soft,
Touch it with your fingertips,
you will never feel it rough.

Look how fine it is, sweetheart. It just slips through your fingers.

KRISHNA: And look over there, dear. [*He points offstage, as if to the river.*]

Look at the waters of the Kālindī,
look how they glisten and they shine,
Sparkling bright as a polished sapphire
that glows with a light of its own.

Yes, the waves ripple and glitter like a fabulous array of jewels that's been sent to adorn this river and make it brilliantly clear that this is the liquid of liquids, the quintessence of everything that flows.

RADHA: Oh my beloved, wellspring of every joy, how the juices do begin to flow. You know, I've just had a strange stirring in my heart, an idea for extraordinary game. Listen:

Listen my darling, love of my life,

A wave just flooded my heart, just now—
something unique, something sudden and new,
Something stirred when I saw your sight
and some thoughts arose and captured my heart:
Thoughts of your gathering the milkmaids around
and giving them pleasure, each, all at one time.[15]

Sweetheart, prove to me that you can do the great circle dance with all the countless thousands of cowherd girls all at once; then I'll be ready to recognize you as that clever crest-jewel and king of connoisseurs everyone says you are. But be careful that nothing pollutes this *rās*. Every heart should be afloat in the mood of the occasion. There's not room for even a speck of jealousy, enmity, pride, or poisonousness.

KRISHNA: Yes, my dear one, my innermost desire, with your help all this will be accomplished. Please just continue to express your wishes as they come to you on the spur of the moment, and I'll do my best to fulfill them.

RADHA: Listen then. Here in Braj among these droves of budding cowherd girls who have fallen in love with you there are all sorts of women. Some belong to your party and some belong to mine and some belong to both. Some stand to the left and some stand to the right. Some have been married and some are as yet unmarried. Some are shy, others jabber away; some are hardboiled, and others think they can control things by sulking away in anger. Some are motivated primarily by friendships, others are more affected by erotic emotions; some want nothing more than to serve, while others are agressive, regular leaders of the pack. Some dwell here eternally and others have earned their presence here by completing spiritual disciplines in past lives. So you see, there are milkmaids of every nature and disposition, and you must dance the great *rās* with all of them.[16]

KRISHNA: Yes, but of all these many hundreds of thousands of cowherd girls only sixteen thousand are eternally with me, and of these there are only two who stand out, you and Candrāvalī. Of those two you are the greater, the one in relation to whom there is no second, the crowning jewel among the young women of Braj, mistress of all, ruler of all. So my dear, in the final analysis I must regard you as above them all. Whatever game I play and in whatever way, it is ultimately you with whom I play, you with whom I unite, most beautiful one.

RADHA: Yes, dear.

KRISHNA: But the problem is that if I were to give you that highest place openly at the time of the circle dance, it's a sure thing that the hearts of the other girls would fill with envy and hatred, and they'd go off into the forest in a huff, nursing their resentments. And if they became contemptuous of me, then the whole mood would be spoiled.

RADHA: Well that's what's going to test how clever you are. If you can manage to dance the great circle dance in such a way that all the girls feel completely satisfied and no one gets jealous of my special position, then it will be a wonderful dance indeed, and I'll believe that you are the clever, matchless sovereign of the emotions that people say you are.

KRISHNA: Mistress of all, dear as life, it's no easy command you've given, but with your grace I will try to carry it out. Nothing you command can be too hard for me, because

You make the impossible possible,
each obstacle you cast aside,
You made me a lifter of mountains,
and with you I can accomplish the *rās*.
You are the source of all my power:
my flute merely echoes your soul;
My form, my essence, each virtue I own
is granted by Radha's grace and love.[17]

[*Once this resolve is firm,* KRISHNA *and* RADHA *retire to their throne and a curtain drops, concealing them and concluding the scene. Soon there is a great flurry in the wings, and* KĀMDEV *appears at the front of the stage. Some troupes liken* KĀMDEV *to those he most easily affects, and represent him as an adolescent boy who leaps cheerfully, aggressively on stage, brandishing his great bow and his flower-tipped arrows. Other companies emphasize* KĀMDEV*'s pride more than his youth, and his enmity to* KRISHNA *more than his energy in the service of love. The* KĀMDEV *we see here is such a one, played by a fully matured man with a great moustache, clad in the rich paraphernalia of royalty. He wears a silken powder-blue turban, red tunic, and loose-fitting deep blue pants, trails a sequined white mantle, and sports jeweled necklaces of various lengths. The amorous bow and arrow are at his side, but his ominous expression makes one aware that these are weapons, not toys. He is accompanied by his general, the similarly arrayed but less stern* VASANT, *whose name means* SPRING. KĀMDEV *speaks with a swagger that reminds one of the sort of role* KANS *and* INDRA *have played in earlier* līlās*—indeed, in this company the same actor often plays all three parts.*]

KĀMDEV: [*soliloquizing, to the* AUDIENCE] Let me tell you about the names they call me. First of all there's Mār, the Marksman. Śiva may have hit me once, but did I come back and clobber him! Pow, boom, baam! And poor old Brahmā: when he sees me coming he quakes in his boots.

I hit, I strike, I knock them down—
there's no marksman like Mār
in the whole wide world![18]

And my second name is Madan, the Intoxicator, because I can level the world's biggest lady killers.[19] My third name is Manmath, the one that churns up the heart. As the verse goes,

Ask Manmath to churn a little milk
and presto: it's turned to whey.[20]

That's right, I take off the butter right away. Whether it's gods or demigods who are concerned, or sages or big ascetics like Kardam and the rest, I just start churning, churning away and suddenly, all that's left of them is a little puddle of whey. [*To* SPRING]

I hit, I strike, I knock them down—
there's no marksman like Mār
in the whole wide world!

How about it, general, is there anyone in the whole universe who can stand up under my attack?

SPRING: No sir, not a soul.

KĀMDEV: [*launching into a paean of self-congratulation*]

In the face of my powerful advances,

Indra forgot the role that he had
as lord over all of the gods,
And set out after an ascetic's wife,
Ahalyā, once under my command.
Grandfather Brahmā, elder statesman,
abandoned all wit and all decorum
And hastened to ravish Sarasvatī,
even though she was his very own daughter.

No lesser lady than Pārvatī
  was another to shed every shred of discretion:
Bitterly smitten, she mimed the ascetics,
  disrobing to lure her lover back.
Even the moon — I blackened his name
  in the eyes of the wife of his own guru.
I've tumbled and turned the entire world to rubble
  and over the ruins raised the banner of love.[21]

So you see, general, that's the way it's always been.

SPRING: Right, sir.

KĀMDEV: That's the kind of ignominious defeat I've brought on the likes of Brahmā, Rudra, Candā, Sūrya, Parāśar, Vasiṣṭha, and Viśvāmitra.[22] Not to speak of all those sages and ascetics and yogis — with them I didn't even have to fight! Cowards! They all ran away before the battle had even begun, willingly choking down their defeat.

SPRING: What do you mean, they just choked down their punishment?

KĀMDEV:

Happiness comes from beautiful women,
  but there's risk in it too: they may take it away.
Some fools have turned, and off they ran
  like cowards away from the battle of love:
Idiots! Look at them cringe from afar,
  heads all shaved and faces blackened;
Shorn of the love that their homes could have offered,
  they go begging at others' for scraps of love —
Well, I keep them out. I guard the door
  against these yogis and fakirs,
Forbidding some ever to cut their hair,
  forcing others to shave themselves bare.
Look at them! Some of them love to breathe smoke;
  others grovel in a graveyard life;
They wander about with a skull in their hands
  and a hope that someone will fill it with food![23]

MUSICIANS:

"Where is there a god who could be my equal?
  For the world dances to the pace I provide."

That was his question to the king of the seasons:
"Is there anyone left to joust with me?"[24]

KĀMDEV: What about it, General Spring, is there any warrior in the world today who's prepared to do battle with me?

SPRING: [*obediently*] No sir, not a one. Your flag of victory has been run up from one corner of the universe to the other, from the depths of hell to the heights of heaven, and out to all the points of the compass. [*Then hesitantly, after a moment's awkward reflection*] But one question, Maharaja: what about the time Śiva reduced you to ash?

KĀMDEV: [*blustering to the defense*] Well, what about it? What happened, I ask you? Didn't I come back and defeat him anyway? What good was all that anger of his? Yes he made ash of me, but what was the result? My influence doubled and quadrupled! Once I was relieved of my body it was all the easier for me to establish my reign in every atom and hair of the universe, so that now I have no rival save for Lord Viṣṇu himself, and so far there's been no chance to test myself in battle against him.

SPRING: No chance? What do you mean, sir? Lord Viṣṇu has come into the world many times, as a fish, a turtle, a boar, a man-lion, and so forth. He's always manifesting himself. Why haven't you come out and attacked him?

KĀMDEV: [*a little taken aback, but trying to save face and deal with this uncomfortable observation*] When was there ever time to take him on? Why, he was practically gone as soon as he got here! What am I supposed to do if he won't even take the time on earth to settle down and get married? How am I supposed to fight with him if he doesn't give me a chance?

SPRING: But didn't he give you that chance, Maharaja? Why, when he was Rām he spent eleven thousand years on earth, and he was married as well. Why didn't you attack him then?

KĀMDEV: Oh but *didn't* I? Who do you think was responsible for the fact that he chased after Sītā all that time?[25]

SPRING: Fair enough, sir. But now you have the chance to test your strength against him in his complete, ultimate form, as the one who makes his home in the Heaven of Cows.[26] For now he's transposed that form to Braj, and manifest himself here as the little cowherding son of Nanda and Yaśodā. Were you aware of that?

KĀMDEV: [*A little worried by the prospect of so imminent an encounter, he masks a moment's hesitation with a rapid, mechanical response.*] Yes, yes I'm quite aware of the whole thing, General. But he's only a boy eight or ten years old, and as you know there's no way for me to enter into the body of a child like that. [*Drawing himself up to his full height and puffing out his chest, insulted now that anyone could have thought of matching him against such a novice, and confident that the case is closed*] So as far as I can see there's no one in the world that stands independent of me. They're all under my thumb.

SPRING: [*acceding, perhaps out of the sense that it is pointless to force the issue any farther*] Well then, Maharaja, you've defeated everyone. All praise to you, World-Victor, Churner of Hearts, you who bear the flowery bow and hold the five flowery arrows in your hands, all praise to you! Those five arrows—the petrifier, the intoxicator, the abra, the cadabra,[27] and the inflamer—any one of them is capable of bewitching gods, sages, and humans, and when you unleash all five of them the whole universe reels from the catastrophe. Everyone is lost. That's the incomparable force your arrows have. And though there's really no need of me, I accompany you as your general, strewing flowers about wherever you have chosen to do battle. But the victory is totally yours. No one can stand before you. Praise to you, eternally!

[*Enter* NĀRAD, *strumming his* tānpurā *and mumbling his habitual mantra. He comes onstage at some distance from where* KĀMDEV *and* SPRING *have been in conversation.*]

NĀRAD: Nārāyaṇ, Nārāyaṇ, Nārāyaṇ. [*Cogitating calmly*] So! Today that world-conqueror and churner of hearts Kāmdev has just about drowned himself in his own pride. There he goes strutting around his capital, Kandarp, trailing his army in glory behind him and quaffing down the liquor of self-satisfaction in great poisonous gulps. Well, why shouldn't he congratulate himself, after all? He has the world's largest ego! Everyone else's pales beside his. [*He strums and chants for a moment, then pauses as an idea dawns on him.*] Nārāyaṇ, Nārāyaṇ. . . . [*Reflectively*] You know, I think I've got a way to defuse that pride of his. Yes, why not? Śrī Krishna, fountain of joy, moon of Braj, has manifested himself playfully in Brindavan these days. I'll arrange it so that the two of them have a chance to meet one another, Madan and Madan Mohan,[28] the Intoxicator and the Intoxicator's Beguiler. That way there's a chance that this Intoxicator will get a little of his own intoxication knocked out of him. All right, on with it. Let's go.

[*He begins strumming his* tānpurā *again and saunters across the stage. As he does so the curtain rises and we see the* GOPĪS *and* RADHA *and* KRISHNA *as a backdrop to the scene that follows.*]

KĀMDEV: What's this? I believe it's Nārad himself.

NĀRAD: Nārāyaṇ, Nārāyaṇ . . .

SPRING: That's who it is, all right, and it seems he's come precisely in order to visit you.

KĀMDEV: Yes, you're right, and what a good thing. If anyone knows who might be able to fulfill my wish for a worthy combattant, surely it's he.

SPRING: Right, Maharaja. He's a great detective, that Nārad. Whatever's going on in the universe, he knows all about it.

KĀMDEV: [*to* NĀRAD] Hail Nārāyaṇ. Hail Nārāyaṇ, Nārad.

NĀRAD: Hail Nārāyaṇ. Blessings on you, world-conquering Kāmdev, you who fly the banner with the crocodile on it. You've been so kind not to include poor old me among your conquests: I'm so grateful.

KĀMDEV: No, no. Quite the contrary. Today I'll be very grateful to you. You may be able, if you'll be gracious enough, to make a wish come true.

NĀRAD: What's your wish?

KĀMDEV: Oh it's not just mine. It's both of ours, yours and mine.

NĀRAD: How's that? I don't know what possible connection the thoughts of an old fool like me could have with the designs of anyone as magnificent as you. But I do know one thing: there's an excellent match for you these days, a regular lion of a youth and a consummate dandy. If you can defeat him, your fame in battle will permeate the universe, and justly so.

KĀMDEV: But Nārad, can there be such a warrior? Why, I've already defeated Brahmā, Indra, Rudra, Candā, Sūrya, Parāśar, Vaśiṣṭha, Viśvāmitra . . .

NĀRAD: As yes, but have you dealt with Lord Viṣṇu?

KĀMDEV: [*skirting the question*] Well, but with the exception of him is there any other?

NĀRAD: Yes. Listen carefully. On the continent of Jambū, in the land of India, in the Braj region, and specifically in the town of Gokul . . .

MUSICIANS: [*forecasting the action in song*]

Fasten a single arrow in your bow:
  and in a second you'll hit him sure.

NĀRAD: . . . in the house of Nanda the cowherd you'll find a wonderfully handsome lad.

KĀMDEV: [*putting two and two together*] Might this be Krishna, the cowherd?

NĀRAD: [*surprised*] Yes, that's the one.

KĀMDEV: But Nārad,

He's just a poor boy who lives in the woods
  and spends his whole day grazing the cows;
He may be enthralling to his herder friends,
  but that hardly makes him a special star!

Really, Nārad, he's just a country lad. He drinks water from the tank and spends the whole day consorting with a bunch of cowherds. Where's the match in that?

NĀRAD: Ah, but Mr. Intoxicator, you've forgotten something very important.

KĀMDEV: And what's that?

NĀRAD: This is no simple boy! He's a lion of a youth, the pride of his lineage and possessed of very fine taste—a real connoisseur when it comes to matters of love: your equal in every way. When the women of Braj were performing a vow to Kātyāyanī, bathing in the river in hopes of obtaining a husband, he brought all their wishes to fruition by stealing their clothing away.[29] Hasn't news of that reached you?

KĀMDEV: Of course it has. I was *there*, after all! I sat nearby with my bow drawn through the whole incident, but I was so charmed with the banter between Krishna and the girls that, well . . . but this time I'll go ahead and shoot. This time I'll conquer.

NĀRAD: [*rubbing it in, but with seeming innocence*] What? You mean you had your bow drawn but it didn't shoot?

KĀMDEV: [*defensive*] Look here, Nārad, there's nothing wrong with my bow. It's as sturdy as they come. It was just that first of all they were just joking around, and when that was over Krishna returned their clothes right away and the game was over. There wasn't any chance to shoot.

NĀRAD: All right, but what about the time the Brahmins of Mathura were holding a sacrifice and their wives gradually edged over to Krishna? Wasn't there time for an attack then?

KĀMDEV: No, it was the same thing all over again. That cowherd Krishna must be afraid of me, because when the Brahmin wives begged to be allowed to stay with him, he turned them all back. He's afraid of me, I tell you. If he'd just break out of that shell of childhood and meet me on the open battlefield, I'd release a rain of arrows so fast you wouldn't even see them leave the bow, and not a one would miss its mark.

NĀRAD: Well that's just the chance you're going to have. Tonight Krishna has stepped out onto the field of battle.

KĀMDEV: [*excitedly*] Where? How? Tell me, quick!

NĀRAD: Come on. Go right away!

KĀMDEV: Where?

NĀRAD: In Brindavan, on the banks of the Jumna, down underneath the great banyan tree, Krishna is playing his flute. You'll find him there. And there all your aims will be satisfied.

KĀMDEV: Good, I'm on my way. But let me tell you something,

Nārad. If he's not there, I'll be doing battle with you instead!

NĀRAD: I'm really past the age. Go on, you'll find him.

KĀMDEV: All right. Hail Nārāyaṇ.

NĀRAD: Yes, yes, hail Nārāyaṇ. Now go!

[KĀMDEV *hurries off with* SPRING *in tow.* NĀRAD *is left alone on stage and concludes the scene with a soliloquy, but one he addresses musingly to* KĀMDEV *as if he were still present.*] Yes, go over there to Govind, for he defeats everyone. He defeated Indra's pride, and stole away Candā's and Rudra's and Brahmā's, and my own as well. And now he'll deal with yours too. [*Turning his eyes skyward and speaking now straight out to the* AUDIENCE] Thank you, thank you, Lord of the needy! You even attend to the gods when they're in need: for the sake of a god you've made yourself appear a man. Yes, now that god's name is finally going to mean something: Mardan, destruction. Whose destruction? Why his own! Well, I'd better get on my way too. I wouldn't miss seeing this for the world. Nārāyaṇ, Nārāyaṇ . . .

[*He exits*]

[*The curtain rises, showing* KRISHNA *seated alone on the throne.* KĀMDEV *makes a blustering entry; his flowery bow is drawn.*]

KRISHNA: Who are you? How'd you get here?

KĀMDEV: Well cowherd, they call me the world-conquering Churner of Hearts, the royal Intoxicator.

KRISHNA: Ah ha! So the all-victorious Kāmdev has made his appearance! And what may I do for you?

KĀMDEV: If you would be so kind, you could give me a good fight.

KRISHNA: But you have to have a fighter to get a fight. Look at me: I'm just a cowherd. I graze the calves all day long. I never learned a thing about fighting.

KĀMDEV: What's this? Nārad said you were a good match for me in battle!

KRISHNA: Well what kind of battle is it you're looking for? From a fort or on the open plain?

KĀMDEV: What do you mean? What's the difference?

KRISHNA: Well, a fort battle is like this. Suppose I should be sitting completely absorbed in yogic trance: I've gathered all my faculties in about me—the will, the intelligence, cognition, and the ego—so that they cut off contact between my self and the outside world. Then suppose you come along and shoot one of your shafts of love at me. If my spiritual concentration then turns to a sexual concentration, you've won a victory in a fort-type battle.

KĀMDEV: I see. And what about the battle on the plain?

KRISHNA: Well, suppose I'm dancing the circle dance with the innumerable women of Braj and you come along and release your shafts of love and have your army waft the sixty-four arts of love about.[30] If I'm won over, then you've scored a victory on the open field, and if I'm not, then the victory is mine. So tell me, which type of battle do you want?

KĀMDEV: Listen, I've seen thousands of those fort battles and the so-called warriors that wage them are all cowards. Here I am stalking around on the open field of life and they rush inside and go sit in their forts! It's as good as admitting defeat. That's no battle, that fort battle. No sir, if you're going to fight with me it'll have to be hand-to-hand combat, right out here in the open.

KRISHNA: All right then, fine. I'll do what I can to satisfy your wish. Come here when the autumn moon is full and I'm performing the great circle dance, and I'll do my best to oblige.

[KĀMDEV *retreats with satisfaction and the curtain falls. When it lifts again we see* KRISHNA *surrounded by three of the same actors who play the* GOPĪS. *Though their garments are unchanged, we are to understand that this time they are playing the role of the* NIGHTS.]

MUSICIANS:

The Nights came in and at Hari's feet
  they bowed their foreheads low;
"Now that we've seen you and met you," they said,
  our master we surely know."[31]

KRISHNA: Who are you? Where have you come from?

NIGHTS: What's this, Lord? You're omniscient but you pretend ignorance and ask us who we are. All right, we'll tell you. We're the nights of summer, spring, fall — all the seasons — and all we want to know is if there is anything we can do to serve you so that you and the numberless women of Braj can be completely carefree as you play out the great circle dance.

KRISHNA: Fine. Perform whatever services you wish.

NIGHTS: Good. Eternal praise to you. [*They exit*]

KRISHNA: [*soliloquizing*] You see, those are the nights I spoke about when the Braj girls were performing their vow to Kātyāyanī. Remember? I said I would grant the wishes of sixteen thousand of them in one night.[32] Now that I've seen these nights, and now that I've heard what it is these girls have on their minds, I'm beginning to get excited about playing the *rās*. Just think how remarkable it is that the great emotion of these simple girls has brought incalculable grace even to the Lord of everything, to God himself, to him whose being is entirely complete. They've managed to transform my completeness into something as yet incomplete.

Who can describe these milkmaids' love?

I who attract whoever sees me —
  now they're attracting *me!*
The sages who swarm around me
  are bees to my lotus feet,
But my mind makes a beeline for *these* girls' hearts:
  it swirls, it swarms, it flees.[33]

Think of it! Here the souls of this world seek happiness in my beautiful form and virtuous qualities, and the wise are drawn to my consciousness. But these girls have reversed the whole process, making bees of my lotus feet, attracting the great Attraction!

The yogis are all enraptured with me,
  their souls find permanent joy,
But where am I to find delight?
  Where to satisfy my heart?

Yes, I dispense joy to all the sages and seers and ascetics and yogis: I am the very form of joy itself. But my heart seeks its joy, too, and I feel the urge to dance the *rās* with the women of Braj who are so full of love in its highest form. That's the first purpose of my great *rās*—to leave behind every striving for God and replace it all with simple love.[34]

Let one autumn night transpire,
  fragrant with bloom and scent;
The queen-of-the-night,[35] every blossom and bud,
  all will play their parts;
And as proud Indra and Brahmā fell,
  Madan will meet his match as well.
He, not I, will fail the test
  this honeyed dance presents.

You know how I defeated Indra by lifting up the mountain, and fooled Brahmā after he had spirited away all my cowherd friends. Now it's Kāmdev's turn. He's going to get so drunk on the liquor of my charms that he'll go completely crazy. Indra and Brahmā and Rudra and all those gods tried to defy me, and now Kāmdev wants to take his turn, too. Well, let him. I'll show him who I really am. That way he'll understand, first, that he's just a drop of love and I'm an entire ocean of it;[36] second, that whereas he is the churner of hearts, I am the one who can churn up the heart of the churner of hearts; third, that his kind of love is never really satisfied until it satisfies itself in me; fourth, whereas his brand of love brings only a fleeting happiness, mine grants a happiness that is eternal, constantly renewed, endless, and fathomless; fifth, whereas his love is of the nature of passion, mine is of a finer stripe—it is a love beyond all qualification;[37] sixth, whereas his love attacks, mine rescues; seventh, whereas his love ultimately brings death, mine brings eternal life; eighth, his love is poison, but mine is ambrosia; ninth, his love is hell, but mine is the divine relaxation of the *rās*. By giving Kāmdev a glimpse of what a sea of love I am in this Krishna avatar of mine, I'll dazzle him and make him fit to serve me. That's the second purpose of my great *rās*—to convert Kāmdev and the love he stands for.

Mothers and fathers and friends could never
quite lose themselves in love,
But the women of Braj fulfilled their hopes
through love in its passionate mode.

I've come to this world to bring happiness to all creatures by means of every possible mood and emotion. That's the whole purpose of descending in this avatar. By playing the role of a child, I've made it possible for Nanda and Yaśodā and the cowherd men and women to taste the joys of parenthood. And by playing all kinds of games with boys like Subal and Śrīdhām, I've given them the chance to taste the fun of friendship. But those are incomplete emotions: the girls have something fuller. Radha, Lalitā, Viśākhā, and the rest are my eternally perfected milkmaids: I am always with them. Others of the cowherd girls are perfected by their spiritual practice. By virtue of having undergone stringent austerities in past lives, they have been given the chance of adopting the bodies of milkmaids in this life, and of approaching my eternal cowherd's feet. Then there are others who undertook the vow to Kātyāyanī, and as a boon they were granted access to the circle dance. But Radha, Lalitā, Viśākhā, and so forth are different: they have constant access to me and are my eternally beloved companions. In them erotic love finds its perfection. And if any imperfection or raw edge remains, my flute will initiate them and remove even that. Still, in the final analysis, it is the grace of Radha, mistress of all, that makes the whole thing possible by endowing these women with love of the highest sort: that is the boon that brings them into the circle of the *rās*. And that's my third purpose in performing the great circle dance—to bring all emotion to its perfection and fulfillment.

I'll churn the Intoxicator, Lust, to a pulp,
and only then relax in sweet love,
Thus showing that the feeling these milkmaids bring
is not lust but love's finest form.

The love the Braj girls feel for me is not called *kām*, but rather *prem*. There isn't a trace of selfish desire *(kāmnā)* in it. The only desire they feel is to satisfy whatever I desire—and even that will be further purified in this great *rās*. That's my fourth purpose in dancing it—to show the difference between selfish and unselfish love. The fifth point is to demonstrate that the ultimate state of religious attainment is to be found right here where these cowherd girls are. They are the standard by which all religion is assessed. Once Brahmā and Śiva and Ūdho saw them, their only aspiration was to share their fate. That's my fifth reason for performing the great *rās*—to show the proper end of religion.

Radha encompasses everything good,
 she has no limit or inner division;
And let me tell you the truth about me:
 I too am Radha's—her lover, her pleasure.

She's the mistress of the *rās*, Radha. The happiness her selfless love showers on it is the culmination of everything wonderful about it. It is the ultimate secret of the *rās*. And it's by dissolving myself in that secret that I'll be able to reemerge in the presence of all the cowherd girls today, visible and manifold. From the outside it will appear that I am a great lover, beloved of all the milkmaids, but the inner truth is that I'm Radha's beloved, Radha's lover, Radha's Krishna, and nobody else's at all. I'll make this plain when I disappear from the others and go off with Radha alone. The *rās* is just my way of beating the drum to announce that she is supreme in the universe. And that's my sixth and final reason for undertaking the great circle dance.

So, then, I have six motives: first, to taste the milkmaids' love; second, to pulverize the self-intoxication of Kāmdev; third, to fulfill the longings of the cowherd girls; fourth, to establish what a difference there is between selfish love and selfless love; fifth, to show that the kind of worship the Braj girls perform is the highest form of religion; and sixth, to demonstrate that Radha's love is the very pinnacle of happiness and good fortune. And the result of it all will be that souls will yearn to taste that love.

I am the one true liquor of love,[38] but the souls of this world go looking for it in any number of mundane liquids and destroy themselves in the search. They quaff down great gulps of passion and desire, and the only medicine that can cure them is the story of my great circle dance. It's the one arrow that always hits its mark.[39]

Take aim with the arrow that never strays;
reach for the cure that cancels disease;
Premānand says that this peerless potion
disperses all hint of selfish desire.

As the story of the milkmaids' love is dramatized, a secret is sure to reveal itself in every heart. It will become clear as day that here is not the slightest hint of satisfying selfish, sensory desires. It's only Krishna's satisfaction that matters. Once you understand that, you'll take it automatically to heart, and pray for the gift of that same selfless devotion. And then you will no longer be tempted to denigrate these cowherd girls by treating them with the honor due a woman. Don't do it: it's a great crime and leads to the most serious difficulties. Rather let grace replace honor, for love flows from grace. It is the unpolluted stream of highest devotion, and once it begins to flow it courses through the heart, cleansing it of every scar that the sickness of selfish passion has left, and transforming it into a temple of love where I can dwell constantly. That's what my great *rās līlā* has the power of doing: it cures the ills of the heart, and transforms it from the victim of yoga's recriminations to a guest at a great banquet.[40]

[*The great soliloquy done,* KRIṢHNA *relaxes a bit and turns his mind to what comes next. We hear him musing as the musicians begin to tune up.*] The enjoyment of the spirit is higher than the enjoyment of the body. Let's see, this is a spiritual game we're going to play, so I'll summon Yogamāyā and we'll get the circle dance underway.

MUSICIANS: [*chanting the first words of chapter 33 of Book 10 of the* Bhāgavata Purāṇa, *where the* rās *is classically described*]

With the support of Yogamāyā . . .

[*Enter* YOGAMĀYĀ. *She is clad in lavender and crimson, wears an elaborate crown, and carries a silver wand, at the end of which a rose emerges.*]

KRISHNA: Yogamāyā, come over here quickly.

[*She crosses the stage to where he has seated himself on the throne, which has been moved to the side and toward the front.*]

YOGAMĀYĀ: Greetings, world-encompassing, lotus-blue Govind, fount of joy. Greetings, you who made Yaśodā flow with the waters of motherly love to support your lotus-blue self. Greetings, you whom the sun's brilliance nurtured and fed. Greetings, lotus-blue Govind, who played with the cowherd boys and joked with them. Greetings, blue lotus that gives such delight to the Braj girls who buzz all around you. Here I am at your service. What can I do?

KRISHNA: I thought of you, Yogamāyā, because today I am going to play the great *rās* with thousands of young women here. It's a task that's impossible from start to finish, and I need you to make it possible. The burden is on you, you see, because I'll be out in the forest tasting the liquid of love. If any problems occur in arranging the whole thing, you will have to solve them—I'll be too involved. But keep this in mind. You mustn't do anything that would obstruct my tasting the mood of the occasion or debase the girls' experience by interjecting an element of worldly love.[41]

YOGAMĀYĀ: I understand perfectly. I stand ready to serve you whenever I can.

KRISHNA: Well, tell me what you have in mind to do.

YOGAMĀYĀ: You're omniscient, of course, Lord, but if you want to hear what I'll be doing, then listen. First of all, when you set your lips to the flute I'll arrange it so that the only ones who hear are those girls whose hearts are filled with amorous emotion[42] for you. The other women of Braj and the men will be completely unaware of what's going on.

No one outside of Braj will hear,
  no god or man or beast;
Indra won't hear, and Rudra won't hear,
  and neither will Brahmā, the voice of the Vedas;

Even in Braj the others won't hear,
  cowherd women and cowherd men,
Mothers and fathers and teachers and friends,
  relatives, servants—they all will be deaf;
No matter how many come dashing to you,
  the others will blissfully stay at home,
And the only ones who hear the call are those
  who will find a husband in dance.[43]

38. Yogamāyā explains her plan

KRISHNA: And after that, what, Yogamāyā?

YOGAMĀYĀ: My second task, Lord, will be to make sure that when the girls hear the sound of the flute and rise to answer its call, their relatives and family won't stop them. What I'll do is to produce a living copy of every girl who departs.[44] That way the real girls can disappear with you, and their husbands and families won't have to wonder why they went crazy in the middle of the night and fled from their houses. There'll be no interference and no recriminations, either against you or against the girls themselves. I'll remove every sharp stone from the path that brings you together—that will be my service.

KRISHNA: Good. Without that my great *rās* could not come to be. And what else?

YOGAMĀYĀ: My third service will be to take the little circle on the banks of the Jumna where you dance and make it so enormous that thousands upon thousands of Braj milkmaids can dance and sport there with complete abandon.

Brindavan is only ten miles by ten,
and then only a fraction of this
Is the Jumna bank, too slight a space
for dancing the circle dance.
Three hundred million herder girls[45]
will dance to conquer the power of lust;
If they all gathered in a single place
they'd link in a line two hundred miles.
Two hundred—no—even more:
this *rās* is even grander by far,
More than all seven continents can withstand.
more than all nine subcontinents can hold.
Never has such a thing been thought.
It requires some magic, a miraculous act
For me to create; and the gods will meet,
says Bihārī, and cheer the great *rās*.[46]

I'll make it so that you have all the room you want to dance with all those countless women, but to the uninitiated eye it will still look like the same little clearing in the forest.

KRISHNA: And for your fourth act?

YOGAMĀYĀ: I'll multiply you when you dance with the girls.

KRISHNA: You'll what?

YOGAMĀYĀ: Multiply you! Just as one flame gives birth to many, I'll make your dark brilliance shine many times.

Just as the fire from a single flame
can repeat, in igniting other lights,
So will I kindle and multiply you,
a Mādhav for every cowherd maid.

One image will seem a multitude,
as root expands to the many branches,
With not a mar, or a shade of difference
between them all, original and copies.
As hundreds of thousands of girls gather,
hundreds and thousands of Krishnas will rise
And live in a tiny place, in a corner of town,
and find room to move and room to dance.
Never has such a thing been thought.
It requires some magic, a miraculous act
For me to create; and the gods will meet,
says Bihārī, and cheer the great *rās*.

KRISHNA: Wonderful, Yogamāyā! And what's the next impossible feat you'll accomplish?

YOGAMĀYĀ: My fifth impossible possibility will be to make your great dance last not one night but one night of Brahmā, that is, 4,032,000,000 human nights.[47]

KRISHNA: But why make it so long? One night for the gods only amounts to six months in human time.

YOGAMĀYĀ: True enough, Lord. But you're not just a god; you're the god of gods, and supremely supernatural. And these Braj girls are supernatural too, and so is their love, and so is the desire that animates their love. The time of the dance will have to be as extraordinary as all of its elements: I have no choice.

KRISHNA: But Yogamāyā, if you make it last 4,032,000,000 nights, won't the gods and the whole universe fall asleep? Won't Sūrya Nārāyaṇ begin to emerge again at the beginning of a new world age?

Yogamāyā: No, no, Sūrya Nārāyaṇ will rise at the proper time, and the universe will keep to its schedule. Nothing will disturb the turning of the Creator's wheel. The time I spread out for you to enjoy the circle dance will be a time to itself.

KRISHNA: But Yogamāyā, what if my mother or father should get up in the night and go over just to have a little look at my face, the way they so often do, and find that I'm not there? Then what?

YOGAMĀYĀ: I've already told you: I'll multiply you into numberless forms. If they get up and peek in on you in the night they'll see nothing strange at all—just you lying in your bed as you always do.

KRISHNA: And what about the girls who come to see me?

YOGAMĀYĀ: The same goes for them. The real milkmaids will be with you and I'll leave copies of them at home as decoys.

KRISHNA: Good. What else will you do?

YOGAMĀYĀ: There's a sixth measure I'll take. As the girls trip out into the forest they're sure to jingle their anklets and let happy little cries escape their throats. But never mind, I'll cast such a magic mantle over the earth that those sounds will go straight to heaven, and the only ones to hear them aside from the girls themselves will be the heavenly musicians and the gods who have gathered in their flying chariots to witness the event.

KRISHNA: Perfect. Now there's nothing to worry about at all, and I can just lose myself in the tasting of emotions. But you be careful to stay alert. You've got a lot to do.

YOGAMĀYĀ: Lord, I always stand ready to perform your every wish. But really, it isn't right for me to get the credit when they say you go to the forest "with the support of Yogamāyā." Actually it is all your doing. But never mind, off I go.

KRISHNA: Yes, you bring Brindā and her helpers[48] and come ready to do your part, and I'll go off to the banyan tree and start calling the cowherd girls with my flute.

[*Both exit*]

[*Curtain. This is the midpoint in the* līlā *and a convenient time to present a tableau for the audience's veneration. It is arranged so that* KRISHNA, *dressed in vivid red, rests on one leg, his other akimbo in the classical fashion, and plays the flute;* RADHA, *clothed in blue, stands at his side a step lower. A second* GOPĪ *is in attendance on his other side. The crowd surges forward to give offerings and obeisances. Many minutes later, when the stream of worshipers has subsided, it is time for the action to resume.*]

Part II. Testing

[*As the curtain lifts we find ourselves in the forest bower where the rās is to take place. The lights have dimmed: it is night.* KRISHNA *stands alone at the side of the stage in the same relaxed pose he struck for the tableau, and now as then he has the flute to his lips. Branches have been brought from trees nearby, and potted plants introduced, many of them flowering, to create a luxuriant wooded atmosphere.* KRISHNA *removes the flute from his mouth a little and addresses it.*]

KRISHNA: Muralī, you are my third Yogamāyā[49] and my dear girlfriend, bound to me with ties of love. You're the one whose call determines who will enter into the circle dance. So it's essential that I take good care of you. Always I've provided hands for you to rest on, soft lips to serve as your pillow, long locks waving in the breeze to fan you, and anxious fingers to massage your feet. I've served you better than the most faithful wife, without missing a day. And now, Muralī, your turn has come: you must bring to completion a task that is as yet unfinished. Help me call the doe-eyed girls of Braj. I'll whisper the name of each one to be called, and you broadcast the summons in the most appealing way. [*Evidently Muralī consents, for* KRISHNA *begins to play as the* MUSICIANS *decipher some of the elements of the message.*]

MUSICIANS:

So saying, he lifted the flute to his lips,
  summoning all with musical sounds:
"Come you womenfolk—Kamalā, Rati,
  Kaumudī, Rūpī, Rasīlī,
Kāmlatā, Gandharvā,
  and wise Vidyāvatī. . . ."
His eyes danced brilliantly as he played,
  matchlessly dark and sweet.

[*This fluting sound is what* KĀMDEV *has been waiting for. He lurches onto the front of the stage even before any of the* GOPĪS *can materialize. For a moment he thinks out loud.*]

KĀMDEV: Ah! So! The time has come when the cowherd Krishna is fluting the message of love to his dear Braj women and summoning them all. Now's the time for me to take out my bow and arrow. Of course it's perfectly obvious that the situation is already in my control, but I'd better stick to proper form, shoot my spell-binding arrow, and reap the victory for all to see. [*With a glint in his eye he crouches and takes aim at* KRISHNA.]

MUSICIANS:

He aimed his arrow in Syām's direction,
ready to penetrate every pore,
But his eye was aimed there too,
so sweet the sight it dizzied him,
And down he fell.[50]

KĀMDEV: [*entirely disoriented as he concentrates his gaze on* KRISHNA *in taking aim*] Hey! What's happening to me? What am I doing with this cowherd boy? I . . . [*After struggling unsuccessfully to release his arrow, he springs with arms wide open as if he himself had been hit, and falls with a great crash to the floor. Shouts of excitement rustle through the* AUDIENCE *as they see* KĀMDEV *laid out on his back before them, practically hanging over the front of the stage. Before their glee dies down,* KĀMDEV'S *wife rushes in and bends over him with extravagant wailing. Through the clamor one hears fragments of narration from the* MUSICIANS.]

MUSICIANS:

Poor woman, disconsolate, weighed with grief,
crying and crying and crying.[51]

RATI: [*from beneath her tears and with formidable gesticulation*] Oh my poor husband! What awful thing has happened to you? [*She shakes him and tugs at him.*] Please, come to! [*Then as her eyes dart around for help she takes cognizance of others present at the event.*]

MUSICIANS:

When she began to comprehend all that she saw
her sadness increased and her heart grew heavy.

RATI: [*looking down at her husband again*] Come on! Wake up! But don't worry. He hasn't even called the girls yet. Here, in the meantime I'll make you some almond halvah. You need the strength. Then you'll be able to go on the attack against this herder boy.

MUSICIANS:

Can't you see? That's no simple boy—
he's invincible, powerful, more than a man.

KĀMDEV: [*stirring groggily as she pleads with him and pokes at his supine form*] Rati . . .

RATI: [*relieved and excited*] Yes, yes, speak.

39. Kāmdev taking aim at Krishna. In the background the *samājī*, with Svāmī Śrī Rām at the harmonium

KĀMDEV: Rati, that's no boy. It's some god descended as an avatar.

MUSICIANS:

His charms do disarm and make the mind reel:
how then to steel the body for battle?

KĀMDEV: [*now quite coherent and annoyed at his wife for having accepted his own former estimation of his powers so completely; what on any other occasion would have seemed encouragement and solidarity now comes across as nagging.*] Look, just what am I supposed to do? One look at that sweet smile and sidelong glance, and I was defeated: my bow and arrow were useless. So how am I going to fight with him?

MUSICIANS:

The very thought makes my mind immobile.
How can I fight him? I haven't the strength!

KĀMDEV: [*languishing hopelessly*] That sly glance from the corner of his eye pricked my heart.[52] When he drew me into his field of attraction with that sweetness of his, what force did I have to counteract his magnetism?

RATI: Now just take it easy for a minute. You'll get your courage back. After all, you're known all over the world as invincible, the world's most heroic fighter. What could a puny boy like that do against the likes of you? Why, all thirty-three hundred thousand gods bow to you, so what's a little kid like that? Come on, get hold of yourself.

Listen, you've only lost one little skirmish.
Why should you despair of your strength?
The whole world knows you as world-conquerer:
Brahmā and Śiva—they tremble with fear.
And look at that frivolous cowherd boy:
what does he know about fighting a war?

Think a minute. All thirty-three hundred thousand gods sit at your feet and that little boy. . . . Come on, get hold of yourself.

MUSICIANS:

Get ready, prepare! The girls are coming.
Seize your bow now and take your revenge![53]

[*The* GOPĪS *begin to filter onstage from all sides. They array themselves around* KRISHNA, *some standing near him, some seating themselves on the floor nearby between the plants. These are not the usual three or four, but eight or ten, as many as the company can muster.*]

RATI: [*poking and shaking* KĀMDEV *a little*] See, he's calling the herder girls, and here they come. Now's the time to get out your bow. Pull yourself together. You were just a little foggy there for a while.

KĀMDEV: [*pulling himself up from the floor with great effort*] You're right, Rati. I just forgot. That cowherd said to me that I should come and do battle with him while his great *rās* was going on. I just got too excited and started to attack while he was still alone. It's no wonder what happened, considering that there weren't even any women on the scene yet.

RATI: Right. That's the spirit.

KĀMDEV: I'll just draw my bow again now and walk away with the victory. [*He crouches again, aiming his weapon.*]

MUSICIANS:

He strung his bow yet once again. . . .[54]

RATI: Now!

KĀMDEV: All right . . .

[*But once again he crashes helpless to the stage, and again to the great satisfaction of the* AUDIENCE. *This time the outcome of the contest is definitive, and he and his wife slink off in ignominious defeat. A verse or two from the* MUSICIANS *drive home the point that nothing is lost:* KRISHNA'S *brilliance is equivalent to that of innumerable* KĀMDEVS. *Once* DESIRE *and* PASSION *have departed, the air is cleared for the* rās, *and the dialogue between the participants can begin. The* GOPĪS *commence by praising various aspects of* KRISHNA'S *beauty, a praise that is seen even more clearly in their appearance than in what they say, for they have arrived in all states of unreadiness. The texts tell how they dropped whatever they were doing when they felt his attraction, and some companies make this vivid by having them appear with pestles or cooking utensils or milking pails, or the fans with which they had been cooling their husbands. In this performance, however, we see only the central symbol of their readiness to come immediately: they all carry mirrors to signify that even the enhancement of their own beauty was of no concern once the call came. Even if they were combing their hair or making themselves up, they ran out the door at the sound of the flute. Their own dishevelment praises* KRISHNA'S *irresistable attraction. He, however, taunts them for the urgency of their arrival, and affects complete nonchalance. He quotes a famous sentence of greeting from the* Bhāgavata Purāṇa*:*]

KRISHNA:

A good welcome to you, my dear fine ladies—
but what are you all doing here?[55]

What about it, girls? [*Proceeding ironically*]

Now why would you come at this strange hour?
To what do I owe the pleasure?
How kind of you to grant me this vision—
you've greatly increased my good fortune!
Is that water or sweat that covers your brows?
—enough to irrigate all of Brindavan—
But now that you're here I'll massage your feet
and use my own garment to fan you dry.[56]

Chaste ladies, dedicated to your husbands, how have I deserved this great act of mercy, that you would make your way through the forest to give me the chance to set my eyes on you? Nothing's gone wrong in Braj, I hope? [*He is suggesting there must have been some great catastrophe to cause such an exodus, and is anxious to offer his hospitality under the circumstances.*] Now don't worry about a thing. Poor things! I stand ready to massage your feet and fan the sweat from your brows with my yellow scarf. Do tell me, is there any other way in which I can be of service?

SAKHĪ 1: Oh girls, this is terrible! Here we've come to make him our husband, and he teases us by calling us chaste! Here we are absolutely bereft unless we have the chance of serving him, and he fires us up by saying how fortunate we are to have husbands! He calls us with his flute, and then asks us what we've come for! And all this innocent concern about what catastrophe may have befallen us, and this nonsense about massaging our feet and fanning our sweat! Friends, what kind of love is this that he goes around stupidly asking what he can do for us?

KRISHNA: Tell me, girls,

You're standing there ragged as a pack of yogis:
What then? Has a lion ravaged the town?

Look at your jewelry, a mass of tangles—
  wasn't there time for proper attire?
The way you came here heaving and panting,
  it seemed you'd been utterly terrified,
And look, you've brought no men as companions:
  was it women alone who encountered disaster?[57]

Take a look at yourselves, girls. Some of you have your jewelry on every which way, some of you have your skirts inside out, with others it's your blouses; some of you have put your anklets on your hands and some of you have your waistbands around your necks. Take a look in those mirrors of yours! And look at that girl over there: she's still holding the rope she uses to tie up her cow at milking time. And look at that one with mascara on only one eye. Some of you have come completely without bangles on your arms. And look at you [*pointing to one of the* GOPĪS]: your shawl is hanging down. And you, your sari's so loose you're about to trip on it. What in the world has happened to you that you've come racing in here with your hair all a mess, and fighting for breath? I must say it's a mystery to me why none of the men came out here screaming for help—were you the only ones affected? What happened, anyway? Did some demon get loose in Gokul? Some cow go berserk? Tell me quick so that I can do something!

MUSICIANS:

Manmohan, there's nothing else gone wrong,
  it's only your love that's driven us wild.
Gokul's endured no great disaster:
  all we've suffered is love's deep wounds.

SAKHĪ 1: [*plaintively, awkwardly; the* Bhāgavata Purāṇa *says the* GOPĪS *dig their toenails in the sand with embarrassment at this point.*] Friends, what are we going to do? Here we've abandoned every worldly propriety, and Syām Sundar is still observing them all! Here we come all this way to meet him, and he tries to put us off. Is there no way for us to tell him what our hearts have endured for him? [*Her glance falls on* MURALĪ *and she thinks she puts two and two together.*] This rival of ours has dashed our chances for love! [*Then sinking into despair*] What are we to do? What are we to do?

KRISHNA: Well girls, I take it from the fact that you've not answered my questions that there really hasn't been any great disturbance in Braj. Then what in the world has caused you to flee here at a time like this? What about it, girls?

SAKHĪS:

Syām, you're trying to ridicule,
  and make us return to our home.

KRISHNA:

But don't forget, they can always be told
  that you simply forgot the way.
Or tell them while going to sell milk in Mathura
  you met with misfortune, some great delay.
Because of a bamboo flute, you can say.

MUSICIANS:

And with that a tiny wink danced across his eye.

KRISHNA: Now come on, girls, turn right around to where you came from and go home. Don't try to avoid the issue. You're the ones who wandered out from Gokul and you're the ones who have to go back. Never mind the fancy talk. Whatever were you thinking of to come out here in the middle of the night?

SAKHĪ 1: [*on behalf of all the* GOPĪS] Now wait a minute, my dear Mr. Mountain-lifter. What's all this? Are you trying to cover up what you've done by using a little of that cleverness you're so famous for? We didn't lose the way coming back from Mathura—you *called* us here! Otherwise how to explain the fact that not everyone came—only the names that lovely, amorous Muralī of yours sang out?

KRISHNA: Well if you were so obedient to my every wish then, what's changed now? Go home! [*Then, singing a couplet from the* Bhāgavata Purāṇa]

By hearing about me and chanting my names,
  meditating and visualizing,
You might possibly find a touch of my presence,
  but not here with me, so go home.[58]

Come on girls, don't just stand there speechless. Use your heads:

Since you often wander through here, you may think
that a place like this offers nothing to fear;
But now it is night, not brilliant day,
and the forest is more a forest, my friends.
Look: you parade around in these woods
blissfully fearless where horrors abound;
Beasts roar and stare and prey,
released by the dark from their secret pens.[59]

Look here, this is a very frightening place. There are wild animals grazing all about and if they get hungry for your auspicious faces, it'll be too late to run! You'd better get going right away.

Perhaps you've been thinking, "While Krishna is here
there's simply no reason to be afraid."
But I've been thinking, "If danger appears
it's myself I'll have to be able to save."
Perhaps you've been thinking, "That celibate boy[60]
will surely respect our marital state."
But I've been thinking, "Fate's not to be trusted,
for impulse runs wild around women at night."

Listen girls, if you've been thinking there's no reason to fear for your safety if I'm around, let me tell you something. You should be scared to death, because when young boys and young girls meet in a deserted forest at night who knows that what will happen! And if you're counting on the fact that I'm still a celibate youth whereas you are chaste, married women, you'd better watch out. The will can be pretty fickle: I wouldn't trust it too far. So I think you'd better go home, girls.

Your parents and brothers, your husbands and sons,
they'll miss you, they'll worry: don't frighten them.[61]
You stand there in silence, as still as a stone—
there's every good reason you've frozen in fear:
Whoever it is you've left at home—
some mother or father or husband or son—
They're sure to come find you, and why will they say
that I've stolen you away and brought you here?

Think of the shame that would come, yours and mine
and not the least theirs: we'd all rather die.

Sooner or later your parents are going to notice that you're not there and come out looking for you, and someone is sure to come and find us here. We'll die of shame if they do. I'll never be able to show my face in Braj again. So please . . .

Perhaps you are thinking: "Krishna has powers—
his mantras have mastered the snake and the mountain.
At his glance our families will be fixed in his spell,
just as we've been when he looks our way."
Why do you heap this crime on my head?
A sin against family is a serious thing.
The mantras you'd mention: all just illusion.
Why are you trying to sully my name?"

Look girls, if you're not afraid because you think I'm some big wizard because of the way I dealt with Kāliya and Govardhan, and you think I'll be able to make you invisible if anyone from your families should appear on the scene, then let me tell you something: you're dead wrong. I won't be able to protect you at a time like that; I'll have myself to think of, lest I be despised as an immoral law-breaker. Come on now, you're a saintly lot, the best really, and saints are merciful: now why not spare your relatives this pain? Please go home.

SAKHĪS:

Isn't there someone to reason with him?
We're simply not thinking the things that he says.
It's just that our lives have been swept off downstream—
our homes and our families, lost in our tears,
And we're left with only one moral standard:
our sole religion is looking at Syām.
Our bodies stand ready to serve him at will;
with a thousand emotions our hearts overflow.

SAKHĪ 1: Can't you see? What mothers and fathers do we poor girls have any more? What standards of womanly obedience can we obey? How can we perform our duties to the family any longer? We've lost all that. It's all washed away with our tears, and now there's only one thing that can

40. *Gopī* listens to Krishna's arguments

save us: to stand in front of your bewitching image and drink in the sight of you like *cakorī* birds.

KRISHNA:

Listen girls, if you ignore the Vedas,
 the path you travel is a pointless one.
Shed your pretenses, do some real worship—
 then you will find your heart's true reward.
Your path, you think, will suddenly bridge
 life's broad, encompassing sea;

But paths have steps—there's order involved—
so you need not come rushing to me.
And girls,
The heart, you know, leads a thousand ways,
and you've wanted to follow its every whim.
Take some advice from someone who knows:
when the heart wants something, don't give in!
Remember, you are women, families' gems:
don't let go of the values of home.
That's where your passion belongs, not out here:
turn homeward and there let love bloom.

I don't care what wastrels or boors your husbands may be, it's they whom you should serve if you have any hope of heaven. So the scriptures decree.

SAKHĪS:

You clamor for right and recall us to duty,
yet you are the one who undermines it all.
We know: when we followed the family path
you did all you could do to lure us away.
What's a real husband, one worthy to serve?
He's one you truly marry and for whom you endure.
False husbands behind, we've chosen to stay
with you who confound us: without you we'd die.[62]

You see, as far as we're concerned, you *are* the eternal way of righteousness. You are the basis of every duty. And when we left duty behind we grasped onto you. Why would you tear us away from the root now and leave us hanging from the boughs and branches instead?

KRISHNA: No, your husbands are in Braj. Go back.

SAKHĪ 1: Lord, there are two possible meanings for *vipati*, the word that describes the dilemma we're in. [*In its usage here, the word means both "disaster," though the form would properly be* vipatti, *and "the state of being without* [vi] *a husband* [pati]."] Either the prefix *vi* can stand for *vikṛti*, "defilement," indicating the defiling husband, or it can stand for *viśeṣ*, "special," indicating the special husband. The husbands we have left behind are the former, husbands of mud, and you are the latter, the husband of consciousness. They are husbands of the body and you are the husband of the soul. They are the husbands of this one birth, but you are the husband of every age—past, present, and future. How then, Lord, can you send us back to our other husbands? Those husbands *(vipati)* are pure disaster (*vipati* or *vipatti*).

KRISHNA:

By hearing about me and chanting my names,
meditating and visualizing,
You might possibly find a touch of my presence,
but not here with me, so go home.[63]

SAKHĪ 1: What's made you so harsh and cruel, so lethal, so unfeeling? [*She lifts her hand toward him, holding a mirror.*] Take this mirror and look at your face. That mouth of yours—which is it: a palace of ambrosial nectar or an arsenal of arrows? And those eyes—you'd better remove the cataracts of injustice from your own before you start lecturing the rest of us on the specks of unrighteousness that that have blown into ours.

In leaving our homes and cleaving to you,
did we do right or did we do wrong?
Even those who choose the renunciant's path,
don't they leave adrift their moral life?
Renunciants cleave to the path of freedom
and think they've left Hari, yet find they still
crave him.
We've rejected them both, our homes and our freedom:
cleaving to you where righteousness leads us.

Teacher of righteousness, it's only fools that desire liberation if it means release from the worship of Nārāyaṇ. We've kicked off that sort of freedom and come to immerse ourselves totally in your service. And what do you do? Instead of sheltering those who come to worship you, you turn around and assault us! All this abuse you've been pouring out—it contradicts the laws of civility, the principles of morality, and the dictates of religion.

SAKHĪ 2: And, moral preceptor [*she quotes from the* Bhagavad Gītā],

Just as the devoted approach me in worship,

so I devote myself to them.[64]

That was the promise that issued from your very own mouth. Now are you going to limit that promise to men, or will you fulfill it for women too?[65]

KRISHNA: Worship? Service? Listen you milkmaids, you've left your husbands only in order to have sex with me. And that's a very serious sin, completely wrong.

SAKHĪ 1: Oh, but Mr. Preceptor, we have your very own promise on this point [*quoting again from the* Gītā]:

Abandon all claims of right and wrong
and come, take refuge with me alone.[66]

Is this another one of those promises that only applies to men, or does it extend to women who love you too?

SAKHĪ 2: And what about when you said [*in the* Gītā] that

Those who draw near me, Kaunteya,
will never endure another birth.[67]

Is it true what you've said, as we've heard in many sermons, that if a soul takes refuge at your feet, you will never force that soul to endure further reincarnations?

KRISHNA: Yes, it's true.

SAKHĪ 2: Just for men or for us women too?

KRISHNA: It's true for all.

SAKHĪ 1:

Think of what he has promised us, friends,
promised and promised beyond our counting:
Remember the time by the river—remind him—
after he'd come and stolen our clothes,
He promised he'd dance us the nocturnal *rās*,
and here he is now, sending us home!
For him there's no sin in forgetting the truth,
but for us who are truthful only sadness comes.

Look at that, friends. It seems for him there's no sin involved in turning truth to falsehood, whereas if we take these false promises as truths, that's a sin against us. Tell me, where's the justice in that?

SAKHĪ 2: Some teacher of righteousness you are! You'd have it that for us to be faithful to you is a sin, whereas for you to leave us in the lurch is a point of merit! Yes indeed, that's excellent!

How did we merit this vale of tears?

So long we've been searching, and finally found you,
 and now you hound us about our return;
You who expound your righteous lessons —
 you're the one who needs to learn!
Deserting us women, who are helpless and trusting:
 is that what you call the moral life?
And further, it's futile: we'd die before leaving.
 Then you'd be guilty of all of our deaths!

KRISHNA: Come, come girls, don't be so brazen. That's no way to act.

SAKHĪ 1: However brazen we're being, you're being just that much worse. Brazen! Listen, in our position there was no way *but* to be brazen. If we hadn't bolted from our lives the way they were, we never could have gotten to you. After all, a certain amount of stubbornness befits the lowly — otherwise you never see them shine. Look how the *cātak* bird refuses any other nourishment, and obstinately waits for the clouds to come forth with rain. People applaud that. So stop being so impossible, and rain a little of the immortal liquid of love on us instead of this poison you keep spewing out.

KRISHNA: Oh come now girls, am I so inaccessible, so savage, so cruel? [*He scans the gathering, but meets no forgiving glance.*] All right, then, suppose I am all those things. But are you such pure, calm streams of translucent water? Maybe I did shoot some arrows at you as I spoke, but what about you? I suppose what you had to say was just a gentle rain of flowers! I may have spoken with a barb now and again, but were you always so sweet and straightforward? Come on, let's let bygones be bygones. Just tell me plainly what it is you want.

SAKHĪ 1: Handsome, all we want you to do is take care of us the way Nārāyaṇ takes care of those who are devoted to him. We feel we deserve that, because as the scriptures say we've left behind all worldly concerns to be with you.[68]

KRISHNA: Girls, if you left worldly things behind, what were you doing coming to me? I'm a sensual being too, you know. You can see me, smell me, taste me, touch me—if you've left everything worldly and sensory behind, what are you doing here?

SAKHĪ 1: No, no, Lord, you're not sensual; you're the one who wipes away every trace of the sensual, everything disagreeable. You're the medicine for our worldly disease, the wholesome food that will drive it away. Are you thinking of withholding that medicine now? Is that just?

KRISHNA: First you lie down with your husbands and then you come sidling up to me: it's all nothing but self-interest.

SAKHĪ 1: [*offended, enraged*] What is this? You keep taking the role of the sensualist and seeing things from the wrong perspective. Over and over again you say the same things. And over and over there's only one answer. If it were sensual pleasure we wanted, then that would be desire. But it's *you* we want, and that's not desire *(kām)*, it's love *(prem)*. Desire serves the senses, but love serves only you; ultimately desire results in nothing but destruction, but love leads to playing in the eternal circle dance. In so saying all we're doing is repeating back to you the very words you swore to us; our speech is pure. And Lord, you know our inner feelings.

KRISHNA: But girls, according to the common understanding a woman's highest duty is the service of her husband. If you depart from that it's a sin, and I'm implicated too.

For married women to act like whores
  is something which is always deplored.
Wicked and worthless, it's abhorrent to all,
  a scandal on earth and a passport to hell.[69]

SAKHĪ 1: Lord, that sermon on woman's duty that you just gave isn't really correct, because scripture considers it improper to sermonize without being asked to do so.

The scriptures say only on request
  should you preach a moral sermon;
Otherwise you should keep your silence
  and practice what you'd preach.

If we'd put you on the orator's box and asked for a discourse, that would have been one thing. But we didn't, so you should have kept your sermon to yourself.

KRISHNA: But the scriptures also specify that if saying something will be beneficial to the person concerned, it's a sin to withhold it.

SAKHĪ 1: [*ironically*] Oh yes, Lord, thank you so much for having deigned to speak! Now if you'd only put a little of that into practice and show us how we can get back on the right track!

Do us one little favor more:
demonstrate our proper role.
Then your sermon will have some weight:
demonstrate to all the world.
Show us what serving a husband means—
demonstrate so we can see.

Come on, Syām Sundar, give us a real lesson in how it's done.

KRISHNA: Now you're making fun of me. I'm a man. How can I show you how a woman ought to serve her husband and sons?

SAKHĪS: By becoming a woman. What else?

KRISHNA: And how am I supposed to do that?

SAKHĪ 1: Do it the way Nārāyaṇ did:

We know you have Nārāyaṇ's powers:
you're a treasure chest of all his wonders.
He once became a seductive woman—[70]
now it's your turn to do the same.
Having taken the feminine form, of course,
the feminine role you'll also adopt;
We'll be your students in all that you do
and learn by example what's womanly, proper.[71]

SAKHĪ 2: Wait a minute, friends. Don't listen to that stupid suggestion! Look, he's already pulled us away from the duties of our sex. If now he goes and becomes a woman he'll leave the duties of manhood completely unattended. Isn't there any god left in the universe these days, or any human, who refuses to follow the example of Śiva, and insists on remaining a man? Once that last real man is gone, girls, we can say goodbye to being women! Think twice! This plan is hardly designed to protect the good; it can only destroy it.

KRISHNA: Girls! Girls! What babble! Here, let me set you on the right track by telling you a story.

SAKHĪS: Fine, Syām Sundar, do.

KRISHNA: All right, listen carefully.[72] Once there was a Brahmin, and he had a wife who was most devoted to him. She served him ceaselessly. Now one day this Brahmin decided to perform a sacrifice, and he worked so hard in preparing it that he fell asleep from exhaustion, and his head fell on his wife's thigh.

SAKHĪS: Yes, and then what?

KRISHNA: Well, just then the woman's son came along playing, and got too close to the fire. At that the Brahmin's wife debated with herself: "If I don't rescue my son, the innocent little thing will fall into the burning pit. But if I get up to save him, I'll disturb my husband's sleep. What to do?" In the end she decided that her son had come to her in the course of performing the actions that life brings with it necessarily, but her bond to her husband was more than a bond of action, it was one of solemn duty.[73] So she left the child to its own devices, and it fell into the fire. But that's not the end. When the Fire-god[74] began reflecting on the strength of this woman's devotion to her husband, a strength sufficient to send him a child to burn up, he began to worry that she might curse him if he did so. So he cooled himself down by transforming himself into a thick sandalwood paste, and the boy was saved. You see what force a woman's devotion to her husband has, girls? I think you'd better get up immediately and go back to Braj and attend to your husbands and sons.

SAKHĪ 1: [*She had been holding her tongue through the whole story. Now she rushes in before anyone has a chance to budge.*] Well, Mr. Pundit, let me tell a story too.

KRISHNA: Fine, by all means do.

SAKHĪ 1: It was like this. Once there lived in a certain village a Brahmin and his wife, and they were very poor. So one day the Brahmin told his wife he was going off to another country to earn some money. But the woman was completely devoted to serving her husband, so she asked, "Lord, if you go off to another country, whose service shall I perform?"

The Brahmin replied, "I'll make a clay copy of myself and you can perform all the daily services and religious duties to it that you would to me." And with that he went away.

KRISHNA: What happened then?

SAKHĪ 1: Well, the poor Brahmin woman locked the door and performed her wifely services to the image day in and day out. After some time the Brahmin returned, but the door was locked. His wife was inside ministering to the image. So he shouted to her to open the door, but she debated with herself as to whether she should go. "If I interrupt my wifely service," she thought, "I will be transgressing my wifely duties. And if I go open the door it's the same thing exactly." Tell me then, wise one, what should she do?

KRISHNA: When she realizes her true husband has come home, she should go open the door, of course.

SAKHĪ 1: [*elated*] Ah ha! Ah ha! [*The other* GOPĪs *soon join in the merriment. Their leader addresses* KRISHNA, *who doesn't see the humor as yet.*] You're the one who said it. Now let's see you follow through.

KRISHNA: What? What do you mean?

SAKHĪ 1: It's obvious, Maharaja. We're just like that woman. All these days we've been performing our wifely services before clay corpses, but now, Lord, we have met our true husband. How can you expect us to go back to those clay copies? Don't forget, Syām Sundar, the teachings of religion take precedence over ethical precepts.[75] From the point of view of ethics, there's no disputing the fact that one should be true to one's single husband, but from the point of view of religion that one husband is none other than you. But we know now, Syām Sundar, that none of us can claim you particularly; you are the husband of each of us.

Look, here's another way of seeing it. In this world the union of a man and a woman is like the confluence of a male river and a female river.[76] The male river will feel, of course, that he is the husband and that the female river is his wife, and she will think the same. But let's not forget that in the ultimate sense both are Brahman, not limited by their conventional, worldly status; and the proof of it is that both of them are as wives to the sea. Both of them consist of a single substance, water, and in that sense the sea, which is the summation of all water, is to them the husband beside which there is no second. Similarly you, Krishna, are the seven seas to us. Whether we be men or women we are like female rivers insofar as you are concerned: you are our husband. And that is why if you prevent us from staying with you, we will all simply die.

KRISHNA: How so, girls? What will you do?

SAKHĪ 1: As the saying goes, "what you think at the end sets the rest in motion."[77] If we die in separation from you, languishing at the thought that we have not united with you in this life, then we'll meet you in the next. And if not then, then in the life after that, and on it will go. But one thing is sure: that meeting will finally take place.

KRISHNA: [*aside*] But Radha hasn't come yet. I'll have to scold them once more. [*Turning to the* GOPĪS] Now girls, don't be so stubborn. Please, go back home.

SAKHĪ 1: Listen Syām Sundar,
You can send us back, but we won't go.

Why would we want to return to Braj
after seeing what the universe wants to see?
There's no one else who can care for us,
so talk all you want, we've no other home.
Fathers? Mothers? Who are they?
We just don't know them any more.
Who has husbands to lure them, or sons?
Where are these homes to which we'd return?
Morals—what are they? And sins?
We're driven mad, we've forgotten them.
We're simple girls and so it seems
no simpler path we know
Than meeting you, Lord, and having done that,
how, says Sūr, could we ever repent?[78]

SAKHĪS: [*chorusing together in one last, exhausted cry*] Syām Sundar, we may die but we're not going back home.

[*As they shout their defiance,* RADHA *appears at the back of the stage, behind the* GOPĪS, *and* KRISHNA *catches a glimpse of her.*]

KRISHNA: All right then girls, all right, don't go. What's it to me? [*Radha moves closer and closer.*] Yes, all right, whatever you want. . . .

[*His attention is entirely riveted on* RADHA, *who floats wordlessly into his presence and raises her calm, clear voice.*]

RADHA: Sweetheart, what's been the delay with the circle dance?

KRISHNA: Syāmā dear, I was waiting for you.

[*At that they embrace by placing their heads first on the other's right shoulder and then on the left.*[79] *Great shouts of acclamation rise from the* AUDIENCE *at this much-awaited moment, and as the curtain falls one hears:*]

AUDIENCE: All praise to Radha! Hail Bṛṣabhānu's darling daughter! All praise to Radha!

Part III. Fulfillment

[At this point the drama undergoes a definite shift. From this point on, dialogue, which has so far predominated, is at a minimum; increasingly action prevails as we move into the circle of the *rās* itself. Some in the audience are weary from the long dialogues they have heard: their dedication has been tested along with the *gopīs*'. Others are excited at the prospect of what will come next, and the result is a general restlessness that the *rāsdhārī* tries to calm by channeling the audience's attention even before the curtain rises again. He leads them in chants celebrating the best-known names of Śiva, who is about to appear.]

RĀSDHĀRĪ AND AUDIENCE: Har Har Mahādev Śambhū! Lord of all, of Benares and the Ganges! Har Har Mahādev Śambhū! All praise to Lord Śankar! Hail Mahādev, Lord of cowherds! [*The curtain rises, revealing* ŚIVA *at the front of the stage. Not far behind him another curtain remains drawn shielding the back half of the stage from view. His is a commanding presence. He stands with his legs spread gener-*

ously apart and holds his arms outward and down in a grand gesture suggesting rigidity: one hand holds his trident, decorated with a red and silver cloth. Though much bejeweled, this is ŚIVA *the ascetic. His legs are painted white to suggest a covering of ash, serpentine bands encircle his arms, and behind his crown are the matted locks of a renunciant. Though he stands, not a muscle moves and*

41. Śiva in meditation

we understand that he is in meditation—in the heights of the Himalayas, as his words will reveal. Presently he emerges from his concentration by uttering his signword and beginning to move around a bit.]

ŚIVA: Infinite One![80] [*He struts pensively back and forth.*] Hmmm. Tonight I don't seem to be able to find Lord Syām

Sundar, that fountain of bliss and hero of all creation, in my field of concentation. What's the matter? Let's see. Let my try again. Infinite One! [*His signword indicates that he is about to retreat from the world of speech and sensory perception again. He stiffens and gazes directly in front of him for a while. Suddenly speech carries him again from trance to action.*] Ah ha! Oh good, there he is! Syām Sundar, that joy and lord of Braj, is in Brindavan, blessed place, and he's playing his big circular *rās* with numberless Braj women. Come on, I've got to go and see this for myself. [*He lifts his conch to his lips and its deep, rough bellow announces his arrival in Braj.*] Infinite One! [*He comes up against the curtain at midstage: it does not rise.*] Hey, wake up!

[*At this, three* GOPĪS *appear from the side of the stage, as if they had emerged from behind to answer his call.*]

SAKHĪ 1: Who are you and what do you want here?

ŚIVA: They call me Śankar, Lalitā, and I've come down from Mount Kailās to see Lord Syām Sundar, fountain of joy and the delight of all Braj, do his *rās līlā*.

SAKHĪ 1: But men aren't eligible to observe dear Syām Sundar's *rās līlā*. If you want to see it you'll have to become one of the milkmaids of Braj. That way you can see it, otherwise not.

ŚIVA: Well if that's what it takes, you'd better tell me what I have to do in order to take on the identity of a cowherd girl.

SAKHĪ 1: Not far from here there's a tank called Mānsarovar. It is possible for people who bathe there to adopt the mindset of a milkmaid girl.[81] So you should go over to Mānsarovar first, and then come back and see Syām Sundar's circle dance.

ŚIVA: Fine. Whatever you say, girls. [*He goes offstage.*] Infinite one . . .

[*While* ŚIVA *is transforming himself into a* GOPĪ, *the curtain rises and we see eight or ten girls with their hands joined circling around* RADHA *and* KRISHNA *and singing happily. Suddenly* KĀMDEV *enters.*]

KĀMDEV: Now at last I've got him. This time I've caught him in the act: his girlfriends are already circling around him. What a wonderful opportunity! I'll just draw my flowery bow. . . .

[*He butts into the center of the circle and, though disoriented by the whirling motion all around him, lifts his bow of flowers and aims at* KRISHNA. *Again it is pointless. He is incapable of shooting, and falls to the stage with a thud even louder than before. His back slaps definitively against*

42. Kāmdev aiming at Radha and Krishna from inside the circle of the *rās* dance

the boards, and his legs bounce back up in a vivid gesture of complete loss of control. The GOPĪS, *a few of them so tiny they are scarcely taller than the mass of garments that lies in their midst, increase their pace, circling all the more joyfully. Predictably, it is but a few seconds before* RATI *runs up, breaks into the circle, bends over her fallen husband, and with much grieving gesticulation sings a song that indicates this is* KĀMDEV'S *last battle.*]

RATI:

Oh my lifeblood! What ill fate!
The earth without you is barren, lost.
I told you before not to fight that boy —
now what future have I but suttee?[82]

My dear husband, what have you done? What got into you to do this again? Now, alas, there's no one who can revive you, no one.

43. Rati lamenting her husband's demise

[*With desperate tears, she slumps down and joins him in a great heap. The* AUDIENCE, *however, takes great amusement at the final downfall of this tragicomic couple, and as the curtain falls there are great laughs of satisfaction. When it rises again, their mood changes to awe and excitement, for at last they witness the scene to which all this has been leading.* KRISHNAS *have been recruited from companies all over Brindavan, often accompanied by a* SAKHĪ. *They expand the circle of the rās to much more than its former size, and make it possible for there to be enough* KRISHNAS *to hold each* GOPĪ'S *hand. Some of the girls, in fact, have* KRISHNA *on both sides. At the rise of the curtain, they have formed an inner and an outer ring, and as their brilliant and varied costumes flash by the front of the stage, it makes a dazzling sight indeed. Crown after golden crown whirls by, and on the inner ring one sees even more. Tradition says that the* GOPĪS *were stunned by the presence of their lover with each of them. Those who witness the spectacle may also be awed at this miraculous specificity, but they cannot fail to be impressed at the same time with the multiple mirage before them, a kaleidoscope of crimson and indigo, white and gold.*]

MUSICIANS:

Eternal, the dance of the circle whirls:
 the milkmaids are linked by twos and twos
 and between each pair a Mādhav.
That's how he dances there, Nanda's boy. . . .[83]

[*Then they announce the* rasiyā *whose theme sets the stage for what is to follow:* KRISHNA'S *various dances.*]

My devotees have me dance many ways.
 I never delay when I hear their call,
 as with Draupadī, in near-naked distress:
My devotees have me dance many ways.[84]

[*The* MUSICIANS *interpolate several verses to suggest the connection between the various incidents to be recalled in the many stanzas of this* rasiyā *and the visual image of* KRISHNA *that the* AUDIENCE *has before it. These verses change the voice: they are not spoken by* KRISHNA *but rather directed to him.*]

That eyeblack you've used to darken your eyes—
 what magic is mixed there? It casts a spell:
Your smiles make you laugh, but they make others die,
 and you disown that disorder, above it all!
That singular beauty, so hard to describe,
 so winsome and subtle and dark,
Is as dear to Syāmā as the life force itself,
 and to all of Braj you're the pleasure of play.[85]

[*Continuing with another song*]
The feathers of peacocks crown your head,
  around your neck a flower garland;
You dance the circle dance with Radha,
  a precious sight, this boy of Nanda.
Have you seen him, friend, our love's delight,
  this deep boy, who buoys up the milkmaids?
The world can't fathom him, take in his brilliance,
  but for us, says Premānand, he bends at the knee.[86]
[*Then returning to the main* rasiyā]
  I never delay when I hear their call,
  as with Draupadī, in near-naked distress:
My devotees have me dance many ways.

Poor Narasī was the subject of scorn—
  so poor he had no birthday gift—
Until I, incarnate, intervened:
  the Dark One, supplier of every need.
When Prahlād summoned me to come
  I made myself a lion-man
And ripped apart the one who threatened him,
  Hiraṇyakaśipu, his father.
I spurned Duryodhan's elegant feast,
  preferring Vidur's weed-like greens instead.
My devotees have me dance many ways.[87]

Two is to praise him as Lord of Dvaraka,
Three for dispersing the three afflictions,
Four for the discus and his other weapons,
Five for the Pāṇḍav brothers he befriended,
Six for becoming our beautiful Syām,
Seven for taming the seven bulls,
Eight for his eight chief queens,
Nine for the newness of the butter he stole,
Ten for his ten avatars.
Time and again I worship little Kānh.
My devotees have me dance many ways.[88]

I dissipated Dhruv's remorse
  by providing a capital for him,
And when he saw such magical force
  all he could do was laugh.
Nāmdev also called and received
  what he wanted most: a roof of thatch.
Certain times all the gods have called,
  as when I became a seductress,
Distracting the demons and stealing away
  the ambrosia I meant to feed to the gods.
My devotees have me dance many ways.[89]

For Mīrā I'm the cowherd boy
  who joyfully lifted the mountain;
Kans knows me as certain Fate,
  and Tulsī Dās as Rām.
I'm the loyal husband of Lakṣmī
  and of the Vedas the subtle essence,
Yet I changed into a little boy
  so Sūr could call me Syām
And I could serve the lovely feet
  of Bṛṣabhānu's daughter:
My devotees have me dance many ways.[90]

As this song reviews the various "dances" Krishna's devotees have put him up to, the action on stage provides a visual representation of the same reality. After the double circle dance has expanded to a great single circle and the *gopīs* and multiple Krishnas have arrayed themselves in a long double row at the back of the stage, each Krishna has a chance to demonstrate some favorite dance. It is as if a single Krishna had quite literally multiplied, and changed his clothes to appeal to various tastes.

The representative of the host company begins the sequence by dancing the pièce de résistence of the *rās* as it is performed daily (and symbolically, eternally), preceding every *līlā*. This is the knee dance, an allegro affair in which

Krishna kneels and pivots from one knee to the other around and around in a wide circle so that his skirts rise to a constant whirl at his waist. The audience roars with delight, and specially honored devotees who have been allowed to sit at the side of the stage toss rose petals on the object of everyone's attention. The *pad* of Premānand that makes reference to the knees is sung at this point.

Then the Krishnas of other troupes take their turns. Sometimes they dance with a *gopī* partner, introducing various balances, swings, and promenades; sometimes they dance alone. Selections vary from showy displays like the one in which Krishna dances quick shuffling steps while twirling a great brass platter on an upturned forefinger, to the slower, more sinuous rhythms of a recently choreographed peacock dance. Here Krishna, clad totally in a deep, shiny blue, holds at his waist an ample spray of peacock feathers long enough to shield his head like a great crown. (His jeweled "peacock crown" only imitates this natural tiara.) He dips his body and cocks his head as he sidles along on his knees, looking for all the world like his prototype in nature. His neck juts in and out; he shakes himself all over, rustling his feathers; and in a climactic gesture he tosses his head suddenly to the ground and the feathers fly over his neck and sweep the earth before him. It is typical for each contributing *rāsdhārī* to be present and lead the musicians in appropriate music as his Krishna dances. And contrary to normal decorum, it is permitted for these various *svāmīs* to accept offerings of money on the spot if anyone in the audience is particularly moved or impressed by the performance of a given Krishna.

One dance in this series does not fall to Krishna. Instead it is introduced by his great rival among Indian dancers, the god who is styled "king of the dance," Śiva. Ever since his bath in the Mānsarovar tank, Śiva has been transfixed with the emotions of a *gopī*, but the chance for him to demonstrate his skill at the dance is too good to miss. The one he chooses is a robust affair in which he jumps from one leg to the other, holding the unused leg as high as he

44. The peacock dance

can in evident imitation of classical representations of the wild *tāṇḍava* dance that is Śiva's favorite. This is a vigorous *gopī* indeed, but he reaffirms his metamorphosed identity by ending with a humble prostration at the feet of Radha and Krishna.

This enactment of the *rās* includes a contribution almost as surprising as the dance of Śiva. It is Krishna who dances, but in a mood not commonly—some would say not properly—thought of as belonging to the circle of the *rās*. The dancer is the Krishna of Girirāj Prasād's troupe, a glowing boy of six or seven, perhaps the youngest taking part, and his dance is the *cor cāl*, the dance of the butter thief. This is more than a dance; it is its own special drama, and Krishna speaks as he moves about the stage.

KRISHNA: Ah Brindavan, my eternal home! It's more excellent than Vaikuṇṭha, more brilliant and beautiful than the Heaven of Cows itself. Why do I feel this intense sense of belonging here? It's shocking but true what they say:

One's mother and one's motherland
are dearer even than heaven.[91]

This is where I was born. I may be worshiped all over the world, but here I am the priest myself:[92] with my very own hands I serve the cows and the cowherd men and women in all their needs. And I serve my mother, too. She gets to put out a big bowl of milk for me and stand over me threatening to give me a good slap if I don't drink it all, and telling me how if I don't, my braid won't grow long. Oh thank God for that motherly love, that rope of love that binds me so tight I can't get loose!

When they won't release me, how can I be free?
They've bound me strong with love's stout cord:
Dark billows emerge, storm-clouds of love,
and my peacock-heart starts dancing feely.
This heart of mine has a mind of its own,
but the milkmaids have caught it and
made it their own.[93]

Some call me the moon of Braj,
others a cloud of joy,
The milkmaids' cowherd love
or Yaśodā's little boy,
Guardian of the whole wide land,
or slayer of the wily Kans. . . .

Oh they call me all those names—Braj's moon, cloud of joy, Nanda and Yaśodā's boy, the death of Kans—the list goes on and on. But the name they don't call me is the one that's the sweetest of them all, the one my daddy calls me. [*He refers both to Nanda and to his own father, who now provides the antiphon.*]

RĀSDHĀRĪ: And what's that, sweetheart?

KRISHNA: It's sweeter to me than crystalline sugar, sweeter than *rasgullahs*:

One name's sweeter than sweets to me,
it's when they call me the butter thief.[94]

[*He titters with joy at the thought of this favorite identity, bounding up and down as he rolls the name over and over in his mind.*] Beloved butter thief, beloved butter thief, beloved butter thief. . . .

[*Now he launches into the stylized movements that go with stealing butter—the dance of the butter thief. He angles and snakes around the floor on his knees, craning his head from time to time over his shoulder to see if he is being watched. Though this is not a dance like the others in the sense that it is without rhythm, it resembles them in that his body is never without motion, always bent for action. The* RĀSDHĀRĪ *supplies him with a little pot of milk sweets, representing butter. As he tastes them he lifts his shoulders repeatedly in delight and offers them teasingly to the* AUDIENCE, *sometimes getting a glint in his eye, withholding what he had seemed to give, and wiggling his thumb in a gesture that says, "too bad for you!" All this inevitably accompanies the dance of the butter thief, and as it proceeds the musicians sing various songs that emphasize the dance motif.*]

MUSICIANS:

He laughs at the prisons
the world has made for him,
Eluding the trances
that saints and yogis spread,
But willingly he's trapped himself
in Yaśodā's ample lap;
The one who is known
as the deathly terror of Time—

Yaśodā made him cry
by tethering him at home.
Thanks be, and thanks a hundred,
to every milkmaid girl
Who chanced upon Brahman,
the indestructible force of the world,
And made him dance.[95]

That for which the caverned yogis concentrate,
having smeared their bodies ashen,
The secret the Vedas failed to fathom,
the rhythm eluding the wisest of the wise,
The name whose sound makes all heads bow
from heaven to earth and in distant hell:
That one was the one who danced for a bowl
of whey from the cowherd maids.[96]

[*After this last and rather extended display of dance virtuosity, Girirāj Prasād's* KRISHNA *rejoins the array of other* KRISHNAS *at the back of the stage. In the center, seated on the throne, are* RADHA *and* KRISHNA *from the host troupe, and at their sides sit eight other* KRISHNAS; GOPĪs *fill in at the edges. The splendor of this unaccustomed row of crowns inspires understandable feelings of awe among the spectators, and the tableau is maintained after the rās is through so that those who have witnessed the event can come forward, touch their heads to the feet of these many* KRISHNAS, *and make their offerings. It is fitting that they must walk through the area where the dance was performed to do so, shuffling among the rose petals and in some measure entering the circle of the rās themselves. When all have had a chance to participate at close range, a tray with lighted lamps is brought, as at the beginning; and* RADHA *and* KRISHNA, *honored with prayers and gifts and light—and each by the presence of the other—go off arm in arm.*]

CHAPTER V

The Coming of Akrūr

Introduction

AFTER THE DANCE is done, after every ounce of human energy is roused and consumed in the *rās*, then what?

It used to be that this was no problem. The entire emphasis of the story was different. Krishna's dance with the *gopīs* was, to be sure, recounted in the oldest version of the Krishna story that has come down to us—that contained in the *Harivaṃśa*—but it was not given anything like the attention that was to be directed to it later, particularly by the writer of the *Bhāgavata Purāṇa*.[1] In fact, the dance was neither given a specific name nor restricted to women, as in later accounts.[2] It was simply a rustic dance open to all. Far from culminating here, the story swept forward to quite a different climax, an epic climax. In the *Harivaṃśa*, the tension mounts slowly as Kans deputes demon after demon to do in his juvenile enemy. There is the bird who upon alighting in Braj turns into a woman with poisoned breasts—Pūtanā, the putrid one; the snake whose poisonous fangs and torrid breath keep human and animal alike from approaching the Jumna, and who would in time scorch all Braj to death—Kāliya, the black one; the horse whose stinging hooves aim for Krishna's chest, and whose jaws threaten his head—Keśī, the hairy one; and many more. Krishna defeats them one by one. At length Kans decides that he has no other choice but to summon the lad to Mathura, where he can confront him with an unbeatable array of foes. He will arrange a great tournament, display the unbreakable—even unbendable—bow he possesses, and pit Krishna and Balarām against the greatest wrestlers in the realm. An elephant will be held in the wings to trample them if that doesn't work.

Kans sends a messenger to Braj—Akrūr, one of his ministers, who relates the news of the tournament. But Akrūr goes on to report on matters entirely outside the scope of what Kans has dictated. He describes how Devakī, Krishna's mother, languishes without that one thing that makes a woman's life worth living: sons. To be barren is curse enough, but to give birth and then have every maternal expectation foiled is far worse. He also relates how Kans subjects his aged father to wicked taunts: Kans has accused the kind old man of trying to undermine the state in the hope of establishing his dynasty. Akrūr begs to know how someone powerful enough to bring even his enemies to salvation by slaying them, someone capable of subduing even Indra, can stand by without relieving the grief of his own parents. That is enough for Krishna. He is ready to leave immediately, and the rest of the cowherds, almost equally affronted, assent as well. They will follow as soon as they can; their anticipation is keen.

Excitement redoubles with every turn of the wheel of the carriage in which Akrūr transports the two brothers to Kans's court. As they ford the Jumna, Akrūr has a remarkable vision of Balarām as the primeval snake and Krishna as Viṣṇu shielded under its great hood. What could more clearly forecast the victory that is to come? There are other signs, as well. Not long after the boys enter the city they chance upon a poor man whose only claim to fame is his responsibility for dyeing the king's clothes. When the youths ask to wear some of these he refuses, understandably, but goes on to abuse them for their ignorance of city ways, and gratuitously opines that their doom is near. Krishna's ire is roused, and he deals him a blow that brings immediate death: guilt as much by association with the wicked king as for his own tactless remarks. A hunchback woman meets a happier end as Krishna straightens her back. And then the boys wander into the royal armory and instantly snap the unbendable iron bow. The sound rumbles through the city like thunder, and the terrified armory guard rushes into the royal quarters with the unsettling news of what has happened. Kans braces himself, a prisoner now in his own city. He mulls it all over in his mind, and realizes that no matter how hard a man tries, it is fate that rules. At last he can hold his secret no longer. In talking with the elephant driver, he reveals that he is not the true son of Ugrasen but only a foster child. His mother, he admits, conceived him by a demon. He stands alone against the world. Daniel H. H. Ingalls translates his words: "Uncared for by my parents, I stand on my strength. More than that they hate me, as do all my relatives. And I shall kill them all, when I have killed this Kṛṣṇa and his brother."[3]

As the boys enter the ring, Kans's eyes redden in anger: Krishna flashes a great tusk, signifying that he has already dealt with the elephant. He expatiates on the rules of wrestling, making the crowd pointedly aware of the vast inequality of the opponents. The crowd swoons at the mismatch, but Kans intends to accentuate its effect by further defying the rules and preventing the drummers from sounding the end of the round. He hopes the youths will tire, but the effect is the reverse. Cāṇūr and Muṣṭik, his champion wrestlers, begin to weaken, and as the Davids emerge victorious and the Goliaths are left broken and crumbled at their feet, Kans breaks out in profuse sweat. Dread signs show themselves. The ground trembles, and a jewel falls ominously from his crown. Trapped and raging, he orders Balarām and Krishna expelled, their father jailed, and their people's cattle expropriated. But the drama rushes to its conclusion against his every effort. Krishna leaps into the stands and drags him down into the ring by the hair, pulling him around and around and around until he lies lifeless.

That is the core of the story of the confrontation between good and evil, as the old Krishna epic tells it. It all comes to a burning focus in the arena of Mathura, only a few paces from the prison where it all started. The hero has escaped his prison and returned to trap the demonic jailer in his own city, freeing the good in the process. The epic logic is impeccable.

But two thousand years have passed since the story was told in quite that way. As reenacted in Braj today, it climaxes in the forest, not in the city; in a dance, not a fight. If a battle is resolved, it is one of passion rather than hatred. Indeed, it is more than possible to sit through a whole cycle of *līlā*s without even seeing the play that depicts what once was the focus of the entire legend, the *kans vadh līlā* in which the great events in Mathura are portrayed.[4] What replaces it? What forms the appropriate sequel to the *rās* in this modern recounting of the Krishna story? What follows its consummation of love? Separation, of course. About this the worshipers of Krishna are sober and realistic.

Two plays of parting and separation have a particular prestige, the *ūdho līlā* and the *akrūr līlā*. The *ūdho līlā* is a great favorite, including as it does both open lament and bitter, yet clever argument. It depicts the moment when Krishna, firmly ensconced in Mathura, sends a messenger, his friend Ūdho, back to Braj to convince the women there that it is pointless for them to grieve so over his loss. They have only to understand that he resides with them intimately as their very souls, as he does in every living creature, and all will be well. The *gopī*s and Yaśodā, hopelessly bereft by the loss of Krishna, have no use whatever for this pale doctrine, and say so in no uncertain terms. By the time Ūdho emerges from matching wits with them, he is convinced that there is an intensity in their identification with Krishna that his message of universal participation does not even begin to comprehend. As the *līlā* concludes, it is Ūdho who is converted, not the women of Braj, and we look back on the union of Krishna and *gopī*s in the *rās*, and realize that the consummation we observed there was incomparably more intense than the union of soul and Soul that Ūdho preaches.

The *ūdho līlā*, an example of which has been translated by Norvin Hein, provides a format for the recitation of some of the most famous poetry in Braj, the *bhramargīt*, or "songs of the bee."[5] Ūdho, the buzzing messenger from Krishna, the black one, is the bee; and the songs are sung not by him but to him. The biting irony with which these simple women of Braj take on their cultured adversary in debate provides in some ways a more pointed glimpse into the ache of separation than would a softer mode of expression. They play dumb, and ask for a full description of this Nirgun he keeps talking about, who is to replace Krishna in their affections. But Nirgun is no substitute bridegroom; it is God conceived without attribute, the placeless Spirit Ūdho would have these women find in their hearts, and a description is precisely what is impossible to offer.[6] Sometimes the irony is less stinging. In the following poem attributed to Sūr Dās, which is often quoted in the *ūdho līlā*, the *gopīs* only belittle Krishna implicitly for not being able to follow up on his much-touted feat of stemming the floods at Mount Govardhan when Indra threatened. Here their plaintive protest is more direct:

"Day and night our eyes rain tears.

The monsoon storms have settled inside
 since Syām has gone away.
Everywhere mascara smears,
 blackening our cheeks and hands.
From within our breasts a torrent spills
 and our blouses never dry:
Our bodies are liquified in tears,
 incessant sadness, passion, and rage."
The women demand to know, Says Sūr,
 "Has he forgotten Gokul?
 And why?"[7]

In some ways the moment of parting itself is even more poignant than the cries of passion and outrage that ring through the *ūdho līlā*, incubated over months and years of longing. And for that we must turn to the *akrūr līlā*. Its skeletal narrative structure has not changed markedly since the time of the *Harivaṃśa*, though there have been some alterations and additions, but its emotional force has been entirely redirected. In the epic account, the people of Braj rallied immediately to Akrūr's call, and Krishna first of all. The women in Krishna's life were not even mentioned. Now everything is turned inside out. It takes the last ounce of emotional strength to pry the hero loose from the attachments of those who love him in Braj; he scarcely escapes. The concern before had been to remind him of his family in Mathura. Now we hear not a word of that, so swamped are we in the grief of his family in Braj. Indeed, it is that impending separation that must be justified, not the years he has spent away from his biological mother and father (if one can use such terms in Krishna's case at all). And Krishna himself must be jarred free from his involvements in Braj. It takes no less a figure than Nārad, the divine messenger and arranger of plots, to accomplish this feat, and even he is not very sure that he will succeed.

No longer a loop in a heroic tapestry, the story has become a testament of grief. When Akrūr first arrives in Braj he has a beatific vision much like that described so poetically in the old *Harivaṃśa*.[8] He sees Krishna and his brother flanked by cow and cowherd. But the moment he explains why he has come, that peaceful, beautifully arranged tableau is distorted into a complex knot of gestures and countergestures, as a smiling face becomes disfigured by weeping. The cowherds bend in front of Krishna, trying to catch his attention, begging him to look at them: if only he would *see* them, surely he would not be able to turn his back and depart. When his mother and father enter the picture they pull even more insistently at the once happy contours of this bucolic scene. The calm and rounded Raphaelite symmetries give way to the oblique, ungrounded perspectives of a Tintoretto as Yaśodā tugs at her son's garments, grasps wildly for him in the indifferent air, and comes crashing to the stage in her unanswered despair. By the time Radha and her friends make their appearance, the principles of composition used in this mannerist canvas are already fixed, but their petitions and shouts of grief expose the subject to another palette. It is typical for these *līlās* to present us three versions of a painting, three phases of a *darśan*, and here we have this triptych again: separation from friends, from parents, and finally from lovers.

The people who observe these scenes are anything but solemn museum-goers who meditate inwardly upon some feature of the painting before them and then pass silently to the next. I remember sitting cross-legged on the floor among the men in the audience on a hot August day as this *līlā* was performed, not far from the stage and not far from the slim, irregular little aisle (sometimes crowded to the point of nonexistence) that ran down the center of the hall, dividing the sexes. The exciting scene depicting Kans's nightmares was scarcely done; it had aroused awe and delight in those who sat around me. Akrūr had barely begun to make his way toward Braj, scarcely uttered a sentence of self-doubt about the propriety of his mission, and the mood in the audience changed utterly. As he acted out the first couplet expressive of his misgivings—only just beginning to entertain the thought that if he brought the boys to Mathura they would surely be killed—I happened to turn to my left. And there I saw several old women so absorbed in the drama that huge tears already rolled down their cheeks, as if from a reservoir that had been waiting to overflow. With every successive line of poetry, every moment of dialogue or change of scene, the feeling around me intensified. Little springs welled up in every direction, gurgling with coughs and the clearing of throats, and soon the whole audience was a marsh of emotion. It was a remarkably humbling experience: I felt no longer one of a great number of discrete individuals but rather a drop in a sea. And from that point on, the action performed on stage seemed only the play of waves across deep currents of grieving that swept through the crowd about me. There have been occasions, I am told, when this play has had to be cut short lest the burden of feeling become too much for the worshipers to bear.[9]

The existence of such a vast store of pain so readily available may seem hard to understand. Lent has long ago gone out of fashion and it takes something like a cult of thanatology to provide a public vehicle for emotions that are otherwise saved for guarded and often strictly individual therapeutic settings. In crowded India, where so much more of life is necessarily lived on the streets in any case, it is not so. But perhaps this level of emotion, and this sort, is not as foreign to us as we suppose. Think of the last time you lost someone, through death or departure or even betrayal: how it ached, how empty you felt. In such moments of loss there is no particular zone of the body that demands your attention with a special ache. Rather the pain is everything and everywhere, so generalized that there is nothing to pin it to and thereby control it. We habitually think of this as a strictly human phenomenon, something emotional rather than biological, a decoration for our being rather than part of its essence. Then we see it in other animals, and we are startled and feel its poignancy even more. There is something heart-rending in the way an animal will scurry frantically around her nest or hole when her mate does not come home. It is so pitiful, so beyond help, and we see ourselves vividly in the desperation.

In the worship of Krishna and Radha all this is taken very seriously. Love's torments are understood as the natural form of religious discipline: *viyoga*, the separation of those who love, is a regimen at once far more natural and far more taxing than its explicitly "religious" cousin, *yoga*.[10] There is a whole field of poetry in Braj dedicated to making this point, to demonstrating how the *gopīs*, separated from Krishna, endure mortifications by virtue of the sundering of their love that are deeper by far than any austerities yoga can concoct. They manifest all the marks of yogic discipline naturally. A yogi must learn through years of practice the art of keeping awake for long periods of time; for the women of Braj separated from Krishna, sleep is out of the question. The one-pointed concentration for which yogis strive is also all too easily theirs: they can think of nothing but their lost love. They go about their daily tasks with the indifference that yogis so carefully cultivate; their egos are mere husks. And in the absence of such self-consciousness they freely hallucinate beyond the confines of the insipid daily world, as yogis desire to do; they hallucinate Krishna, who is their world, even if he is not "there." A total imperviousness guards them from worldly involvements: yogis may desire that adamantine state, but the women of Braj would rather have their hearts burst and break than endure it a moment longer. As for the internal heat *(tapas)* that yogis learn to fan and channel so as to make all this possible, it is theirs without even asking. Love is an unquenchable forest fire, as they often say: robbed of its object it scorches everything in sight.[11]

Obviously there is a certain quotient of irony in all of this, but it is engendered by the tradition's disdain for the term of comparison—yoga, the religion of disciplined aspiration—rather than by the nature of love itself. As one sits among the worshipers at the *akrūr līlā*, where so much of this comes to the fore, one sees that it is scarcely conceit. The painful feelings of separation that the *līlā* brings to focus are real and general. They are the aches that come from simply being alive. Life involves estrangement, as Christian theologians also have emphasized,[12] and it is entirely appropriate that the song of estrangement be directed back toward the Ground of Being from whom we have been parted.

The theological question is, who is responsible? And here the Christian and the Vaiṣṇav make rather different assessments. The Christian tradition has dealt with the fact of existential estrangement under the heading of the doctrine of sin, holding that the onus falls entirely on the human side. God's action conduces rather to healing and reconciliation: that is the mission of the Messiah. Sophisticated Vaiṣṇav theologies, like those of Rāmānuja and Vallabhācārya, approximate this view in some respects, though they rarely place the moral burden of sin so squarely on the shoulders of humanity.[13] This separation is more in the nature of things. But what is striking is that the stories of Krishna (in contrast with the theologies) take a much more complicated view, and sometimes, it seems, almost the opposite. After all, it is Krishna who abandons those who love him, not the reverse.

In the age of the *Harivaṃśa* this parting posed no theological problem. The *gopīs* had not yet come to stand for the force of human emotions directed toward God, and Radha, the sum of these, had not yet materialized. But once that identification had been made, once the *rās* had come to represent the joys of union with the divine, the tradition did not shrink from affirming the narrative consequences. It was Krishna who left his lovers, not they him, and when they cry out against the injustice of it all, there is no hint that they have brought this fate upon themselves through some act of transgression or omission. By their inclusion in the *rās*, indeed, they have already been completely vindicated. It is one of the wonders of the history of religions that their grief and their complaints against God are registered so freely and without apology. What Job is to justice, they are to love.

All this is in the wings for the *akrūr līlā*. It is understandable that Krishna must go to Mathura to serve the cause of righteousness. Nārad is there to remind him that he cannot forever commit himself to the forgetfulness of play in Braj. But he and his brother assure the aggrieved Brajbāsīs that there is no cause for concern, since they will be back in a few days. The immediate plot excuses them: they are merely repeating what Akrūr himself says (quoting Kans) when he comes to take them away. But the fact of the matter is that they never do return. Two days stretch to four and four days to a week, and weeks turn to months and months to years, and still they do not come. The soul waits and waits for God, and the silence is deafening.

Yes, there is a minor reunion. Years later, long after Krishna and Balarām have departed even from Mathura, they do encounter the Brajbāsīs who, like them, have come to auspicious Kurukṣetra on the dangerous occasion of a solar eclipse. There all who love Krishna have one last look at him, and the *līlā* that depicts the episode celebrates a sororal affection between Radha and Krishna's wife Rukmiṇī, queen of Dvaraka. But even that is not a real return. Assurances to the contrary not withstanding—and there have been several theological ones[14]—Krishna never comes back to Braj.

In terms of the information given in the *akrūr līlā* itself, then, it may seem extreme that Nanda and the cowherds and Yaśodā and the girls wail so in the face of the claims they repeatedly hear that the two boys will be returning immediately. But even in this situation, we can understand the foreboding they feel as they imagine the slaughter when Kans gets his hands on Krishna and Balarām. And the broader sweep of the story, which every member of the audience has known since the age of three, justifies their anxiety and grief. As childhood departs inevitably, so Krishna's childhood becomes irrecoverable once he leaves Braj, and all its fluent and joyful attachments with it. He is gone, and what divinity there is in all our childhoods departs with him, an equally final separation. What we feel once this happens is not mere nostalgia. The loss is at once more profound and more valuable. The Gospel of John hints at what is involved with its doctrine of the Holy Spirit. "I will give you another Comforter," says Jesus when he leaves his followers.[15] The text clearly implies that if he had not absented himself, then the wedding of souls human and divine that the Holy Spirit represents and that Christians affirm as fact could not have happened.[16]

Vaiṣṇavs put it even more strongly. It is not, they say, that this presence-in-separation will be altogether comforting. Rather, in the wailing and groaning of separation one knows what depth love has: that sense of presence comes, paradoxically, only in the absence of the object of one's love. To put it otherwise, we do not understand the beauties of the play world in which childhood takes place until we are beyond it, but that fact subtracts neither from their profundity nor from those of our sentiments looking back. Or again, we do not sense the glory of experiencing the divine until we are beset with our own banality.

On the face of it, it may seem that the Christian story and the story of Krishna move in entirely opposite directions. On the one hand, the passions of Christ lead on to the resurrection, and victory succeeds defeat in the specific sense that Jesus becomes present again to those who love him after his departure. On the other hand, through various trials the *gopīs* did find perfect union with Krishna—victory—only to have it smashed by his departure for Mathura, never to return.

As we have suggested, some of these differences are real. But there are analogies between the experience of the resurrected

Christ and that of the departed Krishna for which these apparently contrasting story lines do not prepare us. For Christians too, after all, there is a haunting finality about the departure of Jesus. At that point the unitary story line is lost: it spinters into accounts of resurrection that greatly differ from one another. And for Vaiṣṇavs all is not lost with the parting. Instead, there is the clear sense that the imitative remembrance of Krishna—as in the *rās līlās* themselves—that the reality of estrangement from God all but forces upon us is deeply salutary. It is its own kind of resurrection, creating the possibility of union with Krishna once again, and precisely (yet paradoxically) because of that separation from him that we all share. As in the case of the Church, the Vaiṣṇav community, the *satsaṅg*, comforts. And in the acting out of the *akrūr līlā* it comforts at the point of grief itself, by creating a framework in which those fundamental human feelings of separation can be vividly shared.

Both stories, culminating as they do, respectively, in the resurrection (and ascension) of Jesus and the departure of Krishna to the land from which he came, are open-ended. Victories may be cosmically attained: at Calvary and in the three days in hell that followed; and at Mathura, where Krishna's successful battle with Kans served as the culmination of eons of incarnations in which Viṣṇu projected himself into the world for the sake of relieving the burdens of earth. But the cost is separation. The people who have been touched by the divine presence, in both cases, must go on living their often very imperfect lives in the apparent absence of the divine victor. Both traditions make the affirmation that if such open-ended lives are lived in love (for as Vaiṣṇavs say, *bhāv*, feeling, is everything, the access to and meaning of the divine), the hurt of that separation will be, if not altogether healed, nonetheless redeemed in a way that exceeds even what its healing would have meant.

Christians have understood this centrality of suffering in human life as the way of the cross. Jesus's sufferings redeem our own. For Vaiṣṇavs this redemption comes not through the paradigmatic experience of Krishna as a sufferer, but rather through our confronting with honesty the poverty and suffering of our own lives, emotional and otherwise. But we know that poverty precisely because he has been in our midst and has departed. That is both why we suffer and why the suffering is redeemed. In both cases, Christian and Vaiṣṇav, the confrontation with pain is the access to a deeper, if less predictable, joy. And that is why Vaiṣṇavs have sometimes said that love in separation is even greater than love in union.[17]

The emotional climax of the *akrūr līlā* builds through its three scenes of separation: Krishna's farewells to his friends, his parents, and his loves. This is not mere repetition. As in the worship of Krishna generally, what is crucial here is not so much the plot as the feeling associated with it. This point was made systematically by a group of Vaiṣṇavite theologians living in Brindavan in the sixteenth century as they transferred a particular theory of dramatic aesthetics to its devotional counterpart, insisting that the value of a play lay in the mood *(ras)* it engendered, and that Krishna's play, even in its cosmic reaches, was no different.[18] The sequence of three farewells in the *akrūr līlā* allows the emotions associated with separation to deepen in the audience (and in the players). In this it moves forward in somewhat the same way as an Indian raga is typically developed. The performer goes over the same thematic material again and again, but each time digs deeper into the well of associations and overtones that go with it. The number three itself is significant in music: a repetition in three signifies the culmination of a particular section of a piece or of the entire composition.

It is no accident, then, that when the *līlā* explores two other visions of Krishna these also are expressed in sequences of three. One precedes the great scenes of separation—Kans's fearful visions—and the other follows them—the awesome epiphanies to Akrūr as he takes the boys back to Mathura. Indeed, these two sets of visions balance one another and provide the dramatic framework within which the central visions of the play, the scenes of separation, are set. They are wonderful to the eye, since they are visions in the supernatural sense and must be staged as such, but the verse that surrounds them is only the solid stream provided by Brajbāsī Dās's long narrative poem *Braj Vilās.*[19] The real poetic deepening is reserved for the more natural and human scenes of farewell. When the *rāsdhārī* comes to them he reaches beyond the *Braj Vilās* and enacts the much finer poems attributed to Sūr Dās. It is not merely that such poems are available to embroider these parting scenes, but that through them the *rāsdhārī* hopes to deepen and refine the audience's emotional understanding of what they are seeing.

The moods and meanings of other plays are amplified and given definition by particular ritual occasions with which they are associated—the *līlā* of Krishna's birth with *janmāṣṭamī*, and the great *rās līlā* with the night of the full moon of autumn. The *akrūr līlā*, however, is different. Like the *banśī corī līlā*, it has no such calendrical niche. Yet it is enriched by certain temporal associations. As the hopeful, playful *līlā* of the flute stimulates feelings of anticipation by being placed typically at or near the beginning of a cycle of plays, so the sadness of this *līlā* is enhanced by the fact that it typically comes near the end. The audience has a fresh memory of all that has gone before, and the pilgrims among them know that in the matter of a few days they will have to undergo the same separation from Braj that Krishna himself experiences in the *līlā*. Their separation from Braj will inevitably also be in some degree a separation from him and all the drama of his world. This echoing between Krishna's departure and the pilgrims' own is made doubly poignant by another factor of timing. As they themselves will typically do (and almost always did until train schedules complicated the picture), Krishna sets out on his journey in the early morning.

It is a special feature of both the *ūdho* and *akrūr līlā*s, both of which are played near the end of the *rās līlā* cycle, that they focus upon the experiences of travelers, these figures who give the *līlā*s their names.[20] And Akrūr in particular is more than a traveler: he is a pilgrim. From the point of view of the old epic story, it is his family connections that make him so anxious to set out for Braj, but in the play before us it is not so much that as his pilgrim's urge. He goes to Braj for the same reason every pilgrim goes to Braj, and says as much: he goes to have for himself a vision of Krishna and Balarām leading their bucolic existence. Like every pilgrim, he goes to see a tableau come to life. And he feels the pilgrim's uncertainty as he departs. In his case it is actual dread as he contemplates the reason for his being sent. But his anticipation is even greater than his foreboding, and it drives him ahead. Like every pilgrim to Brindavan, he relishes in his mind what will happen when he arrives: how he will at last have the chance to prostrate himself at Krishna's very feet. As a member of Krishna's family he can hope for even more; he longs for the moment when Krishna will raise him up and embrace him. One wonders if other pilgrims share the same desire, for the swoons are so heartfelt when that embrace is consummated.

Like every pilgrim, finally, Akrūr must go his way. As he crosses the river that separates the magical realm of Braj from the outer world of profanity and struggle, the pilgrim in Akrūr wonders what he has seen, really, and how the vision will accompany him as he moves onward through life. There, as he bathes, the waters of Krishna's magic *(māyā)* wash across him and in the succession from one vision to the next it becomes clear that the Krishna he has seen in Braj, the Krishna who eats a breakfast of butter and dried fruits, is the same Viṣṇu/Krishna who rules the universe. The lesson to Akrūr on that occasion is that he need not fear for the victory of this humble boy. But the lesson to the pilgrim—and perhaps to the pilgrim in Akrūr as well—is that in the last analysis this omnipotent ruler of creation can only be encountered intimately, in this humble guise. Hence the pilgrim need not worry that the vision will fade. As Krishna sustains the universe, so will this intimate, truthful vision be sustained.

Yaśodā, who has prepared this little breakfast for Krishna, has a similar double vision earlier in the play. As she makes her last appeal and Krishna pulls irrevocably away from her insistent grasp, as she loses her immediate connection with him forever, she is overwhelmed with the realization that this child of hers was no ordinary child but God himself. Nārad had told her, but somehow she had been powerless to remember. She laments. She bewails the fact that she has not worshiped him all these years instead of mothering him and even punishing him in the course of bringing him up. She is disconsolate, but we in the audience know that she has worshiped him in a way that no other has done before her or since, with the honest emotions of motherhood: "worshiped the beloved with a kiss," as the Christian carol puts it.[21]

If one senses that such an intimacy is all that matters in the worship of Krishna, then one's pilgrimage to Braj is complete. If one understands that the sight of Krishna eating breakfast communicates the inner nature of the Lord's sustaining omnipotence, then one has genuinely seen the vision Brindavan has to offer. And for all the wrenching sadness that separation from this magical world brings, one can leave in the knowledge that such a vision will not fade, since it baptizes the loves that circle around our lives' commonest and most fundamental points of contact.

Here follows the *akrūr līlā* performed by Svāmīs Śrī Rām and Natthī Lāl on August 15, 1976.

The Coming of Akrūr

MUSICIANS:

Tell us a story to capture and gladden
  the hearts of the saints, a ladder to heaven:
A tale of the Jumna, that joyous ocean
  that lies beside Mathura, flowing and splendid.
The blessings conferred by the sight of that river
  are known to the far distant ends of the earth.
Hurry then, Nārad, to the king of the region . . .[22]

NĀRAD: [*entering alone, strumming the* tānpurā, *the drone instrument he always carries with him, and repeating over and over a name of Viṣṇu as he goes*] Nārāyaṇ, Nārāyaṇ, Nārāyaṇ. [*addressing the* AUDIENCE] Friends, let's hear a cheer for Krishna. Come on [*and the* AUDIENCE *joins him*]: hail Lord Krishna, God himself!

What is a body but a lone and fleeting
  home in a whirling world?—
A palatial pattern of dirt and dust,
  a mansion, a soaring monument of mud,
And blood is its mortar,
  bones its brick.
The instant it stands proud
  the turrets of ambition crowd the skies,

But let it collide with darkening time,
carried along by the carriage of death,
And walls will crack, the building crumble,
doomed to dust and simple rubble.[23]

[*No intervening prose soliloquy introduces the next poem:* NĀRAD *just continues singing. But the* AUDIENCE *will understand that the song that follows prescribes an antidote to the condition described in the foregoing. It designates the repetition of the names of God as the easiest and surest way to salvation in this degenerate age.*]

These are the names to which always
the tongue returns:
Hari Hara Hari Hara Hari Hara Hari Hara.
The self they strengthen;
The guru's test is passed;
They honor the saints
And satisfy God.
Night and day chanting a garland of sighs:
Hari Hara Hari Hara Hari Hara Hari Hara.
Murmur them with abundant faith,
These names will ever support your life:
They father you and mother you,
Transforming these terrible times.
Hari's gracious forms—let them suffuse your mind:
Hari Hara Hari Hara Hari Hara Hari Hara.
Make these names your craving,
Reap the joy they bring,
Sing Hari Hara till love and tears
Arise and flood your eyes:
Hari Hara Hari Hara Hari Hara Hari Hara.[24]

[*With a third song, a version of a* pad *attributed to Sūr Dās,* NĀRAD *links the theme of his first song with that of his second.*]

Soul, fool! You've wasted your life!

All for a smattering of selfish gain
you've traded in life's treasures.
Lured by a couple of cowries,
duped by the glisten of the shell,

You soon amassed quite a fortune in sins,
 and now they weigh you down.
Go ahead, join the world's selfish family!
 Do whatever you please!
But Sūr says unless you sing God's song,
 you'll beat your breast and grieve.[25]

[NĀRAD *concludes his little recital by repeating the names of* KRISHNA *and Śiva one last time and exhorting the* AUDIENCE *to join him in a swell of praise.*] Hari Hara Hari Hara Hari Hara Hari Hara. All together now: hail Lord Krishna, God himself! Listen friends, Lord Krishna, the root of all happiness, became incarnate on this earth to relieve it of its burdens and to do away with evil-doers. But what's happened now? Has he gotten so involved in playing with his friends in Braj that he's forgotten what he came for? I'd better go remind him of his mission. [NĀRAD *walks back and forth plucking at his* tānpurā *until he is joined at the front of the stage by* KRISHNA.]

MUSICIANS:

 Nārad made his appearance then . . .

NĀRAD: Hail! Praise to you, the god who befriends the wretched. Hail!

KRISHNA: Well Nārad, what brings you here?

NĀRAD: Come on, what's this? You know everything and inhabit every corner of creation, Lord. Why do you need to ask?

MUSICIANS:

 Mathura-born, you left for Braj
 as your mother and father slept.

NĀRAD: Hail, Merciful Lord. In the city of Mathura in Kans's prison you took your birth. Then you came over here to Gokul. But Friend of the Wretched, Ocean of Mercy, was that the reason you became incarnate? Have you forgotten what your purpose is on this earth? Why . . .

MUSICIANS:

 That was so Yaśodā could know you as a child,
 and the girls your amorous side.

NĀRAD: Oh yes, that's all wonderful—how Nanda and Yaśodā treated you as their own son and the cowherder girls of Braj became so romantically attracted to you. Yes, wonderful:

really only you understand the logic of these games you play.

MUSICIANS:

But don't forget your devotees' plight.
Go to Kans now. Kill him.

NĀRAD: Lord, Friend of the Downtrodden, Ocean of Mercy, filled with compassion, loving toward those who love you, now is the time to destroy Kans and relieve the earth of the terrible burden it bears. After all, Lord, how much longer had you intended to stay here playing with these cowherders?

MUSICIANS:

Once he'd said his piece, Nārad
paused a second, and then
Hari's response filled the air—
his gracious, ambrosial voice—
"Listen closely, Nārad, sage,
you go now and persuade Kans
To send someone to summon me
to come to Mathura."[26]

KRISHNA: You go to the king over there . . .

NĀRAD: Who? Me?

KRISHNA: Yes, and have him send someone to fetch me immediately.

NĀRAD: Oh I see. Very clever. And then once you get to Mathura, you'll kill the king.

KRISHNA: Right.

NĀRAD: But one thing: if I go off to Mathura now you won't just forget about all this and go back to playing with the cowherds, will you?

KRISHNA: No, no.

NĀRAD: [*introducing a song that has no direct relation to the plot, but is in general appropriate to the plea* NĀRAD *has just voiced, that* KRISHNA *recall the commitments he has made*]

Now that you've taken me as your servant
you'll have to show me the same compassion
That saved so many from deepest need,
as everyone heard and claimed a share—

Slaves all crowding your royal throneroom
with only their plight to offer as gifts.
If I go off empty no one will grieve
my particular fate, but the rumor will spread
That the Merciful One has found his limit,
bankrupt from righting wretchedness.
So if you want to preserve your name—
granted: under duress of tears—
You'll have to fling mercy's treasury open
and let it be looted bare.[27]

KRISHNA: Yes, yes, Nārad.
NĀRAD: May I go then? you won't forget?
KRISHNA: No, don't worry. I'll keep it all in mind.
NĀRAD: [*mumbling as he exits*] Nārāyaṇ, Nārāyaṇ, Nārāyaṇ.

As the curtain rises we find ourselves at the court of Mathura. Shouts of "Hail, Lord Śiva" announce the arrival of Kans, who, as in the *kṛṣṇa janma līlā,* wears a huge mark *(tilak)* at the center of his forehead, indicative of his devotion of Śiva. Attended by his guard, he seats himself on the throne and glowers at the audience with an ominous expression whose darkness is intensified by the color of his *tilak*. This time it is not red but black. He thunders for his chamberlain, Fang, who lumbers onstage holding a great scroll. Evidently he has been keeping the palace records, for Kans demands to know from him how his royal struggle with the two adolescents of Braj, Balarām and Krishna, is going.

Fang's tenure in office has removed some of his sycophancy. He responds with a boredom suggesting contempt for what we thereby conjecture to be a frequent, anxious inquiry on the part of the king. He does not survey the many attempts Kans has made to do the boys in and how they have all failed. Sparing Kans this chronicle of defeats, he merely summarizes: "it's going badly." At that Kans flies into an enormous rage. He jumps down from the throne and flails his arms about, muttering all the while that this cannot be. He repeats his conviction that the Vedas and Puranas redound to his praise, and makes a sweeping arc with his hand to demonstrate that even Vaikuṇtha, Viṣṇu's heaven, can scarcely compare with the glories of his own capital city. The obsequious guard insists that every power ever arrayed against the potentate of Mathura has come to naught, but Kans has Fang's records to remind him of the unpleasant truth. "How can it be so?" he thunders disdainfully, impotently.

At this point Nārad drifts in, as he so often does, to break the impasse. As he announces himself, Kans treats him with a certain deference, addressing him, perhaps hopefully, as his guru. Then he returns immediately to his obsession, raving on about his difficulties in dealing with Nanda's son. Nārad listens patiently for a while, and then makes a suggestion. He proposes that it is useless for Kans to send more envoys to Braj. Obviously that plan of attack is not working. Rather he should bring the youths to Mathura, where Kans himself will be in full control of the situation: then surely he will be able to get his hands on them.

Kans is impressed with the plan. It cheers him so, in fact, that he loses the sense of deference he had expressed for Nārad only moments before. When he observes that whatever his guru says must be for his benefit, it sounds very little like an appreciation for his teacher's concern. In Kans's mouth this remark is just another expression of his megolomania. Vedas, Puranas, gurus—they all exist to serve *him*, and nothing can stop him now. Fang, skeptic that he has become, says there is no point in it. Krishna and Balarām will kill whatever envoy Kans sends to summon them to Mathura. But to no avail; the king simply calls in his minister, Akrūr, to make sure the messenger is the best the kingdom can offer. And every royal expectation is exceeded when Akrūr willingly volunteers his services.

Kans may bloat himself with pride at this most recent display of the devotion of his courtiers, but in fact Akrūr's motives are otherwise. He has a particular pull toward Braj, for he and Krishna are relatives. As a member of Vasudev's family, he thinks of Krishna as his nephew, and much of the interest of this figure as the drama proceeds will hinge upon the tug of war he feels between his official and familial roles, persecutor and protector.

First, however, we observe another struggle. As the scene changes we see Kans sleeping in his bedchamber. He thrashes about and talks aloud, caught in the grip of a nightmare. Suddenly the nightmare becomes as vivid to the audience as it is to Kans himself. Behind a gauze curtain that has been dropped at the rear of the lion's throne where the king slumbers, two forms jump to life: two Krishnas, dressed exactly alike, rise directly behind the throne, draw their swords, and bend over Kans with the threat of impending death. Kans starts awake with a shout and leaps from his bed of terror. The dream figures disappear behind the throne as quickly as they materialized, but he stumbles about the stage, still dazed with fear and staggering along the borderline between his dreaming horror and his waking obsession.

At length he reassures himself, and returns to his lonely bed. But again he begins to cringe and shake and murmur stifled, shuddering sounds. "No! Oh no!" he shouts as two Krishnas emerge again behind the gauze curtain. This time, however, only one is threatening. The other plays his flute with a kind and beautiful air, reminding us that the fear is in the eye of the beholder and that even the threatening gesture of the other Krishna is only a dream projection. Once again the king wakes terrified as the dream dissipates. He wanders crazily about the stage, then returns to his bed.

Asleep again, he generates the process all over—a third negative *darśan*. This time Kans's fearful obsession expresses itself in two Krishnas who appear with their bows drawn on him, the vision expanding as his fear increases. A third archer Krishna is added, then a fourth. This time when the king bolts awake he is still fully in the thrall of his dream. He unsheaths his sword to fend off the phantoms, but it falls useless to the ground as they recede a third time behind the throne. Faltering, desperate, he wobbles away from the throne calling for his guard, but when he hears someone approaching he is so terrified that he lunges for his sword, drawing it on his own protector. The guard starts back and the audience roars with laughter. Coming gradually to his senses, Kans calls for Akrūr, who emerges complaining that it is the middle of the night. As Kans explains about his haunting dreams, however, Akrūr decides he had better depart immediately for Braj, to preserve the royal sanity and in order to find the boys.

MUSICIANS:

Balarām and Krishna graze the herd
    the very first thing in the morning,
So if I want to find them still at home,
    I'll have to leave—right now.

AKRŪR: I've heard, King, that Nanda's two sons get up early in the morning and lead off their cows and calves. So if I wait till morning to start on my journey, I won't find anyone there when I arrive.

MUSICIANS:

I'll get to Nanda's before the dawn
    and bring back the boys in the morning.

AKRŪR: You see, if I leave right now while it's still night, I can have those boys back in Mathura before noon.

KANS: Fine, but listen, Akrūr. [*He refers to himself formally, in the third person*] Don't give anybody the impression that Kans wants them to come to Mathura so that he can kill them.

AKRŪR: No, of course not.

KANS: Tell them this. Remind them of the time Kans asked that Krishna and Balarām fetch a hundred thousand lotuses from the place in the river where the snake Kāliya was living. Tell them how pleased the king was with both boys for completing the task and how now he wants to give them a little baksheesh.

AKRŪR: Fine, that's just what I'll say.

MUSICIANS:

Say just that in summoning them
    and no one will know the truth.

KANS: And tell everyone that King Kans is arranging a fabulous archery tournament, and he doesn't want Krishna and Balarām to miss the event—all that in addition to the little reward he wants to bestow on them. If you say that, no one will guess the truth. [*He is silent for a second, then pro-*

ceeds slowly.] And, Akrūr, if there are any slip-ups you can be sure that I'll pulverize your children. I will crush them!

AKRŪR: No, no, there's no need to worry about anything like that. I'll have the boys here in Mathura in the morning.[28]

KANS: Good. You'll take my carriage so that you can make good time. [*Bellowing out*] World-conqueror! Fang! Where are those two?

[*At the back of the stage a curtain is raised to reveal the same carriage that was used to bring* VASUDEV *for his marriage. Soon the* LIVERYMAN and CHAMBERLAIN *appear, both drowsy with sleep.*]

FANG AND WORLD-CONQUEROR: Yes, Your Lordship.

KANS: [*to* AKRŪR] There'd better not be any slip-up, Akrūr, because if there is, you know what will happen.

[*With that send-off he escorts* AKRŪR *toward the carriage.* AKRŪR *goes behind the curtain, and his shoulders and head appear framed in the front window of the carriage.* KANS *and his courtiers go off, signifying the departure of the coach, and* AKRŪR *is left to soliloquize as he journeys along.*]

MUSICIANS:

Reflecting on his peerless nephew
  and the murderous nature of Kans,
He turned the whole thing over in his mind,
  his mission and what it would mean.

AKRŪR: That evil Kans—what a murderer! And look! Now he's made me his own deputy and advisor in the task of bringing Krishna and Balarām back for the kill.

MUSICIANS:

How can I ever take them there?
  He'll kill them both on sight!

AKRŪR: How can I do it? As soon as that Kans sets his eyes on me he'll murder both brothers on the spot. I can't bring them to be slaughtered like that. No, I just can't bring myself to do such a cruel thing.[29]

MUSICIANS:

How can I turn them over to him,
  knowing what terrors lie in store?

The thought of the elephant, Muṣṭik, and Cāṇūr
floods my eyes with helpless tears.[30]

[*Indeed, tears are already beginning to well up in the* AUDIENCE *as* AKRŪR *continues his sad soliloquy. Here and there one hears coughs.*]

AKRŪR: Just think how it will be! Soldiers and wrestlers and elephants—villainous wrestlers like Muṣṭik and Cāṇūr and Śal and Tośal—they'll be butchering Krishna and Balarām before my very eyes! No, I just can't go through with it!

MUSICIANS:

The merciful lord knows every heart,
perceives each devotee's doubt;
But Akrūr, as he pondered Krishna's plight,
despaired, for he saw no way out.

AKRŪR: Whatever am I going to do? [*Then finding his resolution*] Well, that's that. Whatever happens, I just can't deliver those boys up to their death.

MUSICIANS:

Thinking on Krishna, the insight came:
"He's lord of the universe, master, king."

AKRŪR: Hey Akrūr, wake up! This Krishna is lord of the entire universe! What can Kans do that can even touch him?

MUSICIANS:

To earth he descended to lighten its burdens:
who knows the ends of his awesome powers?

AKRŪR: He's come to earth to lighten loads, becoming incarnate here. Then what can villains like Kans and all his fighters do against him?

MUSICIANS:

My thanks to Kans, my thanks,
for sending me to see
The sight that rendered the holy books silent:
Nanda's little boy.[31]

AKRŪR: [*relieved, chuckling pleasantly*] Yes, I should be giving thanks to this Kans who came up with the idea of sending me to Braj. Once there I'll see something that has proved inaccessible even to the gods. Well, let's go then. Come on, let's go!

MUSICIANS:

With his thoughts in order he hastened
  and spurred his horses on,
And soon on the right a good omen:
  he noticed a herd of deer.
Beyond the fear of murderous Kans,
the son of Suphalak felt measureless joy,
For he thought of the encounter ahead,
  and he thought of Krishna's embrace.[32]

AKRŪR: Oh think of my good fortune! Today I'll be touching the blessed feet of the lord of the universe. And what's more, he'll take my arms and raise me up and embrace me! Think of it!

MUSICIANS:

And there he will stand surrounded by cows
  and his cowherding friends—what a joyous view.

AKRŪR: This very day I'll be seeing that beautiful tableau: Nanda's son at the center, flanked by cowherds and with cows and calves all about. [*With relish*] Oh yes!

MUSICIANS:

When I reach the feet of Nanda's son
  he will lift me and embrace me.

AKRŪR: First I'll fall at his blessed feet, then he'll raise me up and take me to his heart and give me a hug.

MUSICIANS:

When the giver of joy asks how I am,
  my lips will refuse to answer.

AKRŪR: I know how it will be. He'll greet me and ask if everything is all right, and I'll be so moved I won't be able to stammer out a word. Oh I am so lucky! What fortune!

MUSICIANS:

He herds the cows in the Basil Forest,
  the Lord surrounded by all of his friends,
With his plowman brother he radiates joy:
  for those who love him he entered the world.

COWHERDS: [*They enter from all sides, surrounding* AKRŪR'S *coach and signifying that it has arrived in Braj. To the cat-*

tle we must imagine roaming about in the woods they shout:] Hey! Hey! Hey you black ones! Hey you white ones and dappled, pinkish ones! [*They continue their calling as the* MUSICIANS *sing on.*]

MUSICIANS:

There before Suphalak's son: the scene
that satisfies the hearts of saints—
And so stirred with happiness he could not
sit still in his carriage seat.
To Syām he raced, at his feet he bowed,
and from the Sea of Compassion
mercy showered down.
As Akrūr had imagined, it all came to be:
the vision of love, of divine mercy.
Whoever holds fast to the heart of devotion
reaches unhindered devotion's desire.

[*While this is sung,* KRISHNA *appears,* BALARĀM *at his side.* AKRŪR *hurries out from his curtain-carriage and prostrates himself at* KRISHNA'S feet. KRISHNA *politely resists this gesture of submission in the way that is common in India, and raises him up to embrace him as an equal.*]

KRISHNA: Well, uncle, what brings you here? To what do I owe the honor? How are you, uncle? Is everything going fine?

MUSICIANS:

Wonderful, Lord, how wondrous your sight,
how gracious your feet to your devotees.

AKRŪR: At the sight of you, My Lord, everything is happiness.

KRISHNA: But what have you come for?

MUSICIANS:

Taking what Kans had said strictly in secret,
the son of Suphalak revealed it all.

AKRŪR: Lord, I'll tell you what my purpose is today. The king of Mathura is organizing a huge archery tournament today and he's sent me here to summon you and your brother.

KRISHNA: Well and good.

AKRŪR: You'll go then, will you?

KRISHNA: Of course, uncle. We'll both go.

MUSICIANS:

After the words of Akrūr a smile
came dashing across his face,
And excitement pulsed in his brother's arms
at the thought of a demon slaying:
"There's no pretending, it's that very thing
that we've been aching to do."
But the cowherds were dizzy with wonder and worry:
"Gopāl, can what you are saying be true?"

[*Simultaneously the* COWHERDS, *and particularly* MANSUKHĀ, *make gestures to implore* KRISHNA *not to go.*]

KRISHNA: Oh Mansukhā, now don't be like that.

MUSICIANS:

"My mind is made up, and it's too late to argue.
It's time to visit Kans."[33]

KRISHNA: [*to* AKRŪR] Well then, Uncle, let's go as quickly as possible.

MANSUKHĀ: But Kanhaiyā, what are you saying? You can't mean you're going to leave all of us here in Braj and go off to Mathura! Kanhaiyā?

[*As his helpless pleading proceeds, there are more and more muffled sobs and coughs in the* AUDIENCE. *Familiar with all the stories and emotions that go with* KRISHNA'S *friendships in Braj, the spectators can see the whole scene before their eyes, and readily put themselves in* MANSUKHĀ'S *shoes. And it is particularly poignant that he, who is always full of jest and mirth, now has nothing but tears in his voice.*]

KRISHNA: Come on, pal. We'll be back in a few days.

MANSUKHĀ: No, no, don't go. My poor soul won't make it a day without you. It lives on you: what will it breathe?

COWHERDS: [*crowding around* BALARĀM *for a moment, since* KRISHNA *seems adamant*] No, Balarām, don't go. The king who rules there is as wicked as they come.

AKRŪR: There's no need to worry, friends. I'm just taking them to Mathura for two or three days to see this tournament. Then I'll bring them right back.

MANSUKHĀ: No, Kanhaiyā. Tell me you'll . . .

KRISHNA: [*trying gently to move him away*] No, no, you just go home now.

MUSICIANS:

These folk from Braj—these flowers—
will always remain my life-breath.
I swear by my father, they'll not be forgotten,
not for the tiniest moment.

MANSUKHĀ: [*languishing at* KRISHNA*'s side*] Kanhaiyā . . .

KRISHNA: Yes, brother.

MANSUKHĀ: Brother, there you've gone and sworn by your father that you'll never be away from Braj even for a minute. Then how can you go and leave us? How can you go off to Mathura, friend?

KRISHNA: Come on, there's no reason to be so upset. We'll be back in a couple of days. Come on now, brother, go home. [*At this point* YAŚODĀ, *hearing the sounds of grief, comes on and adds a new dimension to the scene.*]

MUSICIANS:

Gopāl's mother, a simple soul,
doesn't quite know what's happening.

KRISHNA: Look, Mother, our uncle has come.

YAŚODĀ: [*confusedly*] What?

KRISHNA: Our uncle has come.

YAŚODĀ: Who?

[*Her foggy old age adds both to the intensity of her concentration on her son—here she depends on him to understand what is going on—and to the piteousness of her position. Almost at the sight of her, the weeping in the* AUDIENCE *intensifies, spreading like a contagion. Women in particular are moved at the impending separation of mother and son, but men participate in this grief as well, partly because they have* NANDA *to identify with, too.*]

KRISHNA: Our uncle.

MUSICIANS: [*suggesting that the knotted gathering we now see on stage is merely a part of the great assembly one should be imagining*]

Fretful and frantic, Nanda and all
of Brindavan gathered; and from the town
They came as a torrent and left behind,
abandoned, their work and their homes.

YAŚODĀ: [*In typical Indian fashion she impresses upon* AKRŪR *that he should have come long ago, as if she were helpless to influence the itinerary of so great a one.*] Akrūr, how are you? To what do we owe your visit? It's been such a long time since we've seen you—since my son was born, in fact. Why in the world haven't you come before? Have you lost the way? Do tell, what good fortune brings you here?

MUSICIANS:

Then Nanda joined his hands to greet him,
asking after the visitor's health.

NANDA: To what do we owe the pleasure, Akrūr?

AKRŪR: You know how it is in Mathura, Nanda. This business of running the government never leaves me any free time. But today I'm here on a special mission. The king is sponsoring a huge archery tournament and your sons Krishna and Balarām are invited to come see the ceremonies. I've come to summon them to Mathura.

NANDA: [*a bit stunned*] What's that? To Mathura?

MUSICIANS:

Since they gathered the lotus flowers
from Kāliya's dangerous pool,
The king has wanted to find a way
to give them a little reward.

AKRŪR: Nanda, ever since the day Krishna and Balarām retrieved those lotuses from the black hole in the Jumna where Kāliya lived, the king has been very pleased with your sons. Now he wants to tip them, he wants to give them a little present, so he's sent me here to summon them to Mathura.

MUSICIANS:

So I've hurried here early and eager to see them,
and with them together we'll meet.

45. Nanda

AKRŪR: So there's no need to worry: in two or three days they'll be safely back in your hands.

MUSICIANS:

When the people of Braj heard this message,
their eyes were blinded by tears.

YAŚODĀ: [*moving to* NANDA's *side, appealing to him*] Husband, I don't understand this at all. Just think of the times that wicked Kans has tried to kill these boys. Poor little Kanhaiyā was only ten days old when he sent that demoness Pūtanā to come get him. [*Defiant now, and a bit frantic, afraid that somehow everyone is missing the point*] Since when have such feelings of compassion sprung up in that villain's heart? You just tell me!

NANDA: Yes, yes, you have a point there, Wife. Frankly I can't find any reason for it at all. It must be some sort of trick.

MUSICIANS:

A fearful tremor stirred inside
the hearts of Yaśodā and Nanda:
They gestured to Hari and the plowman Rām
and motioned them to their side.[34]

YAŚODĀ: [to NANDA] Husband, I'm just not going to let Kanhaiyā go, that's all. [*To* KRISHNA] Kanhaiyā, Kanhaiyā dear, come over here, son.

KRISHNA: [*not moving*] Yes, Ma, what is it?

YAŚODĀ: Over here, Kanhaiyā.

KRISHNA: [*Still he resists.*] Listen Ma, I'm going to see the big festival in Mathura.

YAŚODĀ: Now don't talk like that, son. My poor little baby, don't talk like that.

KRISHNA: No, Ma, it's all set.

MUSICIANS:

Syām was firm, his mind was sure:
from friends and loved ones he severed his ties.

YAŚODĀ: [*Having had no success in appealing to* KRISHNA, *she turns to his brother.*] Balarām.

BALARĀM: Yes, Ma.[35]

YAŚODĀ: Why don't you come over here, son?

BALARĀM: Well . . .

MUSICIANS:

Mukund has no fetters,[36]
nor yoke to constrain him:
Eternal and boundless, and of constant joy,
there'll be no destroying of him.

YAŚODĀ: [*turning to* NANDA *almost frantically*] Husband, look, do you see what's happening? These two little boys who so often came home from the woods calling for their mother and jumped in my lap—now they won't even look in my direction. Balarām!

MUSICIANS:

Born to love those who also love him,
  Krishna felt shame, but heroic duties pressed;
He cast down his eyes, avoiding every glance,
  and wavered little as a stone.

46. Yaśodā begging Krishna not to leave

YAŚODĀ: [*still to* NANDA] What has this Akrūr done to these children of yours? Kanhaiyā won't even turn his eyes in my direction!

MUSICIANS:

Mother Yaśodā ran to him, distraught . . .

[YAŚODĀ *lunges to the floor at* KRISHNA'S *feet, weeping, imploring.*]

KRISHNA: [*fending her off gently but coolly*] No, Ma, we have to go.

YAŚODĀ: [*hands raised in a gesture of petition*] No, son, don't say that, sweetheart. I can't stand to have you out of my sight, son. [*She slumps to the floor again in helpless tears.*]

MUSICIANS:

. . . Fell at his feet disconsolate.

KRISHNA: Ma, we're only going for a little while. We'll be back in three or four days.

YAŚODĀ: Akrūr . . .

AKRŪR: [*answering softly, respectfully*] Yes, Queen of Braj.

YAŚODĀ:

Son of Suphalak, to you I plead,
I beg you, slavishly.

Give ear to my request. . . .

AKRŪR: What is it?

YAŚODĀ:

If you knew with what pains I've cared for them,
Syām and Balarām, the stars in my eyes.

Oh Akrūr, how I've suffered for these two boys, what troubles I've had bringing them up and watching out for them. How can you just walk in and remove them from my sight?

What do they know about breaking a bow,
or watching a wrestling match?

Akrūr, what in the world is an archery tournament going to mean to two little boys like this? Since when have they ever witnessed anything like that?

Take along Nanda and Upananda
instead; leave the boys with me.[37]

Akrūr, see if you can interest my husband in going. Take him with you if you want, but I beg you—look, my hands are joined in prayer—I beg you not to take Krishna and Balarām.

MUSICIANS:

What do they care about tournaments,
these innocent little boys?
It's all a part of a kingly ruse,
or so it sounds to me.

YAŚODĀ: I'm telling you what I know in my heart is true, Akrūr. There's something fishy about this project.

MUSICIANS:

Consign me, would you, to a life like a widow's?
  Rob me of Krishna and I'm bankrupt, lost.
Take Nanda, my husband, instead of the boy,
  for who'll go on living without Nanda's joy?[38]

YAŚODĀ: Take my husband—my very life—to Kans if you must, but Akrūr, I won't sacrifice my life and wealth, this boy of mine. I won't hand over that life. I won't!

AKRŪR: Queen of Braj, don't be so uncomprehending. It's all so simple. They're just going to be gone a couple of days to see the tournament. They'll be back before you know it.

KRISHNA: [*to* NANDA] Here, Dad, you take care of these cows now. They're yours anyway.

NANDA: [*stricken to tears at the thought of having his most precious gift to his son, his very livelihood, returned to him*] No, no, son. These cows are yours!

MUSICIANS:

Nanda, to you I entrust these cows,
  your cows really—I've herded them so little.
Nanda, to you I entrust these cows.[39]

KRISHNA: Here, Dad, now you herd these cows of yours.

NANDA: Kanhaiyā, what's come over you? How can you say such a thing?

MUSICIANS:

Memories of milk and curd and raising a ruckus
  will never fade—you've fathered me and mothered—
Though my leaving must seem like when a crow tends
  the borrowed nest of the cuckoo's young
And watches them fly away.

KRISHNA: [*turning to* YAŚODĀ] Listen, Ma, I know I've been pretty hard to deal with. Please forgive me.

YAŚODĀ: [*She can scarcely force a word through her tears. It is much more difficult to accept this loving acknowledgment than it was to fend off the brusque, wooden manner in which her son had addressed her before.*] Oh Kanhaiyā . . .

MUSICIANS:

As poor Yaśodā pours forth her heart
 and dissolves in tears, still Krishna says more:
"Who in this world can really claim fatherhood?
 Where is the genuine son?"
Thus Sūr's Lord departed from Braj,
 pretending to sever all ties.

YAŚODĀ: [*Sobbing, she slumps to the ground.*] No, no, my little darling.

KRISHNA: Come on, Ma, don't cry. Patience, Ma, we'll both be back in a few days' time.

BALARĀM: Get up, Ma, come on.

AKRŪR: Queen of Braj, be reasonable. What sense is there in being so distraught?

BALARĀM: Just a few days, Ma . . .

YAŚODĀ: Balarām! [*Coughing through her sobs*] Balarām, you're the older brother. You explain to him.

MUSICIANS:

You and Balarām don't want me any longer,
 but without my boys I'll die.

YAŚODĀ: My dear, my sweet son, my only reason for living is to set eyes on you.

KRISHNA: Patience, Ma, it's just for two or three days.

Take heart, my Ma, don't cry,
 for what's the point of tears?
The world is false, right down to bare bone,
 including mothers and sons.
Even intimate friendships are made for self-gain;
 no one aids another. . . .[40]

[*interrupting himself to comfort his wailing mother*] Come on, Ma, don't cry. Take heart, Ma, don't cry.

Ten birds may flock to a single tree,
 taking shelter there for the night,
But when morning comes they all fly away:
 each searches alone for its food.

[*bending over* YAŚODĀ, *trying to urge her to rise*] Come on, Ma, it's just a couple of days. . . .

YAŚODĀ: [*lifting her face with difficulty, her tears making the cloth of her sari cling all about her head*] Oh Kanhaiyā, don't you see? I won't be able to live a minute without you, my little darling.

AKRŪR: [*reaching over to help*] Queen of Braj, if . . .

47. Radha's grief

YAŚODĀ: Where's your mercy, Kanhaiyā? Have you no mercy? Kanhaiyā, without you [*sobs*], without you, son, I'm going to die. Son, I know I'll never see you again. [*She slumps down again with bitter weeping.*]

KRISHNA: Patience, Ma, patience.
AKRŪR: Queen of Braj, I just can't see why you are so upset.
YAŚODĀ: Oh Akrūr . . .
KRISHNA: [*to* AKRŪR] Come on, Uncle, let's go.
YAŚODĀ: Akrūr:

Son of Suphalak, I beg of you:

A lonely pauper — look at me —
Manmohan's my only wealth,
In blind old age my only crutch,
and that you'd yank away.
Son of Suphalak, I beg of you . . .[41]

Akrūr, I prostrate myself at your feet. [*She does so.*] I'm your slave. I beg you . . .

AKRŪR: [*attempting to lift her up*] Queen of Braj . . .

YAŚODĀ: Akrūr, look how I've brought them up to be such nice big boys — Krishna and Balarām — to be staffs and supports for the darkness of my old age. Don't snatch them away. Make your name have some meaning, Akrūr: don't be cruel. [*Stretching out her hands*] Please, put a little morsel of kindness in my poor beggar's bag.

You would entice away my jewels
with a king's kingly carriage;
I know that king and why he's sent you:
he wants to crush my son.
Son of Suphalak, I beg of you . . .

Akrūr, Akrūr, don't take away my Kanhaiyā.

AKRŪR: Don't worry now, they'll be back in three or four days.
KRISHNA: [*chiming in*] Be a little patient, Ma.
YAŚODĀ:

None of us here can live without him —
so closely together we're bound —
If he is crushed, then crushed are we all
and Braj is reduced to dust.

KRISHNA: [*to* AKRŪR] Come on, Uncle.

AKRŪR: [*Sadly, slowly, he summons them and turns away from the sobbing heap in the middle of the stage*] All right then, boys, let's go.

[*Instead of going off at the back, toward the carriage, the three of them thread their way off the front of the stage, down into the* AUDIENCE, *and go off through a door at the side of the hall. This means that when* YAŚODĀ *raises her last plea to them it is directed toward the* AUDIENCE *as well—indeed, more directly than ever before. Suddenly the* AUDIENCE *must bear the full weight of* YAŚODĀ'*s grief: none of the other players remains to deflect it. She appeals now to everyone present, including them directly in the drama.*]

YAŚODĀ: Please, isn't there anyone in this Braj who will stop him? Stop my Kanhaiyā!

MUSICIANS:

Time and again Yaśodā cries,
"Do no Braj folk care enough for me
To stop them from taking my son?"[42]

YAŚODĀ: [*raising her arms dramatically, as in a Piétà*] Oh, oh, look, my Kanhaiyā's gone now! Can't anyone stop him?

"What earthly use could Kans have for my child,
off there in Mathura?
Son of Suphalak, are you man or the Reaper
come to take my life?"

MUSICIANS:

Time and again Yaśodā cries . . .

YAŚODĀ: Kanhaiyā! Kanhaiyā! [*And then, through her deepest grief, an insight dawns, a remembrance only this drastic separation seems able to stir.*] O alas, yes, now I recall something—how Nārad once said I should never regard this child as my own son. He's the fullest Brahman. Oh Kanhaiyā, now I know that you are Brahman Itself, son, the Soul above all. Oh my darling boy, if only I'd given you a jewel-studded throne to sit on! If only I'd worshiped you! And instead I went and tied you to that mortar! Ever since then you've been getting ready to leave me.

NANDA: [*reaching down to comfort her*] Wife . . .

YAŚODĀ: Husband, go bring Kanhaiyā back.

NANDA: Well, you know how stubborn he is. But all right, I'll try. Don't worry. I'll go to Mathura and bring him back.

You go home now and I'll follow him to Mathura. [*Then musing sadly to himself, as old people will*] So stubborn, that boy.

[*Exit* NANDA *and* YAŚODĀ]

[*Curtain. When the curtain rises again we see* AKRŪR *and his two charges seated in the coach. His head shows at the front window and theirs at the back. At the front of the stage a knot of* GOPĪS *is gathered, unaware as yet of the presence of the carriage.*]

MUSICIANS:

From Nanda's house the news fans out . . .

SAKHĪ: I heard today, Kiśorī Jū, that Akrūr has taken our sweetheart to Mathura. Come on, let's go see what's happened.

RADHA: Yes, friend, let's go in a hurry. [*They turn and go toward the back of the stage, where they find the coach.*]

SAKHĪS: [*to* KRISHNA] Hey sweetheart, dear as life, where are you going? Are you deserting us?

RADHA: Why are you leaving me, dear?

KRISHNA: Now, now, Radha, there's no need to be upset. It's just a matter of a couple of days and we'll be back. Don't worry, girls.

SAKHĪS: No, don't leave us. Why, without you . . .

MUSICIANS:

We bow at your feet, we women, and beg:
abandon your plans for Mathura.
We'll lose our hearts and our true homes in Braj
when we lose your lotus feet;
You'll strand us and leave us, fish washed on the shore,
floundering in the net of love.
When you played your flute, we were thrilled, hooked, and lost:
abandon your plans for Mathura.[43]

SAKHĪS: Syām Sundar, without you Braj will be empty and bleak. Lord, what will we do if you leave? How will we stay alive if you go?

MUSICIANS: [*giving the* AUDIENCE *a reminder of the time that passes in the course of such entreaties, and that the morning, with the inevitable departure it signals, is at hand*]

Thus the whole night ebbed away
until the first chirps of dawn.

SAKHĪS: Syām Sundar . . .

MUSICIANS:

They call it love, but in love I've found
nothing but purest pain.
I've torn through the town with a drum
and a warning:
"Love is abroad; let no one succumb."
When my eyes look out, they see pain all around,
in torment my body moves,
And no one shows me a whit of pity:
pain, your name is love.[44]

[*They continue with another song.*]

None who finds love is happy:

The moth, in love, has been drawn to the flame
and burned herself to death.[45]

SAKHĪ: Girls, let me tell you a thing or two. Love is nothing but trouble. Look at the moth, how it fell in love with fire and got burned up in the process. But perhaps someone else had a better reward. . . .

MUSICIANS:

The bumblebee, in love with the lotus,
boxed herself inside.
The doe felt love at the huntsman's call,
only to face the bow.[46]

SAKHĪ: Think of the poor deer, how they love the strains of the "deer" raga, and what reward to they reap? Hunters go into the woods singing that raga, and when the deer run toward them the poor things find a shower of arrows aimed against them. That's their reward, friends.

And we who fell in love with Mādhav—
deserted without a word.
To love the Lord of Sūr is to suffer
unendurable pain.

[to KRISHNA] Where are you going, Lord, that you're leaving us? You've left Braj barren and empty. Please, please Syām Sundar.

[There are other cries of grief and petition from these little GOPĪS, *but they are all but inaudible. These as yet young, unpracticed players are so genuinely moved by the emotion of the situation in which they find themselves that*

48. A spectator

they simply cannot produce any further lines. All one sees is four little pink bundles bent over at KRISHNA'S *feet, begging him with the most touching intimacy not to go.* RĀDHA, *who is older, is clearer with her gestures and more in control, though she also cries very genuine tears. She raises her hands piteously, as* YAŚODĀ *has done before her. Her friends try to comfort her, but they are so shaken themselves that they cannot begin to restore her to a standing position. There are sputters and coughs, and the curtain falls as the* MUSICIANS *repeat an earlier couplet.*]

MUSICIANS:

When my eyes look out, they see pain all around,
in torment my body moves,
And no one shows me a whit of pity:
pain, your name is love.

[*Curtain. Presently* AKRŪR *appears in front of the curtain, alone.*]

MUSICIANS:

Akrūr was entirely lost in thought:
"Have I done the right thing or not?"

YAŚODĀ: [*unseen: spoken backstage as a voice from* AKRŪR'S conscience] Akrūr, it's an evil thing you've done because . . .

MUSICIANS:

To his mother and father I've brought despair
and to every village woman grief;
Now if I take him to Kans I fear
there'll be a murdering.

AKRŪR: What am I doing? I've already left his mother and father in a state of complete desperation, and here I am taking the boy and his brother on to be murdered in Mathura! What is this?

MUSICIANS:

How can I turn them over to him,
knowing what terrors lie in store?
The thought of the elephant, Muṣṭik, and Cāṇūr
floods my eyes with helpless tears.[47]

AKRŪR: Alas, what in the world am I going to do? [*He fidgets and pounds his head with his palm.*]

MUSICIANS:

Damn, damn, damn! What stupidity!
They must go back with me to Braj.

AKRŪR: Oh Akrūr, you idiot! How could you be so stupid? Come on!

MUSICIANS:

Let them kill me, imprison my family!
—such thoughts swirled through this mind.

AKRŪR: That's right, by God. So what if that monster Kans kills me? So what if he destroys my family? Whatever the consequences, I'm not going to lead these boys to their destruction. I'm turning back.

MUSICIANS:

Pondering this, he reached the Jumna,
alighting from the coach.
The gracious Lord dwells in every heart,
removes each devotee's doubt.

[*As these lines are sung,* KRISHNA *and* BALARĀM *emerge at the front of the stage as if they had alighted from the carriage, and join* AKRŪR.]

"We're hungry!" Hari announced,
"Our breakfast time has come.
And after you've bathed in the Jumna waters
it'll be breakfast time for you too."

KRISHNA: Say, Uncle, we're really hungry. Let's all have some breakfast.

MUSICIANS:

Hearing a voice so sweet to the ear,
Akrūr was filled with attention;
He offered both brothers dried fruit
and a simple breakfast meal.

AKRŪR: Krishna, your mother gave me this butter especially for your breakfast. You go ahead and eat while I take my morning bath. Then I'll join you.

KRISHNA: [*hungrily, reaching out for the little pot* AKRŪR *has produced*] Right!

[KRISHNA and BALARĀM *retire to the wings to have their breakfast. The curtain rises, revealing a tank at the front of the stage that represents the Jumna. The curtain on which the carriage is painted has been moved to a position just behind the tank, giving the impression that it has stopped at the bank of the river and emptied its passengers.* AKRŪR *lowers himself into the river and begins his ablutions in the time-honored Indian fashion, with a prayer of* saṃkalp *or intention, in which the worshiper orients himself in time and space before the divine presence, and states what he intends to do in the rite that follows. It is a logical time for* AKRŪR *to reflect on his orientation and intentions more broadly. He pretends to lift water from the river—the tank is in fact dry—into hands held palm open, and allows it to fall back into the Jumna as he says the* saṃkalp. *Then he proceeds to the actual bath, which he takes in the familiar Indian way by dunking his head under the surface of the water and then bobbing up again.*]

MUSICIANS:

As he bathed in the Jumna his heart overflowed
in a heavenward prayer of intention,
And as his head dipped beneath the flow
he saw an amazing vision,
For it seemed he could see in the Jumna depths
Balarām and Krishna in their carriage seats.

[*As* AKRŪR *goes down for a long dunking, disappearing from sight at one end of the sunken tank,* BALARĀM *and* KRISHNA *pop up for a moment at the other end. When* AKRŪR *reemerges, they dip down out of sight.*]

AKRŪR: Hey, what's this I'm seeing in the water? What are that fine carriage and Krishna and Balarām doing here? What is this?

MUSICIANS:

Is it the coach's reflection
or a touch of Hari's magic?

AKRŪR: What is this? A reflection of my carriage in the water, or is this some trick the Lord is playing?[48]

MUSICIANS:

It may be a dream, but I seem to be awake—
perhaps I'm going mad!

AKRŪR: Is this a dream I'm seeing or is my mind just too overburdened? I don't understand at all. Well, I'll go on with my bathing.

MUSICIANS:

Again he dipped beneath the water,
again the image of the coach.

[*This time when* AKRŪR *disappears from sight into the tank,* KRISHNA *and* BALARĀM *appear with their pot of butter, calmly sharing their breakfast. When* AKRŪR *appears again from the other end of the tank, anything but calm, they drop down out of sight.*]

AKRŪR: Oh no! It's the same thing all over again! I could see Krishna and Balarām eating their buttery breakfast—but there they are having their breakfast over by the coach! [*He gestures just offstage.*] What is this, anyway?

MUSICIANS:

One minute here and the next minute there—
it sends my mortal mind reeling.

AKRŪR: I just can't believe my eyes! Am I seeing things? [*He bobs down into the tank a third time.*]

MUSICIANS:

Just when Akrūr was at the end of his wits
Syām showed his very own form.

[*This time the* KRISHNA *who emerges from the river is played by an older boy, so as to give a more regal impression, and he bears all the paraphernalia to support this role. Two false arms hold the conch and discus—the two accoutrements that invariably identify Viṣṇu/Krishna in his supernal form—and two divine personages attend him. Stage right we see* ŚIVA*: a crown surmounts the tangled locks of an ascetic, and his hand bears the trident. And at stage left stands* BRAHMĀ, *represented simply as an old man. The divine tableau remains visible this time when* AKRŪR *emerges excitedly but reverently from his end of the tank.*]

AKRŪR: Hail, hail, hail!

MUSICIANS:

This time what did he see in the water?
All of the gods at Hari's side.[49]

AKRŪR: [*sighing with satisfaction and awe*] Aaah! Ah-ha-ha!

MUSICIANS: [urging the AUDIENCE to voice their participation] Shout it out: Hail, Lord Krishna, God himself!

AKRŪR: What is this sight I have before me? It's Nārāyaṇ with four arms, and Śiva and Brahmā and all thirty-three hundred gods! And the Lord Nārāyaṇ is holding in his four arms the conch and the discus and the lotus and the club. O thank you! Now I understand! Oh I do understand! Hail to you, Lord, all praise! You are my refuge—I run to you for refuge, refuge, refuge!

49. Akrūr's vision at the river: Krishna with four arms attended by Brahmā and Śiva

MUSICIANS: [*as if addressing* AKRŪR]

How happy are you, so overjoyed,
when moments ago you were sad.

[*Interrupting the action to urge the* AUDIENCE *once again to join them in a great shout*] Praise God, who cares for those who love him! [*Then recapitulating*]

How happy are you, so overjoyed,
when moments ago you were sad.

KRISHNA: What's this, Uncle? Just a little while ago you were overcome with sadness, and now look at you!

MUSICIANS:

Now I know who you are, My Lord:
  sovereign of all, king of the world,
Who made everything, and always sustain
  that which lies in your hands.
Knowing your strength my fear of Kans
  is banished, and that too of Kuvalayāpīḍ:
With your might you can slay all foes,
  and sever them from posterity, Lord.

KRISHNA: What's that, Uncle?

AKRŪR: Huh? Oh, My Lord, there's no need to ask me any more questions. Now I know. Now I know! You're the one who makes the whole universe go round, you originated the whole thing. So what harm can possibly come to you from doing battle with the likes of Kans and Kuvalayāpīḍ? You're the master of them all.

[*With this triumphal affirmation, the curtain closes and the stage is prepared for the scene to come, which will be the last. The tank is covered over again so that no one will fall in as the* AUDIENCE *surges forward at the end to have* darśan. *This is done in a second, and the curtain rises to reveal* AKRŪR *and the boys seated in the carriage.*]

AKRŪR: Well, Krishna, here we are at a grove by the side of the river. You rest here a moment, and then we'll go on to Mathura. I'll have you there before noon.

KRISHNA: All right, Uncle.

[*These are the last words of the* līlā, *and a slight change of position prepares for the onrush of devotees.* BALARĀM replaces AKRŪR *in the front window of the carriage so that he and his brother can receive the adulation of the worshipers. Thus the* AUDIENCE *is treated to a close vision of* KRISHNA and BALARĀM *precisely as they appear in this dramatic setting, rather than in some more standard pose. At the end the* AUDIENCE *walks right into the play.*]

Notes

Chapter I. Pilgrimage to Brindavan

1. Members of the Nimbārk Sampradāy, one of the sectarian communities represented in Brindavan, hold that their ancestors were present in the area at the time of Caitanya's arrival, but there is no creditable document to support the claim. Surely the region was not entirely deserted, but the oldest buildings still standing in Brindavan were constructed by Caitanyites.
2. Caitanya deputed Gopāl Bhaṭṭ to go to the Gaṇḍakī River in north central Nepal, where the *śālagrām* stone is found, and there the manifestation took place. Rādhā Ramaṇ appeared in the rarest variety of *śālagrām*, called *dāmodaraśilā*, a large stone having circular fossil formations at the center and an indentation at the top containing a thread of gold. For further information on stories relating to this event, see Allan A. Shapiro, "The Birth-celebration of Śrī Rādhāramaṇ in Vrindaban," M.A. thesis, Columbia University, 1979, pp. 8–10, 130. On the *śālagrām*, see Gustave Oppert, "Note sur les Sālagrāmas," *Compte-rendus des séances de l'Académie des inscriptions et belles-lettres*, 1900, pp. 472–485. A classical theological description of divine self-revelation in the form of an image is that of Rāmānuja. See Katherine K. Young, "Beloved Places *(ukantaruḷinanilaṅkaḷ)*: The Correlation of Topography and Theology in the Śrīvaiṣṇava Tradition of South India," Ph.D. dissertation, McGill University, 1978, pp. 150–176.
3. From the time of its earliest mention, Golok is conceived as that idyllic realm where Krishna dwells with his cows, a region so exalted that it is inaccessible even to Indra, king of the gods (Parashuram Lakshman Vaidya, ed. *The Harivaṃśa*, Vol. 1 [Poona: Bhandarkar Oriental Research Institute, 1969], 62.28–33). The exaltation of its pastoral simplicity is reinforced in more recent documents, where Golok is ranked not only above the realms of the other gods but also above the heaven where Viṣṇu/Krishna reigns in his lordly four-armed form, Vaikuṇṭha (*Brahmavaivarta Purāṇa* [Bombay: Veṅkateśvara Press, 1909–1910], 4.4; Cheever Mackenzie Brown, *God as Mother: A Feminine Theology in India* [Hartford, Vt.: Claude Stark, 1974], pp. 58–60).
4. The daily regimen at the temple of Rādhā Ramaṇ closely resembles

the schedule followed in the temples (more accurately, *havelīs*) of the Vallabh Sampradāy, one of the great Vaiṣṇav communities of north India, where the classical eight watches are also observed. Whereas it is customary in Vallabhite *havelīs*, however, for all but one of these *darśans* to be public, the tradition of Rādhā Ramaṇ is to add a public *darśan* to the list rather than subtract one. The seventh watch is expanded into two *darśans*: in one the worshipers have a chance to see Rādhā Ramaṇ in his informal household dress *(aulāī)*, and in the other to see him just after he has taken his evening meal, which is distinguished from its midday counterpart, as in the Vallabh Sampradāy, by virtue of the fact that in the evening Krishna eats food that has been prepared in *ghī*, clarified butter, whereas earlier in the day he eats food cooked in water or over a direct fire without a cooking medium. Such distinctions in the daily routine of Hindus who can afford them have an even greater savor when incorporated into the divine program. The venerable temples of Bānke Bihārī and Rādhā Vallabh in Brindavan also follow the schedule of eight watches, but with certain alterations. In the former, particularly, fewer of these *darśans* are public; and those that are are much extended.

The eight watches, which are also sometimes celebrated as dramas in Brindavan, are as follows: 1. *maṅgalā*, the auspicious first hour in the morning; 2. *bāl bhog*, the morning snack; 3. *sṛṅgār*, when Krishna appears fully dressed and ready to depart with the cattle; 4. *rāj bhog*, the large midday meal; 5. *utthāpan*, when he wakes from his siesta; 6. *sandhyā*, when he returns home at twilight; 7. *aulāī darśan* or *vyālū bhog*, his evening meal at home; and 8. *śayan*, when he retires for the night. In the Vallabh Sampradāy these designations vary slightly. *Bāl* and *sṛṅgār* are collapsed under the latter term as the second watch, and *gvāl bhog*, a snack Krishna takes with his cowherd friends, is considered the third. At Rādhā Ramaṇ's temple the second and fifth watches are often referred to as *dhūpāratī*, because offerings of incense are made at that time. Caitanyites are careful to note that these eight visible watches do not correspond exactly to the eight divisions of Krishna's day, since the first and last in the latter series are times at night that he enjoys in the private presence of his *gopī* companions.

5. Though most of the edifice that houses the Śrī Caitanya Prem Sansthān is new, part is hundreds of years old; in fact, it is the oldest secular structure surviving in Brindavan today. It was erected by Jai Singh, the illustrious king of Jaipur, for his visits to Brindavan

from time to time during his tenure as governor of the Moghul province of Agra (1721–1728), and may even at that time have been the site of performances of the *rās līlā*, which he is said to have patronized extensively. F. S. Growse, *Mathurā: A District Memoir* (Allahabad: North-Western Provinces and Oudh Government Press, 1883), p. 264; Govindadās and R. N. Agravāl, eds., *Rās-Līlā: Ek Paricay* (Delhi: Bhāratiya Viśva Prakāśan, 1959), pp. 76–77.

6. For a fuller treatment of the *rās līlā* than I can offer here, see Norvin Hein, *The Miracle Plays of Mathurā* (New Haven: Yale University Press, 1972); Govindadās and Agravāl, *Rās-Līlā: Ek Paricay*; Darius L. Swann, "Three Forms of Traditional Theatre of Uttar Pradesh, North India," Ph.D. dissertation, University of Hawaii, 1974, pp. 73–191; and Vasant Yāmdagni, *Rās Līlā tathā Rāsānukaraṇ Vikās* (New Delhi: Sangeet Natak Academi, 1980).
7. In a recent innovation that makes the analogy even more explicit, Krishna clasps a halter of peacock feathers to the back of his waist as he twirls around on his knees. This technique was first adopted in a Delhi version of the *rās līlā* staged under the auspices of Kamalā Lāl, and was brought back to Braj by Svāmī Rāmsvarūp. It is important to note that particularly in recent times there has been a great sensitivity among Vaiṣṇavs to the danger that Krishna's dance with the *gopīs* be understood as sexual in the mundane sense, and the analogy with the peacock is taken as significant in this respect as well. People in Brindavan sometimes say that there is no actual copulation in the course of the peacock's mating rites. Reproduction is supposed to occur as a result of a rare process according to which the male sheds tears that contain his seed and the female swallows them and conceives. To devotees sensitive to the danger of a vulgar interpretation of the *rās*, the subtlety of this process as well as the presence of tears, with the refined emotion they suggest, seem particularly appropriate. Zoologists of a more secular stripe, however, dispute this account of the biological facts and remain unconvinced.
8. Premānand estimates that there are forty or fifty companies in Brindavan and an additional twenty or thirty in the rest of Braj (Premānand, interview, Brindavan, August 18, 1978). Śrīkṛṣṇamurāri Śarmā "Madhukar" presents comparable figures in his "Vartamān Brajrās Mañckā Uday," *Ras Vṛndāvan* 1:4 (1979), 22. Vasant Yāmdagni points out, however, that this includes short-lived and occasional companies. The more professional, continuing companies in

Braj would number about thirty (Yamadagni, personal communication, February 3, 1979).

9. Hein discusses Caitanyite and Nimbarkite claims in *Miracle Plays*, pp. 223–228. Other communities claim seminal contributions for their founders, as well. For claims on behalf of Vallabhācārya, see Svāmī Rāmsvarūp, "Conversation with Sri Swami Ram Swaroop Ji Sharma on the Ancient Heritage of the Ras Lila in Braj," unpublished paper, Brindavan, 1975, pp. 1–2. In regard to Hit Harivaṃś, see Vijayendra Snātak, *Rādhāvallabh Sampradāy: Siddhānt aur Sāhitya* (Delhi: National Publishing House, 1968), pp. 167–175.
10. This is the most general significance of the adaptation of the vocabulary of aesthetics for the systematic description of the life of devotion that was made by Rūp Gosvāmī in his *Bhaktirasāmṛtasindhu* and *Ujjvalanīlamaṇi*. See S. K. De, *Early History of the Vaiṣṇava Faith and Movement in Bengal* (Calcutta: K. L. Mukhopadhyaya, 1961), pp. 166–221; and Donna M. Wulff, "Drama as a Mode of Religious Realization: The *Vidagdhamādhava* of Rūpa Gosvāmin," Ph.D. dissertation, Harvard University, 1977, pp. 54–76.
11. Proportions vary seasonally. At Holī there is a special influx from the Punjab. Bengalis are in evidence from July to November. *Kārttik* (October–November) is a favorite time for Gujaratis, who are usually affiliated with the Vallabhite sect. In the bright fortnight of *Śrāvaṇ*, which comprises the greater part of the high monsoon season, pilgrims from Bundelkhand (extending from southern Uttar Pradesh into Madhya Pradesh) are probably the single most numerous group, with natives of Malwa, in Rajasthan, coming close behind. *Bhādrapad*, nearer the conclusion of the rainy season, attracts great numbers of Rajasthanis from the regions around Jaipur and Tonk: many are on their way farther east to Gaya and Jagannath Puri to perform rites for their ancestors. In all pilgrimage seasons people who live in or near Braj also take part (Rājkumār and Hit Vallabh Gosvāmī, interview, Mirzāpūrī Dharmśālā, Brindavan, August 18, 1978).
12. This duplication of tradition is caused at least in part by the fact that different communities have come to be established in different parts of Braj. Dāūjī and Gokul are Vallabhite, whereas Nandagaon and especially Barsana are predominantly Nimbarkite.
13. Victor Turner, "Pilgrimages as Social Processes," in Turner, *Dramas, Fields, and Metaphors* (Ithaca: Cornell University Press, 1974), pp. 171–172. Originally published as "The Center out There: Pilgrims' Goal," *History of Religions* 12:3 (1973), 195–196.

14. Radha's overwhelming presence in the temple of Rādhā Vallabh means that no reference is ever made there to Krishna's lordly side. Garuḍa, the divine bird who functions as Viṣṇu's vehicle, sits atop a great pillar and heralds the presence of Viṣṇu/Krishna in every Vaiṣṇavite temple in South India, and even in Brindavan this symbol of Krishna's divine side survives on the handle of the bell one rings at the time of *āratī*. In the Rādhā Vallabhī community, however, Garuḍa is altogether absent, as is the royal conch that figures significantly in the worship of such temples as that of Rādhā Ramaṇ. Though this inclination is particularly strong among Rādhā Vallabhites, these two symbols are also omitted in the temple of Bānke Bihārī.
15. The *banjārau līlā*.
16. The term *paṇḍā* is mostly likely a debasement of Sanskrit *paṇḍita*, "pundit." Sometimes, however, it is said to derive from Sanskrit *piṇḍadāna*, which refers to the offering of rice balls for the sustenance of one's deceased ancestors. The rite is thought to have particular effect if observed in great pilgrimage centers such as Gaya, Benares, and Mathura, and the Brahmins who direct these rites came to be called *paṇḍās* in the course of time. Their command of genealogy was necessitated by the nature of the *piṇḍadāna*. *Piṇḍadāna* is not traditionally practiced in Brindavan, but the term is used in the loose sense to refer to Brahmins who facilitate the aims of those who come to places of pilgrimage.
17. The oldest *paṇḍā* lineages are probably those belonging to the indigenous Sanāḍhya Brahmins. The next oldest are the Gauḍ Brahmins, with their connections to Bengal, and in more recent times Gautam and Sārasvat Brahmins (interview, G. C. Ghosh, Brindavan, August 17, 1978).
18. Many people in Brindavan disagree, but the pilgrim is not apt to find this out. The traditional site of Kāliya's hole is some distance away, beyond the old temple of Madan Mohan, where there are a number of *kadamb* trees. An old stone labels the *ghāṭ* as such. This site is identified with Kāliya's head, and there is another several miles upriver where one can "see"—again in stone—the end of his tail. The problem with the traditional site for Kāliya's hole *(kālīdah)* is that the river has changed course, leaving the spot dry most of the year, and unconvincing even in the rainy season. Hence in recent times *paṇḍās* have begun to refer to a spot where the Jumna currently flows as *kālīdah*. Puranic references to the story are *Harivaṃśa*, 55.1 ff.; *Viṣṇu Purāṇa* (Bombay: Nirnaya Sagara Press,

1914), 5.7; *Śrīmadbhāgavata* (Varanasi: Paṇḍit Pustakālay, *vikram* 2022 [A.D. 1965]), 10.16; *Padmapurāṇa*, edited by R. S. V. N. Mandlic (Poona: Ānandāśrama Press, 1893), 6.272.129–134. Subsequent references to the Puranas will cite these editions.

19. *Śrīmadbhāgavata* 10.22.10–20.
20. This avenue of interpretation is explored, for instance, in the commentary on the *Bhāgavata Purāṇa* that is most easily available today, that which accompanies the Gita Press edition. See Muṇilāl et al., translators and commentators, *Śrīmadbhāgavatamahāpurāṇam*, vol. 2 (Gorakhpur: Gita Press, 1971), 269–270.
21. Many in Brindavan would dispute that claim, because once again there is an alternate site some distance up the river. Circumambulatory tours of Braj identify the theft of the clothes, the *cīr haran*, with this latter site, and it is called specifically Cīr Ghāṭ. The *paṇḍā* at the Brindavan site argues, however, that scripture says the incident took place in Brindavan. This overlooks the fact that the term "Brindavan" in the Puranas connotes the *tulsī* forest generally, not a particular location in it, and certainly not a town. Such debates reveal the tenacity with which people hold that for every incident there must be one identifiable, accurate site; at the same time, however, they are aware that extraneous factors sometimes go into determining such sites.
22. The tale, though one of the best known in the epic, is not included in the older layers of the *Mahābhārata*, and is listed as an interpolation (to *Sabhā Parvan* 68.40) in the critical edition. Franklin Edgerton, ed., *The Mahābhārata*, vol. 2 (Poona: Bhandarkar Oriental Research Institute, 1944), p. 304.
23. The story is found in *Harivaṃśa* 67.1 ff.; *Viṣṇu Purāṇa* 5.16; *Śrīmadbhāgavata* 10.37.1–26, and *Padma Purāṇa* 6.272.149–157.
24. Margaret Stevenson, *The Rites of the Twice-Born* (New Delhi: Oriental Books Reprint Corporation, 1971; originally published 1920), p. 214. Diana L. Eck, "Banāras, City of Light: The Sacred Places and Praises of Kāśī," Ph.D. dissertation, Harvard University, 1976, pp. 398–400.
25. Cf. Diana L. Eck, "Gaṅgā: The Goddess in Hindu Sacred Geography," in John S. Hawley and Donna M. Wulff, eds., *The Divine Consort: Rādhā and the Goddesses of India* (Berkeley: Berkeley Religious Studies Series, forthcoming).
26. On the antiquity of the worship of Mount Govardhan, see Charlotte Vaudeville, "The Govardhan Myth in Northern India," *Indo-Iranian Journal* 22:1-2 (1980), 1–12. Also relevant is my "Krishna's

Cosmic Victories," *Journal of the American Academy of Religion* 47:2 (1979), 201–221.

27. Echoes of the *sāṃkhya* analysis of experience are evident here and elsewhere in Yogīrāj Brahmacārī's exposition. He accounted for the points of difference by explaining that his teaching was practical, whereas that of the *sāṃkhya* system was not. Interview, Brindavan, August 5, 1978.
28. Ibid.
29. Kiśorīlāl Gupta, ed., *Nāgarīdās (Granthāvalī)*, vol. 1 (Varanasi: Nāgarīpracāriṇī Sabhā, 1965), 16–31.
30. Even a standard work as recent as the sixteenth century fails to mention Brindavan, though it describes Mathura as that place in which the benefits of bathing in the Jumna are doubled. Richard Salomon, ed. and trans., "The Sāmānya-Praghaṭṭaka of Nārāyaṇa Bhaṭṭa's *Tristhalīsetu*: Critical Edition and Translation," Ph.D. dissertation, University of Pennsylvania, 1975, p. 371. For Śrīdhara's earlier statement of the same evaluation, see Salomon, "*Tīrtha-Pratyāmnāyaḥ*: Ranking of Hindu Pilgrimage Sites in Classical Sanskrit Texts," *Zeitschrift der Deutschen Morgenländischen Gesellschaft* 128:2 (1978), 105, 111.
31. This logic has been mitigated, however, in the tradition of the great circumambulatory route that binds together all of Braj, the *braj-yātrā*, for there one finds the familiar phenomenon according to which one sacred spot is said to exist in essence in another place. Thus Braj has its Ganges, its Badrīnāth, and so forth. On this pattern of "spacial transposition" see Eck, "Banāras," pp. 15ff. On the *braj-yātrā*, see Prabhudayāl Mītal, *Braj kī Sāṃskṛtik Yātrā* (Mathura: Sāhitya Sansthān, 1966).
32. Status, hierarchy, and morality continue to play a role in the earthly Brindavan; Brahmins officiate in the temples and on the stage, the wealthy and well-placed are given special seats at the *līlās*, and at the highest levels of society women are strictly secluded from public view.

Chapter II. The Birth of Krishna

1. Sculptures from the Upper Śivālaya at Badami and from Sādaḍī and Kekind seem clearly to represent Nanda and Yaśodā holding Krishna and Balarām. Some have argued that this is also the proper identification of sculptures from Deogarh, Badami, Pattadakal, Osian, Amritapura, Abu, and Citor, which would otherwise be

identified as Vasudev and Yaśodā exchanging their babies. See Hawley, "The Butter Thief," Ph.D. dissertation, Harvard University, 1977, chapter 2.

2. In older texts, the term Gokul refers not to a specific encampment but to the entire area. In current Braj usage, however, the term is usually more circumscribed, though the *rās līlās* sometimes preserve the older meaning.
3. In one aberrant account, Balarām is old enough to stand at his side and facilitate the exchange. This is the story as told by the Jain writer Puṣpadanta. Ludwig N. Alsdorf, tr., *Harivaṃśupurāṇa: Ein Abschnitt aus der Apabhraṃśa-Welthistorie "Mahāpurāṇa Tisaṭṭhimahāpurisaguṇālaṃkāra" von Puṣpadanta* (Hamburg: Friederichsen, de Gruyter, 1936), 85:3.
4. George Grierson, "Modern Hinduism and Its Debt to the Nestorians," *Journal of the Royal Asiatic Society* [hereafter *JRAS*], 1907, p. 323.
5. Ibid., pp. 316, 324–325.
6. See, for example, the work of Freud's student, Otto Rank, *The Myth of the Birth of the Hero,* translated by F. Robbins and Smith Ely Jelliffe (New York: Vintage, 1964; originally published 1914).
7. *JRAS*, 1907, p. 323.
8. Ibid., pp. 315–316.
9. J. Kennedy, "The Child Krishna, Christianity and the Gujars," *JRAS*, 1907, p. 980.
10. Ibid.
11. Arthur Berriedale Keith, "The Child Kṛṣṇa," *JRAS*, 1908, pp. 169–175.
12. The connection between Vallabhācārya and the southerner Viṣṇusvāmī is impossible to demonstrate, since we know nothing of the latter's work, and there is no reliable lineage to connect the two. The link between Caitanya and Madhva is equally fanciful, though it is possible that Mādhavendra Purī, Caitanya's teacher's teacher, provides a real connection to vernacular traditions in the South (see Friedhelm Hardy, "Mādhavêndra Purī: A Link between Bengal Vaiṣṇavism and South Indian *Bhakti*," *JRAS*, 1974, pp. 23–41.) And although Rāmānand seems to have had Śrī Vaiṣṇavite (and therefore southern) ancestors, the legendary association between him and Kabīr seems more than doubtful.
13. Aside from the isolated reference in the *Chāndogya Upaniṣad* to Krishna as son of Devakī *(devakīputra)*, which dates well before the time of Christ, there is the fact that the *Harivaṃśa* account,

dating in its completed form to something like the first to third centuries A.D., contains much more archaic material. See Daniel H. H. Ingalls, "The *Harivaṃśa* as a *Mahākāvya*," *Mélanges d'Indianisme à la mémoire de Louis Renou* (Paris: Éditions de Boccard, 1968), pp. 393–394. The fact that Śiśupāla's speech in the *Mahābhārata*, in which he refers disparagingly to various aspects of the childhood of Krishna, is retained in the critical edition and is therefore quite early is also relevant, even though he makes no specific reference to Krishna's birth. Edgerton, ed., *Mahābhārata*, vol. 2, 38.1–11.

14. Grierson, "Modern Hinduism," p. 316.
15. For a recent statement on the subject published in the West, see A. Faber-Kaiser, *Jesus Died in Kashmir* (London: Gordon and Cremonesi, 1977). A much more bizarre and extreme effort to tie Christian history to Hindu is that of Purushottam Nagesh Oak, *Christianity is Chrisn-nity* (New Delhi: Institute for Rewriting Indian History, 1978).
16. This is the view, for instance, of Śrīpād Bābā of Brindavan, personal communication, 1976.
17. On this point, see Edward C. Dimock, Jr., "Religious Biography in India: The 'Nectar of the Acts' of Caitanya," in Frank E. Reynolds and Donald Capps, eds., *The Biographical Process* (The Hague: Mouton, 1976), p. 113. Also Geoffrey Parrinder, *Avatar and Incarnation* (New York: Barnes and Noble, 1970), pp. 117–127, 209–213, 223–239.
18. One can perhaps see this most succinctly in the twenty-five *tattvas* of the *sāṃkhya* system.
19. An elegant exposition of the congruence between the importance of drama in Vaiṣṇavite theology and the prominence of its conception of the avatar is to be found in Donna M. Wulff, "Drama," pp. 14–25.
20. A standard formulation of this point is that of Rūp Gosvāmī, later taken up by Kṛṣṇadās Kavirāj. See O. B. L. Kapoor, *The Philosophy and Religion of Śrī Caitanya* (New Delhi: Munshiram Manoharlal, 1977), p. 107. Cf. also *Śrīmadbhāgavata* 1.3.28: *kṛṣṇastu bhagavān svayam*.
21. The remaining *gopīs* are understood as expansions *(kāyavyūha)* of Radha's energy, whereas she is the very nature of energy itself *(svarūpaśakti)*—energy being understood as female.
22. This is the system used in the *Bhaviṣya* and *Bhaviṣyottara Purāṇas*, upon which most subsequent treatments depend. See Albrecht

Weber, translated by E. Rehatsek, "On the Kṛishṇajanmâshṭamî, or Krishna's Birth-Festival," *Indian Antiquary* 6 (1887), 161–172. Gopāl Bhaṭṭ, however, places the date in *bhādrapad*. Gopāl Bhaṭṭ: *Haribhaktivilāsa, with the Digdarśinī Commentary of Sanātan Gosvāmī*, edited by Purīdās Dās (Mymensingh: Śacīnāth Rāychaudhurī, 1946), *vilāsa* 15.

23. The ritual texts place great emphasis on this point; fasting is one of the two major aspects of the festival. See Weber, "Kṛishṇajanmâshṭamî," p. 167.
24. That is, *kaccā* food is forbidden. See McKim Marriott, "Caste Ranking and Food Transactions: A Matrix Analysis," in M. Singer and B. Cohn, eds., *Structure and Change in Indian Society* (Chicago: Aldine, 1968), pp. 133–171.
25. The others are *durgāpūjā, mahāśivarātri*, and *dīpāvalī*. *Janmāṣṭamī* is part of another calendrical quartet as well—the four *jayantī*s. These mark the birth or appearance days of four of the avatars of Viṣṇu/Krishna: Narasiṃh, Vāman, Rām, and Krishna himself.
26. The restriction of such special *darśans* to once a year is a relatively new practice in this temple, and is what makes its worship distinctive today. I am grateful to Allan Shapiro of Columbia University and to Rādhā Dāsī of Brindavan for a description of this occasion, at which I have not yet myself been present.
27. The other occasion is the day commemorating the manifestation of Rādhā Ramaṇ to Gopāl Bhaṭṭ, which occurs on the full moon of the month of Vaiśākh. See Shapiro, "The Birth-celebration of Śrī Rādhāramaṇ in Vrindaban."
28. Again *vaiśākh purṇimā*, as in the previous note.
29. By Mahmud of Ghazni in his invasion of Mathura in 1017 A.D. and by Sikandar Lodi half a millennium later. Both Muslim rulers inflicted great destruction on Mathura. The exact extent of the damage to the temple of Keśav Dev, the temple on this site, however, is unknown, for it had been restored by the time Bernier and Tavernier visited the city in the middle of the seventeenth century. See Charlotte Vaudeville, "Braj, Lost and Found," *Indo-Iranian Journal* 18:3–4 (1976), 200–203.
30. This is a version of the second major feature of the festival to which the *Bhaviṣyottara Purāṇa* and related texts refer. There the central concern is the erecting of a small shed for the mother and child. Or the rite may be simplified so that a pot replaces the miniature shed and a golden image of Krishna is placed on top of it. Weber, "Kṛishṇajanmâshṭamî," pp. 173–174, 176–177. See also below.

31. The special honor paid to the mother of Krishna on this day is as old as the *Viṣṇu Purāṇa*, but there it is Devakī herself who receives the adulation of the text rather than Yaśodā. *Viṣṇu Purāṇa*, 5.2.7–21. In the *Harivaṃśa* this *stotra* is addressed to Nārāyaṇī.
32. Kānh is a vernacularization of the Sanskrit name Krishna, and the term used here, Kanhaiyā, is an affectionate diminutive for Kānh.
33. But not, its builders point out, unlike the sort of stage described in Bharata's ancient *Nāṭyaśāstra*.
34. These verses, in *caupāī* meter, are quoted from the beginning of the description of Krishna's birth as given in the *Braj Vilās* of Brajbāsī Dās, a mid-eighteenth century work upon which many of the *rās līlās* freely draw. The *rāsdhārīs* quote selectively, however—in this case four verses of six are recited—and it is rare for an entire *līlā* to be structured entirely on the basis of the *Braj Vilās*. Brajbāsī Dās, *Braj Vilās* (Bombay, Śrī Veṅkateśvara Press, 1876), p. 13.
35. The Sanskrit quotation is *Manusmṛti* 8.15. *Manusmṛti*, vol. 2 (Calcutta: Udayācal Press, 1971), 697. A *dohā* of Premānand transposes the sentiment into Braj Bhāṣā.
36. Although such sacrifices involved ritual slaughter in ancient times, it has been many centuries since this has been the case in Vaiṣṇav circles, and there is certainly no such implication here.
37. This is the beginning of one of the best known poems from the *Sūr Sāgar*. "Ratnākar" et al., eds., *Sūr Sāgar* (Varanasi: Nāgarīpracāriṇī Sabhā [hereafter NPS], 1972 [vol. 1] and 1976 [vol. 2]), *pad* 224.
38. All these formulations belong traditionally at the beginning of ritual sequences. The first set, concerning auspiciousness, are *maṅgala* verses. The second, concerning the Vivifier, or more literally Savitṛ, the Sun, is the *gāyatrī mantra* that is a required feature of the dawn and twilight prayers of Brahmins and other twice-born castes. For this I have used the translation of Raimundo Panikkar, *The Vedic Experience: Mantramañjarī* (Berkeley and Los Angeles: University of California Press, 1977), p. 38. The original is *Ṛg Veda* 3.62.10. *Svāhā* is a word of unclear etymology whose chanting accompanies the offering of some substance—usually *ghī* (clarified butter) or water—into the sacrificial fire. The Lord of Mount Kailāsa is Śiva.
39. This familiar quotation is usually said to derive from the *Manusmṛti*. Standard editions, however, do not contain it. The final line is a formulation that occurs a number of times in the *Mahābhārata*, but nowhere in connection with the other verses recited here.
40. These verses refer to an episode in the *Mahābhārata*, the so-called

"Pāṇḍavagītā," but are not part of the standard text. They are the words of Duryodhana responding to Krishna when the latter tries to persuade him that he and his Kaurava kinsmen should give their Pāṇḍava cousins back some of their land and prestige in order to avert total war. Duryodhana, the chief villain of the epic, refuses. See S. K. Belvalkar, ed., *The Mahābhārata*, vol. 7 (Poona: Bandarkar Oriental Research Institute, 1947), 6.119.

41. The reference is to the very early days of Kans's life, when his father called in Brahmins as a matter of course to determine the horoscope of the newborn boy. When it was revealed that the boy would bring disaster to his father, Ugrasen determined to set him in a basket lined with sacred *kans* grass (whence the popular derivation of his name) and set him afloat on the Jumna. Nārad soon intervened, so that no wrong done to Kans could justify any of his later actions, but Kans here recalls his father's unmagnanimous intentions. It was as a result of this act of deliverance that Nārad became, as some *rāsdhārī*s say, Kans's guru, a role he assumes later in the course of this *līlā*.
42. These lines and those included in the following speech of Kans were originally composed by Premānand for his *Gītā Nāṭak*, but the *rāsdhārī* has introduced them here, where they are also appropriate.
43. This is a particularly vivid example of a tendency one often sees in *bhakti* texts to parody the myopic misunderstanding that the Upaniṣadic identification of *ātman* and *brahman* makes possible. I am grateful to David Shulman for emphasizing the point.
44. As in Jewish ceremony, a Hindu wedding is solemnized under a temporary canopied pavilion *(maṇḍap)*; there can be no proper marriage without it. The fact that Kans would disregard the erection of a *maṇḍap* indicates his very great haste, and reminds the audience of his boorish distaste for ritual propriety.
45. It is customary for the groom to return to the home of his in-laws within a week of his marriage in order to untie one strand in the temporary pavilion that has been erected for the wedding. After that the marriage pavilion can be dismantled. The ceremony is called *maḍhā jhā̃knā*, "glancing again at the pavilion."
46. *Braj Vilās*, p. 13. The first two verses comprise a *dohā* and the last two a *soraṭhā*. These meters always occur together in the *Braj Vilās* because they balance one another so well: in the former the causura falls slightly after the middle of the line and in the latter slightly

before. The *rāsdhārīs* quote *dohās* and *soraṭhās* from the *Braj Vilās* with great frequency because they are pivotal. Brajbāsī Dās uses them to announce or summarize narrative incidents, and fills in the details with *caupāīs*.

47. This expression carries a reminder of the famous incident in which Śiva reduced his adversary Kāma to ash with the concentrated, laser-like heat he had stored in his third eye by means of his ascetic austerities. The third eye, the eye of inner vision, is said to appear in the center of the forehead of those who are adept in contemplation. Kans's forehead mark is intended to remind us of this piercing vision of Śiva, to whom he declares himself devoted. Through his figure of speech here he arrogates to himself the powers of the god himself.

48. *Braj Vilās*, p. 13.

49. Dilīp was the ruler made legendary by his devotion to the cow. Although he was able to endure twenty-one days standing at attention with his bow drawn for her protection, he, like all mortals, had to die, and that is the reason for his being cited here. Svāmī Natthī Lāl maintained in an interview on August 2, 1978, that this is all that is intended in the citations that follow, but others feel there is more implied in this traditional list. Droṇ was the Brahmin who instructed both warring factions in the *Mahābhārata* in archery, and was later drawn into the battle himself. He would have been invincible but for the fact that Dhṛṣṭadyumna (not Karṇa, as here), in order to avenge his own father's death at the hands of Droṇ, met Droṇ in combat with the news that his son had been killed. Droṇ was so unnerved that he could not fight. His death may be celebrated here because he is said upon death to have given off a glow as intense as that of the sun and to have been assumed into the heavens. Rāvaṇ is mentioned because, though the archenemy of Rām, he was nonetheless of heroic stock. Furthermore, when Rām ultimately killed him, the divine touch transported him to the ranks of the saved. Vasudev holds out the same promise, implicitly, to Kans. Indeed, we in the audience, knowing who it is that is to be born, are aware that the parallel is closer than even Vasudev imagines, for Krishna is the avatar to follow Rām, and Kans is his greatest enemy. The mention of Bali confirms this pattern as another archenemy of Viṣṇu/Krishna, this time in his dwarf avatar, who was killed and saved with the same blow.

50. *Braj Vilās*, p. 14.

51. Ibid.
52. The threefold repetition of a promise solemnizes it.
53. *Braj Vilās*, p. 14.
54. NPS 713. This song is customarily sung in the *janmāṣṭamī* season at the temple of Rādhā Ramaṇ.

Chapter III. The Theft of the Flute

1. The motif of the stealing of the flute, though it does not have puranic sanction, is not new. It is included in Rūp Gosvāmī's sixteenth-century drama *Vidagdhamādhava*, where Radha is also involved, but in rather a different way. See Wulff, "Drama," pp. 109–114.
2. In ancient times the interdependence of gods and humans was clearly recognized in discussions of the nature of sacrifice. See, for instance, Thomas J. Hopkins, *The Hindu Religious Tradition* (Encino, Calif.: Dickinson, 1971), pp. 32–35. In modern times one frequently hears quotations of a *sākhī* attributed to Kabīr in which the poet asks whether God is superior to the guru or vice versa, since without the guru there would be no access to God. See, for example, Bālakṛṣṇa Śarmā "Navīn," ed., *Cayanikā* (Calcutta: Macmillan, 1973), p. 27.
3. W. Norman Brown has studied the act of truth in various articles. The most recent is "Duty as Truth in Ancient India," originally published in *Proceedings of the American Philosophical Society* 116:3 (1972), 252–268, and reprinted in Rosane Rocher, ed., *India and Indology: Selected Articles by W. Norman Brown* (Delhi: Motilal Banarsidass, 1978), pp. 102–119. An earlier treatment is that of E. W. Burlingame, "The Act of Truth (Saccakiriyā): A Hindu Spell and Its Employment as a Psychic Motif in Hindu Fiction," *JRAS*, 1917, pp. 429–467.
4. The butter-thief *līlās* bear comparison with the flute *līlā* in this respect. Krishna's soulful singing of the song, "I didn't eat the butter, Ma," turns the tide and concludes the play in the *maṇikhambh* and *mākhan corī līlās*. The force his sentiment has upon those who love him, once his situation is embattled, makes all the difference and constitutes an emotional "act of truth," whatever juridical distortions it may entail.
5. All of the *līlās* in the *mān līlā* family have this as their subject, as do the recently composed *kākmāl* and *subal beś līlās*.
6. As in the *gaure gvāl* and *subal beś līlās*.
7. As in the *anurāg līlā*.

8. The *maināvārī* and *rangrejin līlās*. These are briefly described in Norvin Hein, *Miracle Plays*, p. 176. Other plot summaries in Hein's list reveal a host of similar motifs.
9. Cf. also the *mundarī* or *mundariyā corī līlā*, summarized by Hein, p. 174.
10. This is the point at which the theology of Brindavan aligns itself most closely with the great Indian traditions of nondualism, but many theologians of Brindavan would be reluctant to stress the connection.
11. The *dān līlā*.
12. The *naukā līlā*.
13. The *maṇikhambh, mākhan corī* (or *corī mādhurī*), and *yamalārjun uddhār* (or *ūkhal bandhan*) *līlās*.
14. Further exploration of this topic may be found in Hawley, "The Butter Thief," Ph.D. dissertation, Harvard University, 1977, pp. 622–673, and "Thief of Butter, Thief of Love," *History of Religions* 18:3 (1979), 203–220.
15. Discussions of the theology of the Rādhāvallabh Sampradāy are scarce in English and other European languages. See Charles S. J. White, *The Caurāsī Pad of Śrī Hit Harivaṁś* (Honolulu: University Press of Hawaii, 1977), pp. 28–31. The standard work is in Hindi: Snātak's *Rādhāvallabh Sampradāy*. English translations of the literature of the Rādhā Vallabhīs may be found in White, *Caurāsī Pad*, pp. 55–108, and in Growse, *Mathurā*, pp. 201–206.
16. This school, whose philosophical position is most prominently formulated in the philosophy of Jīv Gosvāmī, describes the relation of Radha and Krishna as "inconceivable difference and nondifference," *acintya-bhedābheda*. On the philosophy of Jīv Gosvāmī, see De, *Vaiṣṇava Faith*, pp. 254–480; Surendranath Dasgupta, *A History of Indian Philosophy*, vol. 4 (Delhi: Motilal Banarsidass, 1975; originally published 1922), pp. 396–437.
17. Lakṣmī, the consort of Viṣṇu, is Radha's heavenly antetype, just as Viṣṇu is Krishna's.
18. *Phulvārī līlā*.
19. *Rādhācaranspars* and *kākmāl līlās*.
20. Radha has not always been accorded such exaltation, and the story of her rise from an unnamed favorite among the *gopīs* to her present position is a long and significant one. Two recent studies on the subject are those of Barbara Stoler Miller, "Rādhā: Consort of Kṛṣṇa's Vernal Passion," *Journal of the American Oriental Society* 95:4 (1975), 655–671, and C. Mackenzie Brown, "The Theology of

Rādhā in the Purāṇas," in Hawley and Wulff, *The Divine Consort*, forthcoming.

21. Kālindī is another name for the Jumna. Krishna Dās is the name of the poet, which is typically "sealed," as tradition says *(chāp)*, into the last line of a *pad* as an oral signature.
22. That is, the flute has the power to call all nature to life and responsiveness as it plays, and also to reduce the women of Braj to a state tantamount to lifelessness, in which they lose all power of volition and either stand transfixed or follow dumbly where the flute leads.
23. Brahmā, the Hindu god most closely associated with the creation of the world, is pictured as seated upon a great lotus whose stem emerges from the navel of recumbent Viṣṇu. Brahmā has four faces, one for each of the directional quadrants; they symbolize his control over the created world. The word translated here as "mouths" *(mukh)* means "faces" as well. Brahmā's "preaching" *(upadeś)* refers to his act of issuing the Vedas, of which there are also four. This creation by word and knowledge (which is the literal meaning of the word "Veda") is as primordial as the process of physical creation or emanation, and Brahmā is the author of both. The flute's eight mouths include seven finger-holes for pitch and an opening for the player's mouth.
24. Brahmā's lotus throne is founded upon Viṣṇu, whom Brajbāsīs identify entirely with Krishna. Hence the comparison made here is apt: the *gopī* points out another enthronement that has Krishna as its base, and not one but two.
25. Each Hindu divinity is associated with a particular vehicle, and Brahmā's is the *haṃsa*, a species of goose that flies as high as 35,000 feet, and therefore has the reputation of being able to fly over even the Himalayas. In the heights of that range lies a lake whose name is Mānas, where the *haṃsa* is reputed to quench its thirst. The word *mānas*, however, has a second and more common meaning: "spiritual," or in present-day parlance, "psychological." It is this term that the word "spiritual" translates, connoting the sense both of that rendering and of the otherworldly Himalayan lake. "The Master of Fate" refers to Brahmā, who is designated here by the term "fate" itself, *vidhi*, which he is traditionally thought to command.
26. The wearing of the sacred thread *(yajñopavīta)* is a privilege accorded only the members of the three upper-caste groupings in Hindu society: Brahmins, Kṣatriyas and Vaiśyas. It is draped over the left shoulder and falls to the waist on the right side of the body.

The second distinguishing mark of these upper or "twice-born" castes is that they traditionally keep one lock of their hair uncut, so that it forms a braid that emerges from the crown of the head. In south India particularly, more hair than this may remain uncut, but at least that braid is essential. Because Brahmā is the progenitor and patron of the Brahmin caste, he too is thought of as wearing both the thread and the braid. These symbols of purity and caste identity are allowed to lapse in the life of a Brahmin only if he should choose to become an ascetic: then everything signifying his earthly station is abandoned.

27. The first line of this *pad* is its refrain *(ṭek)*. It has been marked off from the rest of the poem, here and elsewhere, in order to signify that unlike other verses the *ṭek* is customarily repeated during the recitation of a *pad*. Most of these repetitions are at the discretion of the singer, but it is almost obligatory for the refrain or some portion of it to be recalled at the end of the poem.
28. Krishna. Literally, the one who leads the mind astray or who intoxicates the mind.
29. *Grah*, "planet." Often Brajbāsīs will speak about a troubling situation in terms of astrological influences. "What planet have I fallen under?" means "what's the matter with me?" Here, however, the expression is taken in its literal sense as well, and the joke is that the source of the malady, that which casts the evil influence, is far closer at hand than the heavens: it is in Krishna's hands.
30. *Hariyā*, a cow who expends all her energy wandering from one grazing place to another rather than satisfying herself with what lies before her.
31. Just as *bābā* is a familiar honoric for an elder, so *dādā* (translated here as "brother") can refer in a vaguely deferential way to someone only slightly older. Mansukhā frequently uses this term when he refers to Krishna. Equally frequent, however, is the term of abuse, *sāre* (Hindi *sālā*), which both Mansukhā and Krishna occasionally use in addressing one another. It is a familiar term that I have translated variously as "ass," "stupid," and "idiot" below. Literally, however, it refers to the brother of one's wife, with whom a strong joking relationship pertains. In a Hindu marriage the wife is clearly subordinate to her husband, and so by implication is the rest of her family to that of the man she marries. Traditionally, her brother becomes the butt of the banter that this situation can give rise to. He becomes the victim of a great deal of friendly abuse, particularly since it is the brother's obligation to protect his sister's

virtue, and the man who issues the insult implies that she is sleeping with him. Hence "wife's brother" becomes a general term of light abuse.

32. That is, worth is intrinsic.
33. This expression, *dān dakṣiṇā*, refers to the fact that Mansukhā is a Brahmin; one offers Brahmins food on various ritual occasions, and they are notorious for the amounts they shamelessly consume.
34. His use of the term "pundit" in the feminine gender is an odd-sounding locution. Such a term is not out of the question—*paṇḍitāin* would be the correct form—but it is exceptional. Mansukhā's invented term, however, expresses an ironic tone of voice: he denigrates her pretensions by ridiculing the very idea of a female guru.
35. The fun in this is that Mansukhā is too thickheaded to understand that the flute and the *gopīs* are two radically different types of female personalities, two kinds of love Krishna has. Literal-minded, he has taken at face value the jealousy that the *gopīs* direct against the flute as if she were a rival co-wife to Krishna. This leads him to believe that these two loves of Krishna are interchangeable. If one is gone, she can simply be replaced by another: any *gopī* can become *banśī*, the flute. The mention of a two-piped flute *(algozā)* is prompted by the fact that the *gopī* from whom he is proposing it be crafted will have two legs: each one will become a pipe.
36. In the songs at the beginning of the *līlā* we heard a few of the charges the *gopīs* level against the flute. Sometimes they can be even more extreme. The flute has grounds for criticizing the *gopīs*, too, however. Their respectability is clearly compromised by the fact that they run out on their husbands in order to be with Krishna. The *gopīs'* riposte to that, as we have heard, is that the responsibility for such whoring—if such it is to be called—should be laid at the feet of the flute itself, which is the very spirit and impetus of the love that defies the boundaries of propriety.
37. *Mama brāhmaṇa sahasra prabhāva tau naṭatama kaṭatama priyā śānti naimā.*
38. There is humor in this remark. Mansukhā's free associations have led him to list among Krishna's actions one that hardly redounds to the credit of anyone imitating it. The eating of leftover food is abhorred by any person of stature in Hindu society, though it matters not at all to friendly, egalitarian Krishna.
39. A demoness deputed by Kans, originally in the form of a bird, to become a woman upon arrival in Gokul and suckle Krishna to death at her poisonous breasts. Krishna, however, was impervious and sucked every ounce of lifeblood out of her.

40. This is the art of those who have the power to control snakes, from snake-charmers to curers of snakebite. Such practitioners are said to "nail" snakes into a state of docile trance.
41. Heavenly musicians.
42. *Pā*, the fifth tone of the scale. The implication is that it is higher and therefore more audible than the lower tone an elephant would make.
43. In the original the correct sequence should be *sā re gā mā pā dhā nī sā*. Mansukhā sings instead *sā re ga dhā pā nī pī jā*, that is, *sāre gadhā pānī pī jā*.
44. *Bhojan bhaṭṭā laṭṭh gavār*. The first two words of this expression refer disparagingly again to the gluttony of some Brahmins. A *bhojan bhaṭṭ* is an unlearned Brahmin who is in the business, so to speak, only for the food.
45. They combine their familiar way of greeting him as *lālā* Mansukhā *lāl* ("dear friend Mansukhā") with a much more respectful form of address, and the odd juxtaposition suggests that there is more in their approach than meets the eye.
46. Literally, "may you remain fortunate" *(saubhāgyavatī)*. The unfortunate woman is the one whose husband has died, leaving her a widow. She is inauspicious because she is an anomaly: a widow is cut adrift by her husband's death from that which ties her to the structures of society, the man she serves.
47. Even Mansukhā would not be so cruel as directly to wish widowhood upon anyone; there would be no humor in it. He does, however, clearly imply it, and that is the onus of his remark here.
48. Sarasvatī is goddess of music and learning, hence Mansukhā's patroness as a student of the flute. He exalts himself by declaring himself her devotee.
49. *Malāī kai pūā*. A *pūā* is a simple sweet made with fried wheat dough to which sugar or jaggery has been added.
50. Mansukhā is always misspeaking and mishearing. Here he hears the word *saverau* ("morning") as if it were *bakherau* ("quarrel").
51. Sūrya Nārāyaṇ is the sun considered as a divinity.
52. The meter used here combines a *rolā* and a *dohā* in the manner of the *bhramargīt* of Nanda Dās.
53. The earth, the atmosphere, and the heavens form the universe in this most common designation of what we would call "the world." It is significant and typical that Hindus should regard it as multiple and tiered, hence doubly significant that the flute should be said to have gone beyond all three realms. The word used to express this idea is *tāran*, the familiar designation for transcending (literally,

"crossing beyond") the concerns that activate the world as we know it. The reference to Śiva, the great deity of asceticism and gnosis, in the following verse is an allusion to the strenuous efforts of renunciators and spiritual practitioners in pursuit of such transcendence. The sense is that music leads to a level of release to which the assaults of disciplined religious practice have no access.

54. Here, as in much of the play, the term *banśī* ("bamboo flute") is used as a proper name, though there is something approaching synecdoche in relation to the term Muralī, which is always a proper name.
55. Everywhere in India one sees women picking up cowdung and patting it into cakes that can be dried out and used for fuel. It is a perfectly wholesome but rather lowly occupation, and Krishna's mention of it here is a little disparaging.
56. Syāmā, the feminine counterpart of Syām, is a designation for Radha. The terms *śrī* and *jū* (Hindi *jī*) are honorific, and are customarily employed when referring to or addressing Radha.
57. Kiśorī, meaning an adolescent girl, is also an epithet of Radha. Again the double honorific is employed.
58. Logically this line, the refrain, belongs in Krishna's mouth, but the *gopīs* sing it too, since it follows stanzas for which they have responsibility.
59. This is a reference to the episodes in which Krishna stole butter from the *gopīs*. He suggests that their motive in stealing the flute may be retaliation for his earlier act of thievery.
60. The courtroom dialogue in song that begins here is Premānand's invention, and is set entirely in *caupāī* meter.
61. Giridhārī is the epithet for Krishna meaning "lifter of the mountain."
62. Murārī: Krishna as the slayer (literally "enemy") of the demon Mura. See *Viṣṇu Purāṇa* 4.29.

Chapter IV. The Great Circle Dance

1. The earliest description of this battle between Krishna and Kāmdev that I know is provided by the sixteenth-century Braj poet Nanda Dās in his *Rāspañcādhyāyī*. See Brajratnadās, ed., *Nandadās Granthāvalī* (Varanasi: Nāgarīpracāriṇī Sabhā, 1958), 1.97–100. The passage is translated in R. S. McGregor, *Nanddas: The Round Dance of Krishna and Uddhav's Message* (London: Luzac, 1973), p. 72.
2. Though the semantic fields of *kām* and *prem* occasionally overlap

even in the *līlās* themselves (see, for example, note 41 below), they are usually held quite separate. Kṛṣṇadās Kavirāj formulated the distinction with classic brevity, stating that *kām* has to do with love for oneself and *prem* with love for the other, specifically Krishna. *Caitanya Caritāmṛta*, edited by Syāmdās, vol. 1 (Brindavan, Śrīharinām-Sankīrttan Maṇḍal, 1974), 1.4.141. For more on the relation between *kām* and *prem*, see Edward C. Dimock, Jr., *The Place of the Hidden Moon* (Chicago: University of Chicago Press, 1966), pp. 161–164, and Lee Siegel, *Sacred and Profane Dimensions of Love in Indian Traditions as Exemplified in the "Gītagovinda" of Jayadeva* (Delhi: Oxford University Press, 1978), pp. 68–69.

3. See Wendy Doniger O'Flaherty, *Asceticism and Eroticism in the Mythology of Śiva* (Delhi: Oxford University Press, 1975).
4. The fullest example is the *śankar līlā*, which has been translated by Darius Swann, "The Braj Rās Līlā," in Farley Richmond, ed., "Theatre in India," *Journal of South Asian Literature* 10:2–4 (1975), 21–44.
5. This may also be a function of the fact that even by comparison to *kṛṣṇajanmāṣṭamī*, the festival of *rās pūrṇimā* is recent, whereas Hindu religious calendars in general, as Charlotte Vaudeville has observed, are extremely conservative. Lecture, "Krishna and Devī," Harvard University, June 15, 1978.
6. This theological position was first worked out in the *Ujjvalanīlamaṇi* of Rūp Gosvāmī.
7. Premānand, interview, Brindavan, August 18, 1978.
8. These are the opening *ślokas* of the *Mahāvāṇī*. See Rājendra Prasād Gautam, *Śrīharivyāsadevācārya aur Mahāvāṇī* (Brindavan: Bhakti Sāhitya Sadan, 1974), part 2, p. 1. This invocation was chosen as especially appropriate for quotation at the beginning of the *līlā* because it focuses on the interwining of Radha and Krishna. This is obvious in the translation of the first half of the passage, but it is implicit in the second, as well. The first two consonants in the Sanskrit word that begins the last line, *kalātmānam* (referring to Krishna's beauty), if written as a single ligature "kl" in devanagari script, interlock and signify the hidden unity of the divine pair. I am indebted to Premānand for explaining points such as this and for supplying the references for most of the quotations in this *līlā* other than those drawn from the *Bhāgavata Purāṇa* and *Bhagavad Gītā*. Where no reference is given, the poetry is anonymous, either traditional with the *rāsdhārīs* or a more recent currency. Premānand, interviews, Brindavan, August 8–19, 1978.

9. A *dohā* of Nārāyaṇ Svāmī.
10. The word translated as "the devoted" is actually *rasik*, which derives from *ras* and has a comparable range of meanings, everything from "dandy" to "connoisseur" and "esthete." For Vaiṣṇavs it carries the additional connotation that every true worshiper is a *rasik*, since to worship is to taste the mood of Braj, to appreciate Krishna's *līlā*. Krishna, too, is a *rasik*, tasting what the *gopī*s bring. Thus characteristically the divine and the human are brought within the same circle. It is only Krishna, however, who is called *rasikarāy*, the sovereign esthete. The Jumna, considered divine in Braj, earns a similar title, *rasarāj*, as sovereign of liquids, and Krishna is accorded the same title as sovereign of the emotions.
11. Brajbāsīs commonly acknowledge the Jumna and Mount Govardhan as the two ancient foci of worship in Braj, and the river is always conceived as a woman, as ancient sculpture and textual sources confirm. In the last four hundred years or so, Vaiṣṇav artists have indicated the Jumna's preeminent position among women by dressing her in Moghul garments very similar to those worn otherwise only by Krishna himself.
12. A *savaiyā* of Hare Krishna, a contemporary poet living in Brindavan. "Death" is Yama, popularly conceived as Yamunā's (the Jumna's) brother. Hence it is thought that she can intercede with him. "Life" is *bhav*, the sea of existence in which living beings are caught, and is not at all an auspicious presence.
13. These are the soft alluvial sands *(pulin)* that become visible when the river retreats from its monsoon high mark.
14. This *dohā* and the three that follow are compositions of Mādhurī Dās.
15. *Pad* of Brajlāl Bahurā.
16. Most of the allusions in this catalogue will be lost on the average spectator. Simple folk may understand that a reference to the left implies devious or complex behavior, in this case especially the anger of the woman slighted in love *(mān)*: she holds her lover at bay, yet inwardly desires him. The right, by contrast, suggests the sort of *gopī* who is straightforward and cheerful in the expression of her emotions. Some of the other categories, however, require refined theological training to be appreciated fully, for Premānand samples here some of the various types of *gopī*s described in the third chapter of Rūp Gosvāmi's *Ujjvalanīlamaṇi*. The possibility that some of the girls are unmarried is discussed by Jīv Gosvāmī in his *Gopālacampū*. Due to the fact that Brahmā once stole away the

real cowherds of Braj for a year and Krishna left copies in their place, any girl who married in that period of time will not in fact have married, but will only think herself to have done so. Thus, although all the *gopīs* consider themselves unmarried by worldly standards and share the *parakīyā bhāv* that that implies, a number of them are in fact virgins until they meet Krishna: they marry him first *(svīyā, svakīyā)*. The distinction between *gopīs* who are eternally present with Krishna *(nityasakhī)* and those who have earned his presence by virtue of a regimen of purification in past lives is also elaborated by Rūp Gosvāmī. The former group comprises Radha first and foremost, and secondarily the eight principal *sakhīs (aṣṭasakhī)* who express facets of her personality that a single personage cannot present. These eight then multiply by eights to an uncountable number. The latter group *(sādhanasiddhāsakhī)* rise from humanity, as it were, rather than being emanations of divinity, and their number is also vast.

17. Two *dohās* of Premānand, giving expression to the theological formulation of the Caitanya school that Radha is Krishna's *hlādinī śakti*. On this notion see Edward C. Dimock, Jr., *The Place of the Hidden Moon* (Chicago: University of Chicago Press, 1966), pp. 132–134, and Shrivatsa Goswami, "Radha: The Play and Perfection of *Rasa*," in Hawley and Wulff, eds., *The Divine Consort*, forthcoming.
18. This and the other verses in this speech make up collectively a *savaiyā* of Premānand's own composition.
19. This is a pun on a word very similar to the name Madan. The term is *mardan*, and it is used both to mean "destroy" and "powerful man," in this case specifically "lady killer."
20. "Whey" translates the term *chāch*, the watery substance left over after curd is churned into butter. The least valuable component in milk, it is sometimes simply thrown away. Hence it is remarkable that, as a familiar verse by Raskhān relates, the *gopīs* can make Krishna dance just to obtain a little of it from their hands.
21. This *kavitt* of Premānand alludes to four stories related in the puranic literature. The first and third are well known: the story of Śiva and Pārvatī is related in the introduction to this *līlā*, and that of Indra and Ahalyā is described in John Dowson, *A Classical Dictionary of Hindu Mythology and Religion, Geography, History, and Literature* (London: Routledge and Kegan Paul, 1968), pp. 8–9, and Vettam Mani, *Purāṇic Encyclopaedia* (Delhi: Motilal Banarsidass, 1975), p. 17. The second and fourth are tales with an astrolog-

ical significance. The *Śivamahimnastotra* tells how Brahmā became smitten with the beauty of his daughter Sarasvatī and began chasing after her. She transformed herself into an antelope and he followed suit, whereupon Śiva, incensed at the impropriety, hunted down the male with his trident. This scene can be observed in the heavens as the "antelope" constellation *(mṛgaśilā nakṣatra)*. Further on this and related episodes, see Siddheśvarśāstrī Citrāv, *Bhāratvarṣīya Prācīn Caritrakoś* (Poona: Bhāratīya Caritrakoś Maṇḍal, 1964), pp. 528–531. The story involving the improprieties of the moon god Candā (Sanskrit, Candra) with Tārā, the wife of Bṛhaspati, the preceptor of all the gods, is told in Mani, *Encyclopaedia*, p. 171. Hindus associate the tale with the asterism governing Wednesday, Buddh, who is understood as the offspring of this illicit union.

22. The reference to Rudra recalls the story of Śiva and Pārvatī to which Kāmdev has just alluded: Rudra is understood as identical with Śiva. There is no story associated with Sūrya, the sun, and Premānand's script does not mention him: the name simply rolled off Kāmdev's tongue because he had just mentioned the moon (Candā). The story of the sage Parāśar is similar in pattern to all the others: he has been bewitched by the beauty of the daughter of a humble boatman in the course of being ferried across a river. Her name was Satyavatī, and their son was the sage Vyās. The story of King Viśvāmitra's attraction for the commoner Śakuntalā is told in Kālidāsa's play of that name. The mention of Vasiṣṭha seems to be, like that of Sūrya, a mistake, since the marriage of the sage Vasiṣṭha to Arundhatī is a model of conjugal fidelity. Perhaps Vasiṣṭha came to mind because of his close association in legend with Viśvāmitra.
23. *Kavitt* of Premānand. It derives its particular force from the fact that blackening the face with ash and shaving the head are not only practices familiar with yogis but also marks of surrender that traditionally must be adopted by a party defeated in battle.
24. This continues the *savaiyā* referred to in note 18.
25. Sītā is the wife of Rām.
26. Golok. See Chapter I, note 3.
27. Evidently the actor playing Kāmdev had a small lapse of memory and supplied nonsense names to replace two he had forgotten, namely *mādan* and *śoṣaṇ*, "bewitching" and "absorbing," on which see Mani, *Encyclopaedia*, p. 379. The important thing was that the speech continue uninterrupted, which it did.
28. A name of Krishna.

29. This is the *cīr haran līlā* recounted in *Śrīmadbhāgavata* 10.22. It was only after the *gopīs* came out of the water naked before Krishna that he granted their wish that he become their husband by promising them the *rās* dance. Their willingness to come before him without any intervening presence or conceit served as a test of their readiness to enter into the intimacy of the *rās*.
30. These are listed in the *Kāmasūtra*, which, as the name implies, is Kāmdev's textbook. Richard Burton and F. F. Arbuthnot, trs., *The Kama Sutra of Vatsyayana* (New York: Capricorn Books, 1963), pp. 71–73.
31. *Dohā* of Premānand.
32. The reference is to the phrase *tā rātriḥ* at the beginning of the description of the *rās līlā* in the *Bhāgavata Purāṇa*. *Śrīmadbhāgavata*, 10.29.1.
33. A *pad* of Premānand, which is recited in segments of various lengths at relevant points throughout this soliloquy.
34. The last clause is not in the original. I add it here as in the case of each of the arguments that follow, to summarize and clarify the argument.
35. Literally *mallikā*, a flower similar to jasmine, but like the *rāt kī rānī* in that its fragrance persists into the night.
36. Here, as in all the points that follow, with the exception of the fifth, Krishna characterizes not only Kām's love but also his own with the common designation *kām*.
37. *Nirgun prem*, a somewhat surprising term in the context of Vaiṣṇavite theology, and one that *saguṇ* theologians have sometimes therefore interpreted as meaning the love that lacks any demeaning or unfavorable quality *(na heya guṇāḥ nirguṇaḥ)*.
38. In the original, simply *ras*. Cf. *Taittirīya Upaniṣad* 2.7.1: *raso vai saḥ*, "he (or as Brahman, it) is *ras*."
39. The contrast with Kāmdev's arrows is obvious. The understanding of the *rās* as medicine is enunciated in the final verse describing the event, the *phalaśruti*. *Śrīmadbhāgavata* 10.33.40.
40. This is the familiar contrast between two rhyming terms, *yog* and *bhog*.
41. The term is not *kām*, as one might expect, but *lok prem* used in conjunction with *viṣayatā*.
42. *Kānt bhāv*.
43. The term *var* has two distinct senses, both of which are appropriate here: "groom" ("husband") and "boon." The latter refers to the vow of austerity the *gopīs* undertook to appeal to the goddess Kātyāyanī that Krishna be granted them as a husband. It is Yoga-

māyā who facilitates this Vaiṣṇav analogue to the Christian doctrine of election.

44. This interpretation of the *Bhāgavata Purāṇa* was first advanced by the great commentator Śrīdhara. We have already mentioned one use of this interpretation by Jīv Gosvāmī, but it is consistently and generally upheld in the Caitanya school as a way, despite the theology of *parakīyā bhāv*, to keep the savor of the occasion, its *ras*, pure. It is an effort to make sure that Krishna does not consort with used women. Their other marital relations pertain only to copies of themselves; in reality they are with Krishna. See Kapoor, *Śrī Caitanya*, pp. 221–225.
45. Premānand explains that this number is a great multiple of the minimal figure established in *Bhāgavata Purāṇa* 10.20.44. He interprets the compound *vanitāśatayūthapaḥ*, "women in group of hundreds," as meaning minimally three hundred, since a group must contain at least three members. Otherwise it would be called a pair, *dvandva*. Premānand, interview, Brindavan, August 9, 1978.
46. This verse, a *kavitt* by the local poet Bihārī, continues below.
47. According to the Hindu understanding, time runs in great cycles reflecting the diurnal rhythms of the gods, now sleeping, now waking. The world dissolves in the former and regenerates in the latter. See Heinrich Zimmer, *Myths and Symbols in Indian Art and Civilization*, edited by Joseph Campbell (New York: Pantheon, 1946 [Bollingen Series VI]), pp. 3–22.
48. In Caitanyite theology, Brindā, the *tulsī* plant personified, acts as facilitator of the *rās* in her capacity as goddess of place (that is, of Brindavan).
49. Premānand is thinking of three forms of beguiling feminine energy. The first, and the one of which all others are but expressions, is Radha herself: she is primordial. She precedes all creation, and in her union with Krishna is contained the possibility of differentiation, as well. The second is Yogamāyā, who cooperates with Krishna not only in the elaboration of the *rās līlā* but in spinning out all of creation. It too is a grand *līlā*, a great game. The third and most particular beguiler is the flute, whose action is confined to Brindavan, but there it is all-powerful and omnipresent.
50. *Dohā* of Premānand.
51. This fragment and the verses that follow *(caupāīs)* are of Premānand's own composition.
52. The comparison is between the arrows that form the pointed corners of Krishna's eyes and those in Kāmdev's quiver. The latter

have to be consciously loosed, but the former, much tinier and more subtle, act of their own power. Simply to see them is to be wounded.

53. *Caupāī* of Premānand.
54. Fragment from a *caupāī* of Premānand.
55. In Sanskrit, *Śrīmadbhāgavata* 10.29.18.
56. *Savaiyā* of Premānand. The garment to which Krishna refers is the long cloth that he wears hanging from his neck and shoulders, ready to offer protection against the elements. Krishna's scarf is yellow and has a special name on that account: *pītāmbar*. The direct reference to the *gopīs*' sweat and haste in the third verse is an innovation in performance. Premānand's original reads:

    It's only from drinking the dust of your feet
    that all of Brindavan has burst into bloom.

57. *Savaiyā* of Premānand. It continues through the poetic dialogue between the *gopīs* and Krishna.
58. In Sanskrit. *Śrīmadbhāgavata* 10.29.27. In the complete version of Premānand's play, all ten verses of the speech Krishna delivers to the *gopīs* on this occasion are quoted. Here, however, only certain ones have been selected, for the sake of brevity and because the dialogue must be mastered by young boys.
59. An extended *savaiyā* of Premānand intended to convey the force of *Śrīmadbhāgavata* 10.29.18–41 in the vernacular. It continues throughout Krishna's challenge to the *gopīs*, and records their response as well.
60. *Brahmacārī*. In this first of the classical four stages of life a man adopts the regimens of study and sexual continence.
61. In Sanskrit. *Śrīmadbhāgavata* 10.29.20. The *savaiyā* resumes in the verses that follow.
62. This couplet involves a pun on *pati* ("husband") and *vipati* or *vipatti*, the former connoting a false husband, an "unhusband," and the latter, which sounds almost the same as pronounced, meaning "difficulty," here rendered as "confounding." See the commentary that follows.
63. In Sanskrit. *Śrīmadbhāgavata* 10.29.27.
64. In Sanskrit. *Bhagavad Gītā* 4.11.
65. In Sanskrit the masculine gender is used when a differentiation of sex is not made. The *gopī* is asking whether the verb *prapadyante* is to be interpreted in that broad sense, or more strictly confined to men. It is a rhetorical question, since other passages in the *Gītā* make it clear that salvation is extended to all devotees.

66. In Sanskrit. *Bhagavad Gītā* 18.66.
67. In Sanskrit. Ibid. 18.16.
68. She quotes the Sanskrit phrase *saṃtyajya sarvaviṣayān* from *Śrīmadbhāgavata* 10.29.31.
69. In Sanskrit. Ibid., 10.29.26.
70. At the time of the churning of the milk ocean, when gods and antigods were at cross-purposes, Viṣṇu (Nārāyaṇ) became an attractive woman (Mohinī) to distract the antigods from their struggle.
71. This concludes Premānand's long *savaiyā* in dialogue form.
72. This story and the one that follows are traditional in Braj and are also known elsewhere in India. They are a regular feature of the dialogue of the *mahārās līlā*, though in less elaborate forms than Premānand's.
73. In the original the comparison gains force from rhyme: *karma* and *dharma*.
74. Agni.
75. *Mokṣa* over *dharma*.
76. Most rivers are thought of as female and bear names of the feminine gender, but there are a few exceptions, like the Brahmaputra and the Indus (Sindh). These can be called *nad* rather than the familiar *nadī*, and it is these that Premānand has in mind. An example of such a usage can be found in Salomon, *Tīrtha-pratyāmnāyāḥ*, p. 144.
77. A familiar Sanskrit maxim: *ante yā mati sā gatiḥ*.
78. *Pad* of Sūr Dās, NPS 1639 in a substantially different version. Note how this quotation from the greatest Braj poet is used as the final weapon in the *gopīs'* arsenal.
79. This is not a fixed convention. The order may also be reversed.
80. *Alakh*, a term from the vocabulary of the Nāth Yogis. It means literally "bearing no mark," and refers by rights to *nirguṇ brahman*, but is here used by extension to invoke the highest form of divinity, that is, Krishna.
81. Mānsarovar is a site on the other bank of the Jumna from Brindavan, associated with the Rādhā Vallabhī sect. Since members of that sect insist that the only appropriate persona for approaching Krishna is that of a *gopī*, the reference is appropriate for the action at hand. Caitanyites sometimes attribute this transformation to an action of Brindā rather than to a bath in Mānsarovar.
82. Rati's grief is considered highly comic, and consistent with that fact she speaks rhymed prose rather than poetry. In addition to the rhymes she actually speaks, there is an implied rhyme between the

name of the speaker, Rati, and her potential fate, *satī*. The two are logically opposite conditions.

83. From a *pad* of Krishna Dās.
84. This announces the refrain of a *rasiyā* composed by Kalyāṇ, a *rāsdhārī* still alive in Brindavan who uses "Kiśorī" as his *nom de plume*, his *chāp*. On Draupadī, see Chapter I.
85. *Pad* of Syāmā Sakhī.
86. *Kavitt* of Premānand.
87. Narasī Mehtā was a Gujarati saint of the fifteenth or sixteenth century who spent his life in such complete devotion to Krishna that he became penniless. This became a matter of acute embarrassment to his daughter on the occasion of the birth of her first son. In celebration of the event it is expected that the father of the new mother will bring gifts to the family into which his daughter has married. Narasī Mehtā came, however, with only a happy retinue of like-minded devotees, equally impoverished. Seeing his daughter's mortification that they had come empty-handed, Narasī appealed to Krishna, who appeared bearing miraculous cartloads of garments and ornaments, saving the day. The story is found in Nābhājī, *Śrī Bhaktamāl* (Lucknow: Tejkumār Press, 1961), pp. 681–683. Prahlād, also a devotee of Viṣṇu/Krishna, was threatened with his life by his demonic father on that account, but Krishna descended in the form of a creature half-lion, half-man, and tore his father apart, rescuing the son. This is traditionally counted the fifth avatar of Viṣṇu. According to the *Bhaktamāl*, Krishna was to be welcomed by the perfidious Duryodhan with a great feast in his capacity as messenger from the Kauravas. Krishna, however, ignored the invitation and appeared instead at the door of the tiny, rude house belonging to the wise Vidur. Vidur was not at home, however, and Krishna interrupted his wife half clothed in the middle of a bath. He provided her with something for her modesty, and she set about offering him whatever hospitality she could. Alas, there was only a simple plaintain in the house, and she was so disoriented by the magnificence of her visitor that she offered even that in an inappropriate way. She was so distracted that she offered Krishna the peelings rather than the fruit itself, but he accepted her gift willingly as testimony of devotion. Ibid., pp. 102–104.
88. A *kavitt* of anonymous composition that has been current for some years now. In spirit it differs little from the numerical exercise traditional for Passover, *Eḥad mī yode'a*. The poet omits the number

one and begins with two. That he assigns arbitrarily: actually one should bow to a potentate, especially Krishna, many more times. The three afflictions are the ills that affect the universe in each of the three aspects into which a traditional Upaniṣadic formula divides it: the physical realm *(adhibhautik)*, the divine realm *(adhidaivik)*, and the realm of the spirit *(ādhyātmik)*. The standard Indian treatise on medicine, the *Suśruta Saṃhitā*, adopts this classification. The association of the number six with Syām is fanciful. Seven, however, has a logic to it because Krishna is known as tamer of seven bulls in the old Tamil epic *Cilappatikāram* and in several other Tamil texts, and in Sanskrit works of a southern provenance, including the southern rescension of the *Harivaṃśa*, a *kāvya* called *Śaurikathodaya* (2.17–24), and the *Bhāgavata Purāṇa* (10.58.32–55). See Ilangô Adigal, *Shilappadikaram (The Ankle Bracelet)*, translated by Alain Daniélou (New York: New Directions, 1965), canto 17; and Erik Af Edholm and Carl Suneson, "The Seven Bulls and Kṛṣṇa's Marriage to Nīlā/NappiNNai in Sanskrit and Tamil Literature," *Temenos* 8 (1972), 30–35. Krishna had eight chief queens as monarch of Dvaraka, but this grouping also suggests the eight *gopīs* who are eternally in his presence. Indeed, Rūp Gosvāmī saw the former as forms of the latter. The reference to butter in connection with the number nine is a play on words. Fresh butter is *navanīt*, the particle *nava* being cognate with the English "new." *Nava* is also the Sanskrit term for the digit nine.

89. The story of Dhruv's appeal to Viṣṇu/Krishna is told in *Viṣṇu Puraṇa* 1.11–12. See also Mani, *Encyclopaedia*, p. 238. Nāmdev's story contrasts with that of Dhruv in that Nāmdev, the Untouchable fifteenth-century Maharasthrian saint, showed no concern at all for his own status or wellbeing. When he saw his tiny thatched hut afire but only half burned, he regretted that the whole thing was not consumed, and offered whatever he could to sustain the conflagration: so intense was his devotion that he welcomed the fire as the hallowing presence of God through Agni, the fire divinity. When the fire was done, however, he was destitute and called on a thatchmaker to raise a new hut for him. When it was finished everyone was amazed at the workmanship: the artisan was Krishna himself. Nābhājī, *Bhaktamāl*, pp. 337–338. The final incident is that of Mohinī, for which see note 70 above.

90. Premānand's catalogue of the *magnalia dei* concludes with references to three of the most familiar saints of the *bhakti* period in north India: the Rajasthani poet-queen Mīrā Bāī, who most often

appeals to Krishna in the form of Giridhar, the one who lifts Mount Govardhan; Sūr Dās, who often follows his own name in the signature line of his *pads* with that of Syām; and Tulsī Dās, whose poetry is focused primarily on Rām, and includes a version of the *Rāmāyaṇa* in Avadhi. The reference to fate (the term *kāl* may also be fittingly translated "death," an echo of which appears in the Birth of Krishna *līlā* above) alludes to Kans's well-known struggle with the inevitability of his own death. A sustained afterword on the subject is interpolated into the *Harivaṃśa* as Krishna's reassurance to Ugrasen after the death of his son. See Vaidya, ed., *Harivaṃśa*, vol. 1, 78.32n.

91. This familiar quotation, sometimes mistakenly attributed to Vālmīki, is thought of as having been uttered by Rām upon returning to Ayodhyā.
92. The reference is to the affectionate designation of Krishna as Brindavan's "priest of love" *(prem pujārī)*.
93. In this *rasiyā* of Megh Syam, the poet contrasts the peacock's independent dance with the way that Krishna is "made to dance," as the Braj familiarly puts it *(nāc nacāyau)*, by the *gopīs* to whose devotion he is irresistibly attracted in the form of the butter they set out for him. See Premānand's *kavitt* below. The quotation of this passage is appropriate at this point because it establishes a contrast between the peacock dance we have just seen and the butter thief "dance" that we are about to be shown.
94. This concludes the *rasiyā* of Megh Syam.
95. *Kavitt* of Premānand. In the version of the story current since the writing of the *Bālacarita* in perhaps the seventh to ninth century A.D., Yaśodā tied Krishna to a mortar out of exasperation with him for repeatedly stealing butter from the women of Braj and causing them to beseige her with constant complaints. The reference to Krishna as time *(kāl)* recalls the terror Krishna inspired in Kans and his frightening hierophany to Arjuna in *Bhagavad Gītā* 11.32.
96. This *savaiyā*, traditional with the *rāsdhārīs*, takes its final line from a verse of Raskhān.

Chapter V. The Coming of Akrūr

1. For a consideration of the position of the *Harivaṃśa* among the several versions of the Krishna story, and a beautiful recounting of some of its most winning passages, see Ingalls, "The *Harivaṃśa* as a *Mahākāvya*."

2. The name *hallīśaka* is given the dance by an editor of the *Harivaṃśa* but there is no name for it in the text itself.
3. Ingalls, "The *Harivaṃśa* as a *Mahākāvya*," p. 389. *Harivaṃśa* 73.36–37.
4. Although this *līlā* may figure at the end of a full cycle of *līlās* performed elsewhere in India, it is almost always excluded from a series of *līlās* performed in Braj. Svāmī Natthī Lāl, interview, Brindavan, August 2, 1978.
5. Hein, *Miracle Plays*, pp. 179–221. On the *bhramargīt*, see Peter Gaeffke, "Das Motiv der Gottesschelte in der Neuindischen Bhaktiliteratur." *Zeitschrift der Deutschen Morgenländischen Gesellschaft*, 1969, supplement, pp. 924–929; McGregor, *The Round Dance*, pp. 47–54; Kenneth E. Bryant, "The *Bhramargīt* of Sūrdās," paper delivered to the conference on the *sant* tradition, Berkeley, 1978; Hawley, "*Yoga* and *Viyoga*: Simple Religion in Hinduism," *Harvard Theological Review* 74:1 (1981), forthcoming; and numerous considerations in Hindi.
6. NPS 4249. A translation appears in Kenneth E. Bryant, *Poems to the Child-God: Structure and Strategies in the Poetry of Sūrdās* (Berkeley and Los Angeles: University of California Press, 1978), pp. 203–204.
7. NPS 3854. A translation of a slightly different version appears in Hein, *Miracle Plays*, p. 183.
8. *Harivaṃśa* 68.1–17. In the *Harivaṃśa*, however, the time is twilight, whereas in the *līlā* it is just before dawn.
9. Donna M. Wulff, personal communication, and "Drama," p. 44.
10. The term *yoga* does not connote religious practice in all its usages, particularly in more ancient texts, but in the literature of Braj it quite definitely carries this meaning. Yogic practices epitomize the strength of the human longing for divine experience.
11. Examples of these themes may be found in NPS 3599, 3623, 4174, 4184, 4187, 4339, 4408, 4461, and 4501.
12. Paul Tillich, *Systematic Theology*, vol. 2 (Chicago: University of Chicago Press, 1962), pp. 10, 19–78.
13. See John Braisted Carman, *The Theology of Rāmānuja* (New Haven: Yale University Press, 1974), pp. 176–198; cf. also pp. 108–111 on *amalatva*. Helmuth von Glasenapp, "Die Lehre Vallabhâcāryas," in *Von Buddha zu Gandhi* (Wiesbaden: Otto Harrassowitz, 1962), pp. 221–237.
14. Rūp Gosvāmī dealt with the problem in his *Lalitamādhava* by proposing that Krishna's many wives in Dvaraka are but alternate

forms of the *gopīs* of Braj, with Satyabhāmā as Radha. Thus Dvaraka becomes a continuation of Braj, and the problem of abandonment is solved along with the scandal of Krishna's illicit relations, which Rūp seeks to cancel in other ways as well (see De, *Vaiṣṇava Faith*, pp. 585–589). Rūp's nephew, Jīv Gosvāmī, went even further by inventing a legend that Krishna did in fact return to Braj (*Gopālacampū*, chapters 31–36). This departs, however, from the most widely accepted canonical accounts, including the *Bhāgavata Purāṇa*, and Jīv feels he must go to some length to defend his interpretation, since the only puranic source at his disposal is a passage in the late *uttarakhaṇḍa* of the *Padma Purāṇa* (see *Gopālacampū*, chap. 29). A less drastic theological tactic, one adopted by several of the Caitanyite *gosvāmīs*, was to interpret the vision of Akrūr at the Jumna as he returned to Mathura with Krishna and Balarām as signifying that in their sweet aspects *(mādhurya)* these two would never truly leave Braj. Only in their heroic aspects *(aiśvarya)* would they continue on with him: the rest remains in Braj to stimulate the *līlā* of love that is constant there, the *nityalīlā*.

15. John 14.16.
16. John 16.7.
17. For a consideration of the aesthetics of union *(sambhoga)* and separation *(vipralamba)*, see Wulff, "Drama," pp. 289–306.
18. See De, *Vaiṣṇava Faith*, pp. 166–224 and Wulff, "Drama," pp. 54–76. In regard to classical aesthetics, see J. L. Masson and M. V. Patwardhan, *Aesthetic Rapture*, vol. 1 (Poona: Deccan College, 1970), pp. 14–42, and Edward C. Dimock, Jr. et al., *The Literature of India: An Introduction* (Chicago: University of Chicago Press, 1974), pp. 128–136.
19. The verses that occur in this *līlā* are selected from *Braj Vilās*, pp. 458–479. Unless otherwise noted, all the poetry in the translation that follows comes from these pages and all, unless otherwise indicated, is in the *caupāī* meter common in the *Braj Vilās*.
20. A third *līlā* in this same category is one that has been popularized in recent years by Svāmī Rāmsvarūp of Brindavan, the *sudāmā līlā*. All three of these *līlās* are considered important enough that they are frequently allowed to extend beyond a single day's performance into a second day.
21. Christina Rossetti, "In the Bleak Mid-winter," set to music by Gustav Holst. In Elizabeth Poston, ed., *The Penguin Book of Christmas Carols* (Harmondsworth: Penguin, 1972), pp. 100–101.
22. This *caupāī* is the same that initiated the *kṛṣṇa janma līlā*. It is

broken off because the line that follows contains a reference to Ugrasen, who is no longer on the throne. The rest, however, is entirely apposite here.

23. This song is of recent and anonymous authorship. Its genre, *śer*, is a loose and informal one that implies the use of Urdu expressions.
24. A popular, anonymous *bhajan* with *kīrtan*, the repetition of the names of God, in its refrain. Hara, "destroyer," is a familiar designation for Śiva, and Harihara images combine the qualities of Śiva with those of Viṣṇu/Krishna.
25. NPS 335, not among the oldest in the *Sūr Sāgar*.
26. The first four lines are *dohā* and *soraṭhā* from *Braj Vilās*, p. 459.
27. Anonymous *śer*.
28. Actually the actor made a slip at this point and said he would return on the morning of the day following.
29. The word he uses for "cruel" is *krūr*. It signifies the fact that his deliberations have to do not only with a particular action but with his entire identity, for his own name is *a-krūr*, literally, the one who is not cruel.
30. Muṣṭik and Cāṇūr are names of the wrestlers Kans sets against Balarām and Krishna, respectively. The elephant he refers to is Kuvalayāpīḍ, the great beast Kans intends to have trample the boys if necessary. Another set of wrestlers is mentioned just below, Śal and Tośal, who fight, respectively, with Balarām and Krishna.
31. In the original this thought is phrased in such a way as to parody one of the most treasured doctrines of the Vedas, which are traditionally understood to include the Upaniṣads. In the *Bṛhadāraṇyaka* and *Chāndogya Upaniṣads*, particularly in the former, great emphasis is laid upon the fact that the ultimate condition of existence (Brahman, God) cannot be described. It has to do with no particular object, and is impregnable by ordinary discourse. In this sense It "is not" *(neti)*, is "not this." In the present *dohā* this term is used in a double sense. On the one hand, it is affirmed that Nanda's son is that ineffable reality the Vedas and Upaniṣads designate as "not" (*nigam neti nandalāl*, with an unexpressed copula understood). On the other hand, *neti* can be understood as a simple negative with the ironic result that the Vedas are devalued for not *(neti)* even knowing that this is the case *(jāy rūp yah dekhi hau nigam neti nandalāl)*.
32. Suphalak (Sanskrit, Svaphalka) is Akrūr's father, and Akrūr is often referred to as his son in this *līlā*, sometimes to emphasize his family

ties to Krishna. As a cousin to Vasudev, he is like an uncle to Krishna.

33. Again the original contains a double meaning. On the one hand, Krishna will "cross over" *(tāran)* the Jumna and visit Kans. On the other, he will visit him with salvation by causing him to cross over the sea of this earthly life: this is another familiar sense of *tāran*.
34. Balarām's emblem is the plow.
35. He refers to her as his mother though in the strict sense she is not, but rather one of his father's co-wives. In Braj, however, the term "Ma" *(mā)* is commonly used even more widely than this, so it is quite appropriate that Balarām so designate Yaśodā.
36. This is the term *māyā* used in the sense of worldly attachments, as it frequently is in the literature of yoga.
37. Upananda is one of the cowherd chieftains secondary to Nanda, according to the *Bhāgavata Purāṇa*.
38. A play on words. *Nanda* means literally joy, as does its alternative form *nandan* (Sanskrit, *nandana*). When Krishna is given the familiar designation Nandanandan, as he is here, it means not only "Nanda's joy" but "Nanda's Nanda." Krishna is the essence of Nanda, what makes him who he is, the joy that gives him his very name. To take away Krishna, then, will be tantamount to taking away Nanda, so he might as well go himself. For a wife to sacrifice her husband so willingly, however, is scandalous, and underlines the extent of her devotion to her son: it is his absence that will truly widow her.
39. This begins the recital of a song attributed to Sūr Dās, a version of which appears in NPS 3609. It continues until the line in which the name of the poet is mentioned.
40. To many who hear the poem that begins here, one that contains no signature line, its point of view will ring false. This is just the sort of position *(māyāvād)* that is so roundly criticized in the religion of Braj. Krishna takes up this line of argument only as the last weapon in his arsenal, as at the end of the poem attributed to Sūr Dās above, where it is also suggested. There, however, it is qualified with a double meaning, for indeed Krishna is not quite the son of Yaśodā and Nanda, either in the literal or in the theological sense: he is their foster son.
41. Manmohan: "beguiler of the heart," that is, Krishna. These are the first lines of a *pad* whose author is not named.
42. These are the first words of NPS 3591.

43. Anonymous folk song.
44. The first half of this sequence is a *dohā* of Mīrā Bāī. I have not been able to determine the author of the second half, also a *dohā*.
45. This is the opening of NPS 3906, which continues in the next two quotations as well.
46. Indians feel that the response elicited by certain raga modalities are not limited to the human race. The "deer" raga, *rāg baravā*, is one such: it is thought that deer respond to its tones, hence it becomes by tradition a weapon in the hands of hunters.
47. Here Akrūr repeats a line of self-examination he has recited before.
48. The terms "magic" in the poetry and "trick" in the prose translate the important philosophical term *māyā*, which when used by nontheists means broadly "illusion," and when used by theists the supernatural, magic-like powers of God.
49. The three forms of Godhead that are visible to Akrūr – Viṣṇu, Śiva, and Brahmā – go together to form a sort of trinity *(trimūrti)* that represents to Akrūr all possible manifestations of divinity.

GLOSSARY

Akrūr: literally, "not cruel," the name of the minister whom Kans sends as an emissary to Krishna and Balarām

akrūr līlā (akrūr āgaman līlā): rās līlā depicting the arrival of Akrūr in Braj

Allahabad (Prayāg): pilgrimage city at the confluence of the Jumna and the Ganges

āratī: ceremony of waving lamps or candles before an object of veneration

Aurangzeb: stringently orthodox and iconoclastic Muslim ruler who occupied the Moghul throne from A.D. 1659 to 1707.

Balarām (Sanskrit, Balarāma): Krishna's elder brother

Bānke Bihārī: "lithe playboy," a title of Krishna and the name of one of the most important images in Brindavan and of the temple that houses it

bańsī: Krishna's bamboo flute

bańsī corī līlā: rās līlā depicting the theft of Krishna's flute

Barsana (Barsānā): town in Braj where Radha was born and raised

bhādrapad (bhādra, bhādõ): month in the Hindu calendar falling in August-September

Bhagavad Gītā: the "Song of the Lord," that is, Krishna's advice to Arjuna on the occasion of the latter's having to take up arms against his own kinsmen; a classic Hindu text that forms part of the *Mahābhārata*

Bhāgavata Purāṇa: ninth- or tenth-century Purana whose depiction of Krishna's life subsequently became the standard scripture for Vaiṣṇavs

Bhajan Āśram: charitable institution in Brindavan where widows are paid and fed to sing the *mahāmantra*

bhakti: devotion, love, love of God or by God

bhāv (Sanskrit, *bhāva*): feeling, an emotional state

bhramargīt (Sanskrit, *bhramaragīta*): "songs of the bee," or rather, songs to the bee; *pads* describing the *gopīs*' hostile reactions to Krishna's messenger, Ūdho

Brahmā: high god in the Hindu pantheon, who presides particularly over the origin of the world; conceived in Braj as a sort of grandfather

Braj: deriving from the Sanskrit *vraja*, cowherd encampment; hence the grazing country where Krishna grew up, in the environs of (but considered by many not to include) Mathura

Brajbāsī: native of Braj

Braj Bhāṣā: dialect spoken in Braj, and for four centuries the most familiar idiom for Hindi poetry

Braj Vilās: poetic narrative of Krishna's youthful adventures, written by Brajbāsī Dās in A.D. 1743 and patterned on poems in the *Sūr Sāgar*

Bṛhadāraṇyaka Upaniṣad: one of the earliest and most massive *Upaniṣads*, probably completed before 500 B.C.

brindā (Sanskrit, *vṛndā*): a bush or small tree that is a member of the basil family and is commonly called *tulsī*. It gives its name to the forest where Krishna grazed his cattle, Brindavan

Brindā: personification of *brindā* and guardian goddess of Brindavan

Brindavan (Brindāvan; Sanskrit, Vṛndāvana): literally "basil forest," where Krishna is said to have danced the *rās*; now a pilgrimage center consecrating the spot, on the Jumna north of Mathura

Bṛṣabhānu (Sanskrit, Vṛṣabhānu): Radha's father and headman of the village Barsana

Caitanya: Bengali Brahmin saint (A.D. 1486–1533) considered by his followers an incarnation of Radha and Krishna, who rejected traditional brahminical learning in favor of simply reciting the names of Krishna. Caitanyites consider that he founded Brindavan itself; his deputies established Vaiṣṇavite learning and ritual there.

Caitanyite: pertaining to Caitanya or his thought or to the religious community that takes him as its founder

cakorī: mythological female bird said to feed only on moonbeams

Candrāvalī: the *gopī* whom Radha considers her chief rival for Krishna's affections

Cāṇūr (Sanskrit, Cāṇūra): one of the wrestlers to do battle with Krishna and Balarām in Mathura

cātak: mythological bird said to feed only on rain drops

caupāī: meter containing lines consisting of two rhyming segments of sixteen metrical units *(mātrās)* each

Chāndogya Upaniṣad: one of the earliest and most massive *Upaniṣads*, probably composed before 500 B.C.

chāp: "seal," the poet's name frequently included near the end of a *pad* and functioning as a signature

cīr ghāṭ: spot on the bank of the Jumna memorializing the *cīr haran līlā cīr haran līlā*: episode in which Krishna steals the *gopīs'* clothes as they bathe in the Jumna

darśan (Sanskrit, *darśana*): vision, sight; especially the act of seeing a deity

Dāūjī: corruption of "Baladev Jī," that is, Balarām, and the name of the town in Braj that houses his principal temple

Devakī: member of the royal family of Mathura (variously described as Kans's sister, cousin, or aunt) who gave birth to Krishna

devanāgarī: system of notation in which Sanskrit, Braj Bhāṣā, and Hindi are written

dohā: rhymed couplet in which each line contains 24 metrical units *(mātrās)*

Draupadī: wife of the five Pāṇḍava brothers in the *Mahābhārata*

Dvaraka (Dvārakā): city on the west coast of India over which Krishna ruled after he had completed his adventures in Braj and Mathura

gandharva: heavenly musician

ghāṭ: riverbank that serves as a place for bathing and/or washing

ghī: clarified butter

Giridhārī: "lifter of the mountain," that is, Mount Govardhan; a title of Krishna

Gokul (Sanskrit, Gokula): place where Krishna spent his infancy, now identified with a particular village across the Jumna from Mathura

Golok (Sanskrit, Goloka): "heaven of cows," the highest heavenly realm according to Braj theology

Gopāl (Sanskrit, Gopāla): "protector of cows," "herdsman," a title of Krishna

Gopāl Bhaṭṭ (Sanskrit, Gopāla Bhaṭṭa): sixteenth-century Brahmin from south India designated by Caitanya to ritualize the worship of Krishna in Brindavan; the first priest of Rādhā Ramaṇ

gopī: one of the cowherding women or girls of Braj

gosvāmī: honorific title of the families whose hereditary right it is to tend the great temples of Brindavan and surrounding Braj. The title is usually interpreted as meaning "master of the senses," and is reserved for the priestly lineages that became established in Braj by transplant from elsewhere in India in the sixteenth century.

Govardhan (Sanskrit, Govardhana): the sacred mountain of Braj, located west of Mathura

Govind (Sanskrit, Govinda): "keeper of cows," a title of Krishna

Gujar: cattle-raising people, originally nomadic, who live in west and north India

Har (Sanskrit, Hara): "destroyer," a title of Śiva

Hari: name of Viṣṇu/Krishna, variously interpreted

Haribhaktivilāsa: ritual manual composed by Gopāl Bhaṭṭ about A.D. 1541, which governs ritual practices in the temple of Rādhā Ramaṇ and in the Caitanya Sampradāy

Harivaṃśa: Sanskrit epic or Purana which contains the oldest full account of the Krishna narrative (first to third centuries A.D.)

havelī: temple of the Vallabh Sampradāy, but technically the household shrine of any of the scions of that community

Indra: tempestuous chief of the gods in Vedic times who, though he retained the title, was demoted in subsequent periods of Indian religious history

janmāṣṭamī (śrīkṛṣṇajanmāṣṭamī): festival of Krishna's birth, celebrated on the eighth day of the waning half of the month of *bhādrapad*

Jīv Gosvāmī (Sanskrit, Jīva Gosvāmin): sixteenth-century theologian and disciple of Caitanya

Jumna (Sanskrit, Yamunā): second major river of the Gangetic plain, which flows through Braj and borders Brindavan; considered a female divinity by all, and by some a wife of Krishna

kadamb (Sanskrit, *kadamba*): fragrant, blossoming tree that figures in the *līlā*s in which Krishna steals the *gopī*s' clothes and in which he tames Kāliya.

Kailās (Sanskrit, Kailāsa): the Himalayan mountain upon whose peak Śiva meditates

Kālīcaran: hereditary priest to the court of Mathura

kālīdah (Sanskrit, *kāliyadaha*): the hole in the Jumna where Kāliya dwells (or dwelled)

Kālindī: name of the Jumna that portrays her as daughter of the sun

Kāliya: black water snake whom Krishna subdues and banishes

Kāmdev (Sanskrit, Kāmadeva): god personifying *kām* (Sanskrit, *kāma*), love in the sense of desire, particularly sexual desire

Kānh: corruption of "Krishna" and familiar name for him

Kanhaiyā: affectionate diminutive of "Kānh"

Kans (Sanskrit, Kaṃsa): demonic king who usurped the throne of Mathura; archenemy of Krishna

kārttik (Sanskrit, *kārttika*): Hindu month overlapping October and November

Kātyāyanī: name of the Goddess

Kaunteya: matronymic of Arjuna, to whom Krishna preached the *Bhagavad Gītā*

kavitt: meter containing rhyming lines of thirty-one syllables each, in which the caesura falls after the sixteenth

keśī ghāṭ: the principal bathing place in modern Brindavan, named for the battle Krishna is thought to have waged there with the horse demon Keśī

kīrtan: repetitious singing of the names of God, specifically of Viṣṇu/ Krishna

Kiśorī (Śrī Kiśorī Jū): title of Radha meaning "adolescent girl," implying that she is the paradigm of all such

kṛṣṇa janma līlā: *rās līlā* depicting the birth of Krishna

Kuvalayāpīḍ (Sanskrit, Kuvalayāpīḍa): mad elephant in Kans's keeping who was to attack Krishna

Lakṣmī: consort of Viṣṇu, hence an antetype of Radha

Lalitā: Radha's closest girlfriend, who figures as Sakhī 3 in "The Theft of the Flute" and Sakhī 1 in "The Great Circle Dance"

līlā: "play," both in the sense of "fun" or "game" and in the sense of "drama"; the portion of the *rās līlā* depicting particular adventures or episodes in Krishna's life

Madan (Sanskrit, Madana): "intoxicating," a title of Kāmdev

Mādhav (Sanskrit, Mādhava): a title of Krishna whose derivation is disputed. Usually it is taken as a patronymic referring to Madhu, a putative Yādav ancestor of Krishna.

Mahābhārata: great Hindu epic that describes the rivalries between the Pāṇḍava brothers and their cousins, the Kauravas

Mahādev (Sanskrit, Mahādeva): "the great god," title of Śiva

mahāmantra: the "great mantra" containing three names of Viṣṇu/ Krishna (Krishna, Rām, and Hari), in whose chanting Caitanya located the sufficient cause of salvation

mahārās līlā: the "great *rās līlā*," depicting the story of Krishna's circle dance with the *gopīs*

Manmohan (Sanskrit, Manamohana): "beguiler of the mind (or heart)," a title of Krishna

Mānsarovar (Sanskrit, Mānasarovara): tank on the left bank of the Jumna revered by the Rādhāvallabh Sampradāy

Mansukhā: Krishna's awkward, fun-loving friend and the most familiar *vidūṣak* in the *rās līlā*s

Manusmṛti: the *Laws of Manu*, a classical text governing morality and social custom

Mathura (Mathurā): ancient trading and pilgrimage center on the Jumna south of Delhi, at the heart of (but by many not considered a part of) Braj

māyā: magic or illusion, depending upon one's point of view; that power by means of which Viṣṇu or Brahman adumbrates the phenomenal world; often personified as female

Mirzapur (Mirzāpūr): city in eastern Uttar Pradesh

Mukund (Sanskrit, Mukunda): name of Viṣṇu/Krishna

Muralī: Krishna's flute personified as a woman

Murārī (Sanskrit, Murāri): "foe of Mura" (a demon), a title of Krishna

Muṣṭik (Sanskrit, Muṣṭika): one of the wrestlers to do battle with Krishna and Balarām in Mathura

Nanda: Krishna's adoptive father, husband of Yaśodā and Rohiṇī, usually understood as chief among the cowherds of Braj

Nanda Dās: sixteenth-century poet writing in Braj Bhāṣā

Nandagaon (Nandagāõ): "Nanda's town," a village in Braj where Nanda is thought to have lived after he left Gokul

Nandanandan (Sanskrit, Nandanandana): "Nanda's joy," a title of Krishna

Nārad (Sanskrit, Nārada): musical seer who functions in Vaiṣṇavite literature as the emissary of the gods in the human realm, preeminently an arranger of events

Nārāyaṇ (Sanskrit, Nārāyaṇa): a title of Viṣṇu

Nimbarkite: pertaining to the saint Nimbārka (ca. A.D 1200 ?) and his thought, or to the religious community that takes him as its founder

nirgun (Sanskrit, *nirguṇa*): "without qualities," the view that God cannot be positively conceived

pad (pada): a verse form characterized by few fixed poetic conventions, allowing various schemes of end rhyme; typically consisting of six or eight lines, sometimes with refrain, but occasionally much longer

paṇḍā: a Brahmin guide for pilgrims

parakīyā bhāv: sentiments arising out of the situation of belonging to another (*parakīyā*), which some consider to be the *gopīs*' status as they approach Krishna: married women

Pārvatī: wife of Śiva

prasād (Sanskrit, *prasāda*): "grace": food or drink left over from the table of a deity, which becomes by virtue of that contact grace to be consumed by devotees

prem (Sanskrit, *prema*): selfless love

Premānand: the most influential poet alive in Braj today, and a frequent contributor to the *rās līlā*

Purana (Sanskrit, *purāṇa*): one of a group of texts that recount the great events which happened of old (the literal meaning of the word), among them the story of Krishna

Pūtanā: demoness with poisoned breasts whom Kans deputed to suckle Krishna

Radha (Rādhā): the most beloved among Krishna's milkmaid amours, often considered as not different from Krishna himself

Rādhā Ramaṇ: "the lover of Radha," Krishna in image form, whose worship in Brindavan dates to A.D. 1542. Rādhā Ramaṇ's temple is the central focus of worship for the Caitanya Sampradāy

Rādhā Vallabh: "the beloved of Radha," a title of Krishna, and the name of one of Brindavan's most important images and of the temple that houses it—the central place of worship for the Rādhāvallabh Sampradāy

Rādhāvallabh Sampradāy: the religious community inspired by Hit Harivaṃś in the sixteenth century, whose theology emphasizes the supremacy of Radha

Rādhikā: diminutive of "Radha"

raga (Hindi, *rāg;* Sanskrit, *rāga*): the basic unit of organization of classical Indian music, combining mode and melodic pattern

Rām (Sanskrit, Rāma): Rāmacandra, usually counted the seventh avatar of Viṣṇu and the last to precede Krishna; occasionally also Balarām

Rāmānuja: eleventh-century Vaiṣṇav theologian of south India who is claimed as the founder of the Śrī Vaiṣṇav Sampradāy

ras (Sanskrit, *rasa*): literally liquid, taste, or flavor; hence mood, an aesthetic and/or devotional sentiment

rās (Sanskrit, *rāsa*): Krishna's circle dance with the *gopīs*, whose enactment is included as a permanent part of every *rās līlā*

rāsdhārī: leader of a troupe which performs the *rās līlā*, whose sung lines connect the various dramatic episodes and moments within them

rasgullah: a favorite white, milk-based sweet

rasik (Sanskrit, *rasika*): enjoyer, connoisseur (one who appreciates *ras*), dandy; of which Krishna is the ideal type

rasiyā: general term to indicate folk poetry in Braj Bhāṣā

Raskhān: seventeenth-century poet writing in Braj Bhāṣā

rās līlā: a musical drama depicting Krishna's sacramental circle dance with his cowherdess lovers (*rās*) and one of a number of episodes (*līlās*, "plays") in his life story

rās maṇḍalī: troupe that performs the *rās līlā*, members of which are normally drawn from a single Brahmin family

rās pūrṇimā: the full moon of the autumnal month of *kārttik*, which is celebrated as the occasion on which the original *rās līlā* took place

Rāspañcādhyāyī: Nanda Dās's vernacular interpretation of the five chapters of the *Bhāgavata Purāṇa* which describe the events surrounding the *rās līlā*

Rati: personification of passion, Kāmdev's wife

Rohiṇī: wife of Nanda and co-wife of Yaśodā, who gave birth to Balarām

rolā: a rhymed meter in which a line contains twenty-four metrical units *(mātrās)*, with the final syllable heavy and the caesura following the eleventh *mātrā*

Rudra: volatile Vedic deity who became so closely associated with Śiva in the course of time as to be considered an aspect of Śiva

Rukmiṇī: the chief queen of Krishna as king of Dvaraka

Rūp Gosvāmī (Sanskrit, Rūpa Gosvāmin): sixteenth-century Sanskrit scholar sent by Caitanya to Brindavan; author of systematic theologies and Radha-Krishna plays, and first priest in the temple of Govindadev

sakhī: "friend," one of Krishna's and Radha's *gopī* companions

samājī: adult members of the *rās līla* troupes who act as musicians

Śambhu: name of Śiva

sāṃkhya: ancient philosophical system which classifies the world into twenty-five elements, two of which are primordial: matter and spirit

sampradāy (Sanskrit, *sampradāya*): teaching tradition, religious community. The four major Braj *sampradāy*s have a hereditary leadership that was established in the sixteenth (or in the case of the Nimbārkīs, possibly seventeenth) century

Sarasvatī: goddess of music and learning

savaiyā: a general term referring to a group of syllabic meters with fixed orderings of feet within each line.

śer: loose, informal genre of poetry imported into Braj Bhāṣā from Urdu

Śeṣ (Sanskrit, Śeṣa): the primordial serpent who both cushions and shields Viṣṇu

Śiva: great god of the Hindu pantheon, who combines the contradictory properties of pure asceticism and pure eroticism, but who in Braj is usually understood as prototype of the former

soraṭhā: couplet containing lines of twenty-four metrical units *(mātrās)*, each of which rhymes at the caesura

śrāvaṇ (*sāvan*; Sanskrit, *śrāvaṇa*): Hindu calendrical month that falls in the monsoon season, coinciding with parts of July and/or August

Śrī Caitanya Prem Sansthān: "Institute of Love" dedicated to Caitanya; in its hall *rās līlā*s are performed

Śrīmadbhāgavata: see *Bhāgavata Purāṇa*

Śrī Vaiṣṇav Sampradāy: the religious community, principally active in south India, that looks to Rāmānuja as its founder

Sudāmā: serious, penurious Brahmin friend of Krishna's youth
Suphalak (Sanskrit, Svaphalka): father of Akrūr
Sūr Dās: sixteenth-century devotee of Krishna who is commonly considered the greatest Braj poet
Sūr Sāgar: the principal and oldest collection of poems attributed to Sūr Dās
Sūrya, Sūrya Nārāyaṇ: the sun, considered as a divinity
svāhā: Sanskrit term of invocation that accompanies ritual offerings
svakīyā bhāv: sentiments arising out of the situation of being someone's own (wife). Some theological traditions understand this to be the *gopīs*' status in relation to Krishna
svāmī: the familiar title accorded to *rāsdhārīs* in Braj, literally meaning "master"
svarūp (Sanskrit, *svarūpa*): the "very form" or "own form" in which Krishna manifests himself as the actors in the *rās līlā* take on the roles of Krishna, Radha, and the *gopīs*—particularly the former two
Syām (Sanskrit Śyāma): "the dark one," a title of Krishna
Syāmā (Śrī Syāmā Jū): the feminine counterpart of "Syām"; hence, Krishna's opposite number, that is, Radha
Syām Sundar (Sanskrit, Śyāma Sundara): "the beautiful dark one," a title of Krishna
tablā: two small drums of different pitches played together
tilak (Sanskrit, *tilaka*): the mark of auspiciousness or beauty with which Indians typically decorate their foreheads
tīrtha: literally a place for "crossing over," a pilgrimage spot
tulsī (Sanskrit, *tulasī*): see *brindā*
Ūdho (Sanskrit, Uddhava): messenger Krishna sends from Mathura to Braj to urge the *gopīs* not to pine after him, but rather to recognize his presence in their hearts
ūdho līlā: rās līlā depicting the mission of Ūdho to the *gopīs* on behalf of Krishna, now guardian of Mathura and resident there
Ugrasen (Sanskrit, Ugrasena): legitimate king of Mathura and apparent father of Kans
Ujjvalanīlamaṇi: Sanskrit treatise on aesthetics by Rūp Gosvāmī, in which the supremacy of the erotic sentiment in its religious setting is established
Upaniṣad: one of a group of ancient treatises emphasizing interior knowledge and correspondences between various levels of reality
Vaikuṇṭha: heaven ruled by Viṣṇu; in Braj the symbol of beneficent hierarchy

Vaiṣṇav (Vaiṣṇavite): pertaining to Viṣṇu/Krishna or his worship; a devotee of Viṣṇu/Krishna

Vallabhācārya: sixteenth-century saint and philosopher who traveled to Braj and whose descendents became the leaders of the Vallabh Sampradāy

Vallabhite: pertaining to the thought of Vallabhācārya or to the community that takes him as its founder

Vallabh Sampradāy: religious community that takes Vallabhācārya as its founder

Vasant (Sanskrit, Vasanta): personification of Spring, Kāmdev's general

Vasudev (Sanskrit, Vasudeva): kinsman of the royal family of Mathura and father of Krishna

Veda: literally, "knowledge," the collective name of the most ancient Hindu scriptures

Vidagdhamādhava: Sanskrit drama of Rūp Gosvāmī depicting Krishna and his world of *gopīs*

vidūṣak (Sanskrit, *vidūṣaka*): comic personality in a drama

vīṇā: ancient stringed instrument

Viṣṇu: great god of the Hindu pantheon, for Vaiṣṇavs the ultimate summation of divinity. Krishna is either considered one of his avatars or, more familiarly in Braj, coextensive with him.

Viṣṇu Purāṇa: Vaiṣṇavite Purana composed in about the fifth century

Yamunā: see Jumna

Yaśodā: wife of Nanda and Krishna's adoptive mother

Yogamāyā: personification, in female form, of Viṣṇu's miraculous power

Bibliography

Adigal, Ilangô. *Shilappadikaram (The Ankle Bracelet)*. Translated by Alain Daniélou. New York: New Directions, 1965.

Alsdorf, Ludwig N., tr. *Harivaṃśupurāṇa: Ein Abschnitt aus der Apabhraṃśa-Welthistorie "Mahāpurāṇa Tisaṭṭhimahāpurisaguṇālaṃkāra" von Puṣpadanta*. Hamburg: Friederichsen, de Gruyter, 1936.

Archer, W. G. *The Loves of Krishna*. London: George Allen & Unwin, 1957.

Ashton, Martha Bush. "Yakshagana: a South Indian Folk Theatre." *The Drama Review*, 13:3 (1969), 148–155.

——, and Bruce Christie. *Yakṣagāna, a Dance Drama of India*. New Delhi: Abhinav, 1977.

Awasthi, Suresh. "The Ramayana Theatre Tradition in India and Southeast Asia." *Quarterly Journal of the National Centre for the Performing Arts* (Bombay) 1:1 (1972), 47–60.

Bakshi, Sri Ram. "Indian Theatre: A Preliminary Checklist." Lawrence: University of Kansas, n.d., mimeographed.

Banerjea, J. N. *The Development of Hindu Iconography*. 2nd ed. Calcutta: University of Calcutta, 1956.

——. "Hindu Iconography (Vyūhas and Vibhavas of Viṣṇu)." *Journal of the Indian Society of Oriental Art* 14 (1946), 1–74.

Bhandarkar, R. G. "Allusions to Kṛishṇa in Patanjali's *Mahâbhâṣya*." *Indian Antiquary* 3 (1874), 14–16.

Bhanot, Rājendra Kumār. *Hindī Nāṭak mẽ Nāyak kā Svarūp*. Delhi: Bhāratīya Granth Niketan, 1974.

Bhāradvāj, Jagadīś. *Kṛṣṇa Kāvya mẽ Līlā-Varṇan*. New Delhi: Nirmalkīrti Prakāśan, 1972.

Bharata. *The Nāṭyaśāstra*. Translated by Manomohan Ghosh. 2 volumes. Calcutta: Asiatic Society of Bengal and Manisha Granthalaya, 1961 and 1967.

Bhaṭṭ, Gopāl. *Haribhaktivilāsa, with the Digdarśiṇī Commentary of Sanātan Gosvāmī*. Edited by Purīdās Dās. Mymensingh: Śacīnāth Rāychaudhurī, 1946.

Bhattacarji, Sukumari. *The Indian Theogony*. Cambridge: Cambridge University Press, 1970.

Bhattacharya, Asok K. "On the Identification of the Colour Called

Śyāma." *Journal of the Oriental Research Institute of Baroda* 24:1–2 (1974), 440–443.

Bhattacharya, S. K. *Kṛṣṇa-Cult*. New Delhi: Associated Publishing House, 1978.

Brahma-vaivarta Purāṇam. 2 volumes. Translated by Rajendra Nath Sen. New York: AMS Press, 1974. Originally published 1920.

Brahmavaivarta Purāṇa. Bombay: Veṅkateśvara Press, 1909–1910.

Brajbāsī Dās. *Braj Vilās*. Bombay: Śrī Veṅkateśvara Press, 1876.

Brajratnadās, ed. *Nandadās Granthāvalī*. Varanasi: Nāgarīpracāriṇī Sabhā, 1958.

Brown, Cheever Mackenzie. *God as Mother: A Feminine Theology in India*. Hartford, Vt.: Claude Stark, 1974.

Brown, W. Norman. "Change of Sex as a Hindu Story Motif." *Journal of the American Oriental Society* 47 (1927), 3–24.

———. "Duty as Truth in Ancient India." *Proceedings of the American Philosophical Society* 116:3 (1972), 252–268.

Bryant, Kenneth E. "The *Bhramargīt* of Sūrdās." Paper presented at the conference on the *sant* tradition, Berkeley, 1978.

———. *Poems to the Child-God: Structures and Strategies in the Poetry of Sūrdās*. Berkeley and Los Angeles: University of California Press, 1978.

Buddhaprakash. "Kṛṣṇa [An Ethnological Study]." *P. K. Gode Commemoration Volume*. Vol. 2. Poona: R. N. Sardesai, 1960, pp. 36–57.

Burlingame, E. W. "The Act of Truth (Saccakiriyā): A Hindu Spell and Its Employment as a Psychic Motif in Hindu Fiction." *Journal of the Royal Asiatic Society*, 1917, pp. 429–467.

Burton, Richard, and F. F. Arbuthnot, trs. *The Kama Sutra of Vatsyayana*. New York: Capricorn Books, 1963.

Carman, John B. *The Theology of Rāmānuja*. New Haven: Yale University Press, 1974.

Citrāv, Siddheśvarśāstrī. *Bhāratvarṣīya Prācīn Caritrakoś*: Poona: Bhāratīya Caritrakoś Maṇḍal, 1964.

Dasgupta, Surendranath. *A History of Indian Philosophy*. 5 volumes. Delhi: Motilal Banarsidass, 1975. Originally published 1922.

De, S. K. *Early History of the Vaiṣṇava Faith and Movement in Bengal*. Calcutta: K. L. Mukhopadhyaya, 1961.

Dhruvadās, Hit. *Śrī Bayālīs Līlā*. Kampur: Brāhman, *vikram* 1916 (A.D. 1859).

Dikshitar, V. R. Ramachandra. "Kṛṣṇa in Early Tamil Literature." *Indian Culture* 4 (1937–1938), 267–271.

Dimock, Edward C., Jr. *The Place of the Hidden Moon*. Chicago: University of Chicago Press, 1966.

——— et al. *The Literature of India: An Introduction*. Chicago: University of Chicago Press, 1974.

Dowson, John. *A Classical Dictionary of Hindu Mythology and Religion, Geography, History, and Literature*. London: Routledge and Kegan Paul, 1968.

Dutt, Manmatha Nath. *A Prose English Translation of Harivamsha*. Calcutta: H. C. Dass, 1897.

Dvivedī, Hazārīprasād. *Sūr Sāhitya*. Delhi: Rājkamal Prakāśan, 1973.

Eck, Diana L. "Banāras, City of Light: The Sacred Places and Praises of Kāśī." Ph.D. dissertation, Harvard University, 1976.

Edholm, Eric Af, and Carl Suneson. "The Seven Bulls and Kṛṣṇa's Marriage to Nīlā/NappiNNai in Sanskrit and Tamil Literature." *Temenos* 8 (1972), 29–53.

Faber-Kaiser, A. *Jesus Died in Kashmir*. London: Gordon and Cremonesi, 1977.

Gaeffke, Peter. "Das Motiv der Gottesschelte in der Neuindischen Bhaktiliteratur." *Zeitschrift der Deutschen Morgenländischen Gesellschaft*, supplement, part 3, 1969, pp. 924–929.

Gangoly, O. C. "Indra-cult *versus* Kṛṣṇa-cult." *Journal of the Ganganatha Jha Institure* 7 (1949), 1–27.

Gargi, Balwant. *Folk Theater of India*. Seattle: University of Washington Press, 1966.

Gautam, Rājendra Prasād. *Śrīharivyāsadevācārya aur Mahāvāṇī*. Brindavan: Bhakti Sāhitya Sadan, 1974.

Glasenapp, Helmuth von. *Von Buddha zu Gandhi*. Wiesbaden: Otto Harrassowitz, 1962.

Goetz, Hermann. "The Earliest Representations of the Myth Cycle of Kṛṣṇa Govinda." *Journal of the Oriental Research Institute of Baroda* 1:1 (September 1951), 51–59.

Gopalan, V. "Krishna Cult in Tamil Nadu." *The Hindu*, December 20, 1970.

Gosvāmī, Jīva. *Śrī Śrī Gopālacampū*. Vol. 1. Edited and translated into Hindi by Syāmdās. Brindavan: Śrīharinām Sankīrttan Maṇḍal, 1968.

Gosvāmī, Rūpa. *Bhakti-Rasāmṛta-Sindhuḥ*. Translated into English by Bon Maharaj. Brindavan: Institute of Oriental Philosophy, 1965.

Gosvāmī, Vallabhlāl. *Śrī Kṛṣṇa kī Vraj Līlāẽ*. Gorakhpur: Śrīrādhāmādhav Sevā Saṃsthān, *vikram* 2025 (A.D. 1968).

Govindadās and R. N. Agravāl, eds. *Rās-Līlā: Ek Paricāy*. Delhi: Bhāratīya Viśva Prakāśan, 1959.

Grierson, George. "Modern Hinduism and Its Debt to the Nestorians." *Journal of the Royal Asiatic Society*, 1907, pp. 311–335.

Growse, Frederic Salmon. *Mathurā: A District Memoir*. 3rd ed. Allahabad: North-Western Provinces and Oudh Government Press, 1883.

Guha-Thakurta, Prabhucharan. *The Bengali Drama: Its Origin and Development*. London: Kegan Paul, Trench, Trubner, 1930.

Gupta, Dīndayāl. *Aṣṭachāp aur Vallabh-Sampradāy*. 2 vol. Prayāg: Hindī Sāhitya Sammelan, 1970.

Gupta, Jagadīś. *Kṛṣṇa Bhakti Kāvya*. Allahabad: Gautam Printing Press, 1968.

Gupta, Kiśorīlāl, ed. *Nāgarīdās (Granthāvalī)*. Varanasi: Nāgarīpracāriṇī Sabhā, 1965.

Hardy, Friedhelm. "Mādhavêndra Purī: A Link between Bengal Vaiṣṇavism and South Indian *Bhakti*." *Journal of the Royal Asiatic Society*, 1974, pp. 23–41.

Harivaṃśa, The. Edited by Parashuram Lakshman Vaidya. 2 vol. Poona: Bhandarkar Oriental Research Institute, 1969.

Hawley, John S. "Pilgrims' Progress Through Krishna's Playground," *Asia* 3:3 (September/October 1980), 12–19, 45.

———. "The Butter Thief." Ph.D. dissertation, Harvard University, 1977.

———. "The Early *Sūr Sāgar* and the Growth of the Sūr Tradition," *Journal of the American Oriental Society* 99:1 (1979), 64–72.

———. "Krishna's Cosmic Victories." *Journal of the American Academy of Religion* 47:2 (1979), 201–221.

———. "Thief of Butter, Thief of Love." *History of Religions* 18:3 (1979), 203–220.

———. "Yoga and *Viyoga*: Simple Religion in Hinduism." *Harvard Theological Review* 74:1 (1981), forthcoming.

———, and Donna M. Wulff, eds. *The Divine Consort: Rādhā and the Goddesses of India*. Berkeley: Berkeley Religious Studies Series, forthcoming.

Hein, Norvin. *The Miracle Plays of Mathurā*. New Haven: Yale University Press, 1972.

Hiltebeitel, Alf. *The Ritual of Battle: Krishna in the "Mahābhārata."* Ithaca: Cornell University Press, 1976.

Holland, Barron. *Popular Hinduism and Hindu Mythology: An Annotated Bibliography*. Westport, Conn.: Greenwood Press, 1979.

Hooper, J.S.M. *Hymns of the Alvars*. Calcutta: Association Press, 1929.

Hopkins, Thomas J. *The Hindu Religious Tradition*. Encino, Calif.: Dickinson, 1971.

Hospital, Clifford G. "The Enemy Transformed: Opponents of the Lord in the *Bhāgavata Purāṇa*." *Journal of the American Academy of Religion* 46:2 (1973), supplement, 200–215.

——. "The Marvellous Acts of God: A Study in the *Bhāgavata Purāṇa*." Ph.D. dissertation, Harvard University, 1973.

Hudson, Dennis, "Bathing in Kṛṣṇa," *Harvard Theological Review* 73: 3–4 (1980), 537–564.

Ingalls, Daniel H. H. "The *Harivaṃśa* as a *Mahākāvya*." *Mêlanges d' Indianisme â la mêmoire de Louis Renou*. Paris: É. de Boccard, 1968, pp. 381–394.

Iyer, K. Bharatha. *Kathakali: The Sacred Dance-Drama of Malabar*. London: Luzac, 1955.

——. "Krishnattam." *Times of India Annual*. 1966, pp. 71–80.

Jaiswal, Suvira. *The Origin and Development of Vaiṣṇavism*. Delhi: Munshiram Manoharlal, 1967.

Jones, Clifford R. "Bhāgavata Mēḷa Nāṭakam, a Traditional Dance-Drama Form." *Journal of Asian Studies* 22:2 (1963), 193–200.

——. "The Temple Theatre of Kerala: Its History and Description." Ph.D. dissertation, University of Pennsylvania, 1967.

——, and Betty True Jones. *Kathakali: An Introduction to the Dance-Drama of Kerala*. San Francisco: American Society of Eastern Arts, 1970.

Jung, Carl G., and C. Kerényi. *Essays on a Science of Mythology*. Translated by R.F.C. Hull. Bollingen Series XXII. Princeton: Princeton University Press, 1969.

Kapoor, O.B.L. *The Philosophy and Religion of Śrī Caitanya*. New Delhi: Munshiram Manoharlal, 1977.

Keith, Arthur Berriedale. "The Child Kṛṣṇa." *Journal of the Royal Asiatic Society*, 1908, pp. 169–175.

——. *The Sanskrit Drama in Its Origin, Development, Theory and Practice*. Oxford: Clarendon Press, 1924.

Kennedy, J. "The Child Krishna, Christianity, and the Gujars." *Journal of the Royal Asiatic Society*, 1907, pp. 951–991.

——. "The Child Kṛṣṇa and His Critics." *Journal of the Royal Asiatic Society*, 1908, pp. 505–521.

Kinsley, David. *The Divine Player: A Study of Kṛṣṇa-Līlā*. Delhi: Motilal Banarsidass, 1979.

Kinsley, David. *The Sword and the Flute*. Berkeley and Los Angeles: University of California Press, 1975.

———. "'Through the Looking Glass': Divine Madness in the Hindu Religious Tradition." *History of Religions* 13:4 (1973), 270–305.

———. "Without Kṛṣṇa there is No Song." *History of Religions* 12:2 (1972), 149–180.

Kirfel, Willibald. "Kṛṣṇa's Jugendgeschichte in den Purāṇa." *Beiträge zur Literaturwissenschaft und Geistesgeschichte Indiens*. Edited by W. Kirfel. Bonn: Fritz Klopp, 1926, pp. 298–316.

Klostermaier, Klaus. *In the Paradise of Krishna: Hindu and Christian Seekers*. Philadelphia: Westminster, 1969.

Konow, Sten. *The Indian Drama*. Translated by S. N. Ghosal. Calcutta: General Printers and Publishers, 1969.

Kosambi, D. D. "The Historical Krishna." *Times of India Annual*, 1965, pp. 27–36.

Kṛṣṇadās Kavirāj. *Caitanya Caritāmṛta*. Edited by Syāmdās. Brindavan: Śrīharinām-Sankīrttan Maṇḍal, 1974.

Kumār, Rājendra. *Paravartī Hindī Kṛṣṇabhaktikāvya*. Allahabad: Śabdapīṭh, 1972.

Lallūlāl. *Śrī Premsāgar*. Benares: Ṭhākurprasād and Sons, n.d.

Lévi, Sylvain. *Le Théâtre indien*. Paris: Émile Bouillon, 1890.

Liṅga Mahāpurāṇa. Bombay: Lakṣmīveṇkateśvara Mudrālay, n.d.

Mahābhārata, The. Edited by V. S. Sukthankar. Vol. 2. Edited by Franklin Edgerton. Poona: Bhandarkar Oriental Research Institute, 1944. Vol. 7. Edited by S. K. Belvalkar. Poona: Bhandarkar Oriental Research Institute, 1947.

Majumdar, Bimanbehari. *Kṛṣṇa in History and Legend*. Calcutta: University of Calcutta, 1969.

Majmudar, M. R. "The Tradition of Folk-Dances in Western India: the Rāsa and the Garbo." *Journal of the Indian Society of Oriental Art* 14 (1946), 75–90.

Mani, Vettam. *Purāṇic Encyclopaedia*. Delhi: Motilal Banarsidass, 1975.

Manusmṛti. 2 volumes. Calcutta: Udayācal Press, 1971.

Mathur, Jagdish Chandra. *Drama in Rural India*. New York: Asia Publishing House, 1964.

Masson, J. L. "The Childhood of Kṛṣṇa." *Journal of the American Oriental Society* 94:4 (1974), 454–459.

———, and M. V. Patwardhan. *Aesthetic Rapture*. 2 volumes. Poona: Deccan College, 1970.

McGregor, R. S. *Nanddas: The Round Dance of Krishna and Uddhav's Message*. London: Luzac, 1973.

Medhi, Kaliram. "Origin of the Assamese Drama." In *Aspects of Early Assamese Literature*. Edited by Banikanta Kakati. Gauhati: Gauhati University, 1953, pp. 189–216.

Miller, Barbara Stoler. *Love Song of the Dark Lord: Jayadeva's "Gītagovinda."* New York: Columbia University Press, 1977.

———. "Rādhā: Consort of Kṛṣṇa's Vernal Passion." *Journal of the American Oriental Society* 95:4 (1975), 665–671.

Mītal, Prabhudayāl. *Braj kā Sāṃskṛtik Itihās*. Delhi: Rājkamal Prakāśan, 1966.

———. *Braj ke Dharma-Sampradāyõ kā Itihās*. Delhi: National Publishing House, 1968.

———. *Braj kī Kalāõ kā Itihās*. Mathura: Sāhitya Sansthān, 1975.

———. *Braj kī Sāṃskṛtik Yātrā*. Mathura: Sāhitya Sansthān, 1966.

Nābhājī. *Śrī Bhaktamāl*. Lucknow: Tejkumār Press, 1961.

Nadkarni, Dnyaneshwar. "Marathi Tamasha—Yesterday and Today." *Sangeet Natak* 12 (1969), 19–28.

Naqvi, G.A. "The Indian Stage: A Select Bibliography." *Cultural News from India* 3:4 (1962), 31–40.

Natya. Folk Theatre Number, 5:4 (1962).

Oak, Purushottam Nagesh. *Christianity is Chrisn-nity*. New Delhi: Institute for Rewriting Indian History, 1978.

O'Flaherty, Wendy Doniger. *Asceticism and Eroticism in the Mythology of Śiva*. Delhi: Oxford University Press, 1975.

Ojhā, Dharmanārāyaṇ. *Sūr Sāhitya mẽ Puṣṭimārgīya Sevā Bhāvanā*. Allahabad: Śodh Sāhitya Prakāśan, 1973.

Oppert, Gustave. "Note sur les Sālagrāmas." *Compte-rendus des sêances de l'Acadêmie des inscriptions et belles-lettres*. 1900, pp. 472–485.

Padmapurāṇa, The. Edited by R.S.V.N. Mandlic. Poona: Ānandāśrama, 1893.

Pal, Pratapaditya. *Krishna: The Cowherd King*. Los Angeles: Los Angeles County Museum of Art, 1972.

Panikkar, Raimundo. *The Vedic Experience: Mantramañjarī*. Berkeley and Los Angeles: University of California Press, 1977.

Parrinder, Geoffrey. *Avatar and Incarnation*. New York: Barnes and Noble, 1970.

Poddār, Hanumānprasād. *Śrīkṛṣṇalīlā kā Cintan*. Gorakhpur: Gita Press, *vikram* 2028 (A.D. 1971).

Poston, Elizabeth, ed. *The Penguin Book of Christmas Carols*. Harmondsworth: Penguin, 1972.

Premānand. *Braj ke Naye Rasiyā*. Brindavan: Vṛjvāsī Pustakālay, n.d.

Raghavan, V. *Some Old Lost Rama Plays*. Annamalainagar: Annamalai University, 1961.

Rāmsvarūp, Svāmī. "Conversation with Sri Swami Ram Swaroop Ji Sharma on the Ancient Heritage of the Ras Lila in Braj." Brindavan, 1975, mimeographed.

Rangacharya, Adya. *The Indian Theatre.* New Delhi: National Book Trust, 1971.

Rank, Otto. *The Myth of the Birth of the Hero.* Translated by F. Robbins and Smith Ely Jelliffe. New York: Vintage, 1964. Originally published 1914.

Redington, James. "The Meaning of Kṛṣṇa's Dance of Love According to Vallabhācārya." Ph.D. dissertation, University of Wisconsin-Madison, 1975.

Renou, Louis. "Research on the Indian Theatre since 1890." *Samskrita Ranga Annual* 4 (1966), 67–91.

Reynolds, Frank E., and Donald Capps, eds. *The Biographical Process.* The Hague: Mouton, 1976.

Richmond, Farley. "Bhavai: Village Theatre of West India." In *Papers in International and World Affairs.* (Series 2). East Lansing: Michigan State University, 1969.

———. "Some Religious Aspects of the Traditional Indian Theatre." *The Drama Review* 15:3 (1971), 122–131.

———, ed. "Theatre in India." *Journal of South Asian Literature* 10:2–4 (1975), entire.

Ridgeway, William. *The Dramas and Dramatic Dances of Non-European Races.* Cambridge: Cambridge University Press, 1915.

Rocher, Rosanne, ed. *India and Indology: Selected Articles by W. Norman Brown.* Delhi: Motilal Banarsidass, 1978.

"Round Table on the Contemporary Relevance of Traditional Theatre." *Sangeet Natak* 21 (1971), entire.

Ruben, Walter. *Krishna: Konkordanz und Kommentar der Motive seines Heldenlebens.* Istanbul: Istanbul Yazilari, 1944.

Salomon, Richard, ed. and tr. "The Sāmānya-praghaṭṭaka of Nārāyaṇa Bhaṭṭa's *Tristhalīsetu:* Critical Edition and Translation." Ph.D. dissertation, University of Pennsylvania, 1975.

———. "*Tīrtha-pratyāmnāyāḥ:* Ranking of Hindu Pilgrimage Sites in Classical Sanskrit Texts." *Zeitschrift der Deutschen Morgenländischen Gesellschaft* 128:2 (1978), 102–128.

Sarabhai, Mrinalini. "Krishnattam." *Mārg* 19:2 (1966), 43–45.

Śarmā, Harbanślāl. *Sūr aur unkā Sāhitya.* Aligarh: Bhārat Prakāśan Mandir, 1965.

Śarmā, Munśīrām. *Sūrdās kā Kāvya-Vaibhav.* Kanpur: Grantham, 1971.

Śarmā "Madhukar," Śrīkṛṣṇamurāri. "Vartamān Brajrās Mañckā Uday." *Ras Vṛndāvan* 1:4 (1979), 19–22.

Śarmā "Navīn," Bālakṛṣṇa, ed. *Cayanikā*. Calcutta: Macmillan, 1973.

Scott, J. E. *Braj: The Vaishnava Holy Land*. New York: Eaton and Mains, 1906.

Sehgal, S. R. *Bhāsa's Bālacaritam*. Delhi: Munshi Ram Manohar Lal, 1959.

Sen, Sukumar. *History of Bengali Literature*. New Delhi: Sahitya Akademi [1960].

Shapiro, Allan A. "The Birth-celebration of Śrī Rādhāramaṇ in Vrindaban." M.A. thesis, Columbia University, 1979.

Siegel, Lee. *Sacred and Profane Dimensions of Love in Indian Traditions as Exemplified in the "Gītagovinda" of Jayadeva*. Delhi: Oxford University Press, 1978.

Singer, Milton, ed. *Krishna: Myths, Rites, and Attitudes*. Chicago: University of Chicago Press, 1966.

———, and B. Cohn, eds. *Structure and Change in Indian Society*. Chicago: Aldine, 1968.

Sitaram, K. N. "Dramatic Representations in South India, with Special Reference to Travancore and Tinnevelly District." *Journal of the Royal Asiatic Society* 54 (1924), 229–237.

Snātak, Vijayendra. *Rādhāvallabh Sampradāy: Siddhānt aur Sāhitya*. Delhi: National Publishing House, 1968.

Spink, Walter. *Krishnamandala, a Devotional Theme in Indian Art*. Ann Arbor: Center for South and South East Asian Studies, 1971.

Śrīmadbhāgavata. Varanasi: Paṇḍit Pustakālay, *vikram* 2022 (A.D. 1965).

Srimad-Bhagvatam, The. Translated by J. M. Sanyal. 2 volumes. New Delhi: Munshiram Manoharlal, 1970.

Śrīmadbhāgavatamahāpurāṇam. Translated with a commentary by Munilāl et al. 2 volumes. Gorakhpur: Gita Press, 1971.

Śrīśrīviṣṇupurāṇa. Translated into Hindi by Munilāl Gupta. 7th ed. Gorakhpur: Gita Press, *vikram* 2026 (A.D. 1969).

Stevenson, Margaret. *The Rites of the Twice-Born*. New Delhi: Oriental Books Reprint Corporation, 1971. Originally published 1920.

Subramanyam, Ka Naa. "Traditional Tamil Drama and the Present Impasse." *Sangeet Natak* 4 (1967), 27–36.

Śukla, Rāmcandra. *Sūrdās*. Benares, Nāgarīpracāriṇī Sabhā, 1948.

Sūr Dās. *Sūr Sāgar*. Edited by "Ratnākar" et al. 1st ed. Vol. 2 (but Vol. 1 never published). Benares: Nāgarīpracāriṇī Sabhā, 1934. Subsequent editions: Varanasi, 1972, 1976; in these editions the two published volumes were renumbered vols. 1 and 2.

Swann, Darius L. "Three Forms of Traditional Theatre of Uttar Pradesh, North India." Ph.D. dissertation, University of Hawaii, 1974.

Temple, R. C. *The Legends of the Panjâb*. 3 volumes. London: Trübner [1883–1900].

Tillich, Paul. *Systematic Theology*. Volume 2. Chicago: University of Chicago Press, 1962.

Tivārī, Śaśi. *Sūr ke Kṛṣṇa: Ek Anuśīlan*. Hyderabad: Milind Prakāśan, 1961.

Tulsīdās, Bābā, ed. *Rās Līlā-Cintan*. 2 volumes. Brindavan: Bābā Tulsīdās, 1958 and n.d.

Turner, Victor. *Dramas, Fields, and Metaphors*. Ithaca: Cornell University Press, 1974.

Upadhyaya, K. S. "Yakshagana Bayalata." *Sangeet Natak* 11 (1969), 37–51.

Vaikuṇṭh Nivāsī, Rañgīlāl. *Braj Bihār*. Mathura: Śyāmkāśī Press, n.d.

Vājpeyī, Nand Dulāre. *Mahākavi Sūrdās*. Delhi: Rājkamal Prakāśan, 1976.

Varmā, Vrajeśvar. *Sūrdās: Jīvan aur Kāvya kā Adhyayan*. Allahabad: Lokabhāratī Prakāśan, 1979.

——. *Sūr-Mīmāṃsā*. Delhi: Oriental Book Depot, n.d.

Vaudeville, Charlotte. "Aspects du mythe de *Kṛṣṇa-Gopāla* dans l'Inde ancienne." In *Mélanges d'Indianisme à la mémoire de Louis Renou*. Paris: É. de Boccard, 1968, pp. 737–761.

——. "Braj, Lost and Found." *Indo-Iranian Journal* 18:3–4 (1976), 195–213.

——. "The Cowherd God in Ancient India," In *Pastoralists and Nomads in South Asia*. Edited by Lawrence Saadia Leshnik and Günther-Dietz Sontheimer. Wiesbaden: Otto Harrassowitz, 1975, pp. 92–116.

——. "Evolution of Love-Symbolism in Bhagavatism." *Journal of the American Oriental Society* 82:1 (1962), 31–40.

——. "The Govardhan Myth in Northern India." *Indo-Iranian Journal* 22:1–2 (1980), 1–45.

——. "Krishna and Devī." Lecture, Harvard University, June 15, 1978.

——. *Pastorales par Soûr-Dās*. Paris: Gallimard, 1971.

Vishnu Purana, The. Translated by H. H. Wilson. Calcutta: Punthi Pustak, 1972. Originally published 1840.

Viṣṇu Purāṇa. Bombay: Nirnaya Sagara Press, 1914.

Weber, Albrecht. "On the Kṛishṇajanmâshṭamî or Krishna's Birth-Festival." Translated into English by E. Rehatsek. *Indian Antiquary* 6 (1887), 161–180.

White, Charles S. J. *The Caurāsī Pad of Śrī Hit Harivaṁś*. Honolulu: University Press of Hawaii, 1977.

———. "Kṛṣṇa as Divine Child." *History of Religions* 10:2 (1970), 156–177.

Wilson, Frances Ann. *The Love of Krishna.* Philadelphia: University of Pennsylvania Press, 1975.

Wilson, H. H., et al. *The Theatre of the Hindus.* Calcutta: S. Gupta, 1955. Partially reprinted from H. H. Wilson, *Select Specimens of the Theatre of the Hindus*, 1871.

Winternitz, Moritz. "Bhāsa and the Mahābhārata and Kṛṣṇa Plays of the Trivandrum Series." *Bulletin of the Rama Varma Research Institute* 5 (1937), 1–15.

———. "Kṛṣṇa-Dramen." *Zeitschrift der Deutschen Morgenländischen Gesellschaft* 74 (1920), 118–144.

Wulff, Donna M. "Drama as a Mode of Religious Realization: The *Vidagdhamādhava* of Rūpa Gosvāmin." Ph.D. dissertation, Harvard University, 1977.

Yajnik, R. K. *The Indian Theatre.* New York: Dutton, 1934.

Yāmdagni, Vasant. *Rās Līlā tathā Rāsānukaraṇ Vikās.* New Delhi: Sangeet Natak Akademi, 1980.

Young, Katherine K. "Beloved Places *(ukuntaruḷiṉanilaṅkaḷ)*: The Correlation of Topography and Theology in the Śrīvaiṣṇava Tradition of South India." Ph.D. dissertation, McGill University, 1978.

Zimmer, Heinrich. *Myths and Symbols in Indian Art and Civilization.* Edited by Joseph Campbell. Bollingen Series VI. New York: Pantheon, 1946.

Index